THE WILD GOURMETS

THE WILD

Adventures in food & freedom

GOURMETS

Guy Grieve & Thomasina Miers

Photography by Jill Mead
Illustrations by Dawn Reade

First published in Great Britain in 2007.

Based on the television series
The Wild Gourmets produced by
Silver River Productions Ltd.

Bloomsbury Publishing Plc, 36 Soho Square,
London W1D 3QY

A CIP catalogue record for this book is available
from the British Library.

The Wild Gourmets is a trademark of Silver River
Productions Ltd.

Designed by willwebb.co.uk
Photography by Jill Mead
Illustrations by Dawn Reade

ISBN-13 9780747591573
10 9 8 7 6 5 4 3 2 1

Printed in Great Britain by Butler & Tanner Ltd,
Frome.

All papers used by Bloomsbury Publishing are
natural, recyclable products made from wood
grown in well-managed forests. The manufacturing
processes conform to the environmental regulations
of the country of origin.

www.bloomsbury.com

Quotation on page 47 taken from *The Immense
Journey* by Loren Eisley, published by Victor Gollancz,
an imprint of the Orion Publishing Group.

(Previous pages) Our camp at Treshnish, Isle of Mull.

To Juliet and to Mark

PART I
LIVING ON THE LAND

PART II
LIVING OFF THE LAND

A year ago we set out on a journey across Britain. Our mission was to live off the land, subsisting on food that we had gathered and prepared ourselves. We were determined to seek out all that we ate using our own bare hands, the skilled nose of Guy's beautiful retriever, Juno, and the occasional streak of cunning. If it was animal we would hunt, kill and butcher it, secure in the knowledge that it had lived free and died fast; if it was vegetable we would identify, harvest and prepare it, confident that it was the freshest produce in the country. We would be in charge of every step of getting our food from field to plate.

We did not set out to pretend we were SAS survival experts. Quite the opposite – luxury was our aspiration. Why live off limpets and pine needle tea when we could eat like kings? Why shiver away at night in a dark crook when we could sleep on thick mattresses of spruce and pine, lulled by the crackle of the nearby fire?

A gastronomic journey without the safety net of shops – at first this felt like a daunting prospect. But we were delighted by how much the land had to offer us, and how we were able to make do with what we found. Armed with a small store of staple ingredients, like coffee (essential), whisky (medicinal), flour and salt, we set out and discovered that we really could find and eat beautiful food.

While we were on the road we set up camp wherever we could, in every kind of weather, often in far from ideal circumstances. All our cooking was done on the campfire, so the recipes in this book have been tested in sometimes stormy, often sodden, conditions. Hunting and gathering largely took place without the comfort of knowing there would be a hot bath or warm bed at the end of the day. At times it was hard, but the feeling of being self-sufficient was ample compensation. We found our different skills worked together to overcome the challenges of bad weather and (sometimes) unsuccessful hunting. When one of us found our spirits flagging, the other would be there to provide support. The result was that the food we ate was imbued with experience and adventure.

Often our spirits were lifted by moments of unexpected bounty, such as the time in Suffolk when we found a remote stand of sweet chestnut trees that were heavy with food. We roasted the sleek nuts later that day and felt nothing but simple happiness. The sea also gave sustenance, such as the frigid morning that we spent pushing nets through the dark waters of Morecambe Bay hunting for brown shrimp. Our efforts were rewarded with a catch of brown shrimp and, as luck would have it, a flounder. A fire was lit and with our newly caught ingredients we had the makings of a feast. It is hard to express how good these meals tasted.

We hope this book will become a friend, helping you along the road of wild food exploration where we left off. We want to encourage you to eschew convenience from time to time in favour of independence, by seeking out the flavours that can be found all around us on this luscious island. Britain is a wonderfully diverse patchwork of wood, meadow, moor, shoreline and mountain. If you can make the time to explore the country, and to learn from it, you will bring back so much more than just perfect ingredients – you will find freedom in your own land.

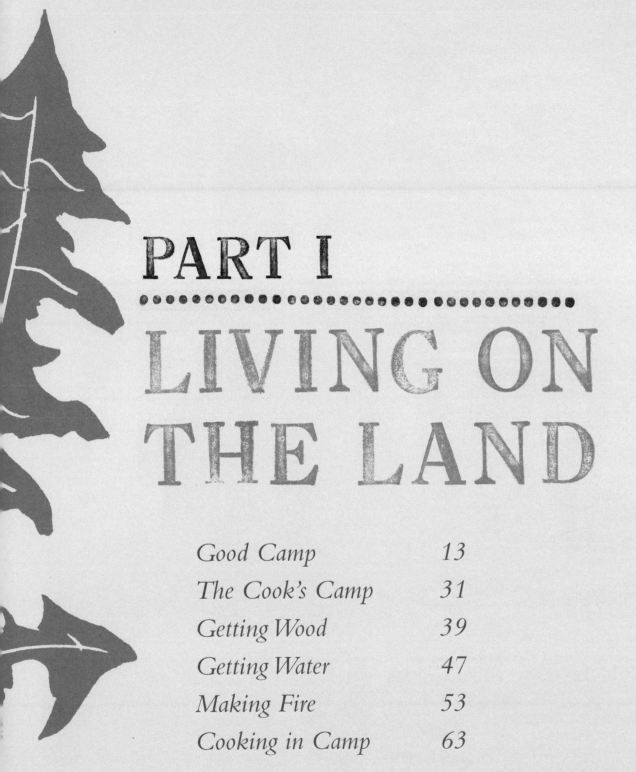

PART I

••

LIVING ON
THE LAND

*'Staying in the
house breeds
a sort of
insanity always'
Henry David Thoreau*

GOOD CAMP

When Tommi and I began our journey around Britain in search of wild grub, it soon became apparent that some old-school thinking was required in order to ensure that we lived as well on the land as well as we did off it. Too often people use the outdoors as some kind of macho testing ground, and the result is an off-putting, uncomfortable and sometimes even hazardous experience. We've all been regaled with tales of friends' disastrous camping trips, which usually go something like this: 'We were flooded out and freezing and we didn't get a wink's sleep . . . But it was great!' For these people, living in the outdoors is clearly all about sadomasochism, whereas I associate camping with comfort, deep relaxation and escape from the petty concerns of modern daily life.

When properly set up, a camp can be a place of utter ease and contentment, where you can happily exist for days, weeks or even months. To achieve this level of comfort, you must be well organised and prepared to work hard. But with some effort and the right attitude, living outdoors can become so good that domestic life can start to feel painful by comparison.

The key to camping in comfort is to approach the outdoors in a flexible manner, without rigid plans and timetables. By all means set out with a mission, but be ready to adapt your plans as you go along or, if need be, abandon them altogether. The beauty of nature is that it is unpredictable, and the joy of rough living lies in your very lack of control over your environment. If you can learn to adjust to whatever comes your way, to bend with the changes, you will have a good time.

Whether you are panning for gold, hunting for mushrooms or hiding from the Mounties, if you are planning to spend some time in the bush, you need to set up good camp. The difference between good and bad camp is like night and day – if your camp is no good you might as well give up, as life will just become too unpleasant and relentless to endure over a sustained period. Camp needs to be a refuge, a place of calm and order, and also a place where you can relax and take it easy. Once you have established good camp, you can happily journey forth in search of food, wood or whatever you desire, knowing that you have a safe haven to return to. In wild country you can take a bearing as you set out and, simply by turning 180 degrees, you will be able to find your way home again. Thus camp becomes rather like the centre of a bicycle wheel, with each of your foraging routes spanning out like spokes as you get to know the surrounding land intimately.

A good sheltered spot in the Lake District. Note that the trees are not wind-bent.

A good location

When making camp, the first thing to decide is where to locate it, and there are a number of factors to consider. The direction of the prevailing wind is the first, and a number of clues will give this away. As a rule the prevailing wind in Britain is from the south-west; however, the shape of the land will greatly affect both the strength and direction of the wind. Camping beneath high ground will often mean that you are besieged by ferocious downdraughts, and headlands or the edges of large hills or mountains also experience accelerated winds. Look around at the trees surrounding your potential site – are they wind-bent, and if so, in which direction? This will help you find shelter from the prevailing wind.

Next look out for natural features that will provide windbreaks: a high wall, a block of forestry or even a slight fold in the land will all give good shelter. It can sometimes be good to set up camp deep within woodland, as the trees will provide great shelter from the wind and weather as well as an endless supply of fuel. Depending on the type of woodland and time of year, however, forest areas may be dank and prone to biting insects. Using woodland as a windbreak can be a good solution: the open ground with its breezier aspect will inhibit the biters, while you will still have proximity to that natural storehouse.

When you have found a place that will be sheltered from the wind, there are a few other considerations. Is there sufficient flat ground to make a comfortable surface for your tent? Is there a risk that the site will become waterlogged should there be heavy rain? Is there an ample supply of firewood within reach?

When looking for firewood, I never choose wood on the ground, as this is usually sub-standard stuff and wet into the bargain. Instead I look for standing dead wood, either in the form of dead branches or, even better, a whole dead tree. This wood is always bone dry and when combined with green or living wood will burn for hours in the stove or fire pit. Also I keep an eye out for useful wood which can supply all sorts of vital tools (see page 41).

The final consideration, and one of the most vital, is whether there is a supply of clean water near by for drinking and washing. Ideally your camp should be near a fresh, fast-flowing supply of water such as a river or stream. A note of caution, however: always bear flooding in mind when considering how close to a river to set up camp. Rivers can rise dramatically with seemingly insignificant rainfall, as they are affected by events taking place a long way upstream.

Clues to the river's behaviour are all around: dry, formerly water-borne flotsam wrapped around the branches of trees and bushes, for example, are telltale signs of flooding. Sometimes trees along a riverbank have scars on their trunks, which show that they have been battered by flood-borne rocks or timber and reveal a sinister side to the character of that sweet babbling brook. Make camp well away from such signs of watery disaster, even if it means hauling your water a bit further. Console yourself with the thought that it is good exercise. I'd far rather heave water carriers about than jog in front of a mirror in a leotard – although each to their own, I suppose.

Heaven is a roof made of canvas

I'm not a big fan of nylon tents. Although obviously useful for one or two nights' camping, they are awful for long-term living. (I do, however, routinely carry a tiny one-man tent and a bivvy bag, in case I get caught out when travelling.) In order to make a true home in the boonies, you need a more substantial structure, with enough space to stand up and move around, and – if you plan to camp out in all seasons – some form of heating. I use a 16 x 14 foot wall tent made of 13-ounce canvas treated for resistance to mildew. Wall tents, so called as they have straight sides like walls, are incredibly comfortable, allowing space to prepare food, cook and hang up clothes, and offering proper defence against the weather. They also have a nice sense of history, conjuring up earlier times when they were the staple means of living for gold miners, trappers and frontiersmen. When my camp is set up, I have the happy feeling that should Mark Twain, John Muir or Henry Thoreau happen to come by, they would feel right at home and happily sit themselves beside my fire or help cut wood for the stove.

It is the stove above all else that lifts the wall tent above those irritating nylon tents that feel more like a condom than a home. Wall tents are built with a stove-jack stitched in, allowing the wise wild gourmet (or WG, as I like to call him or her for short) to install a fine wood-burning stove that will soon become the beating heart of his or her adventure. If you have a good stove, you will be able to live outdoors in all seasons for prolonged periods, no matter what the weather throws at you. I lived in a wall tent for over three months in the Interior of Alaska, and remained comfortable despite blizzards and temperatures that fell as low as the minus 30s.

During our travels in Britain, the threat to our morale came in the form of wind and rain, and here the wall tent and stove really proved their worth, for they allowed us to hang up sodden bits of clothing and kit on a 16-foot line that we hung beneath the ridgepole. Thanks to the stove, everything dried quickly and was ready to use by the next day. Moisture is the nemesis of camping in the temperate world, and must be taken seriously. Camping for any length of time in Britain usually involves some form of soaking, and you must take steps to ensure that your clothing and bedding stays dry, or else you will be in for a very dispiriting and possibly even life-threatening experience. (It is worth noting that British Army survival training in temperate climates is very rigorous, treating wet and windy weather with as much caution as snow, ice and desert conditions.)

I cannot stress enough how important it is when making camp to set out early. The whole process should be enjoyable, and it can't be if you are under pressure, desperately cutting down trees in growing darkness while your family and friends stand around wondering when – or if – they are going to eat.

Setting up a wall tent

It is possible to buy lightweight frames for wall tents. I prefer to use wood gathered from my location, because as well as saving me the bother of transportation, it makes for a more authentic experience. There are two ways of setting up a wall tent. The first is to find two obliging trees that can support a ridgepole hoisted between them, and the second is to create a frame of wood that will support the tent freestanding.

The first method is quicker and achieves a more robust result, but assumes that you are setting up camp in a suitable area of woodland. The second (see page 20) gives you more flexibility when choosing your site, but demands more skill and experience to ensure that the structure is stable. Both need the co-operation of the landowner, whom you must ask if you can cut down young trees to support your tent. If you choose the trees carefully, by thinning the woods you will be doing both the trees and the landowner a favour.

Find two trees from which to hoist your ridgepole. Use stone or wood for weighing down the sides of the tent.

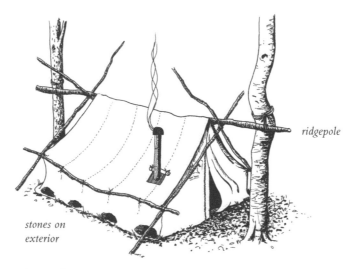

ridgepole

stones on exterior

A wall tent between trees You need to find two straight trees, approximately 18 to 20 feet apart with dry and reasonably flat ground in between. (The dimensions here are for my 16 x 14 foot wall tent, but obviously you should adjust dimensions according to the size of yours.) Ideally these trees will allow you to position your wall tent so that the entrance will be at 90 degrees to the prevailing wind.

You then need to cut a ridgepole, which means cutting down a slim, straight tree. Ideally this should be a spruce, but plenty of other young deciduous and coniferous trees are suitable, as long as they are straight, stiff and not too 'whippy', and able to hold their shape well under pressure. To cut down the tree I use a saw, and I always carry a lightweight boy's axe for knocking off branches. The ridgepole must be approximately 18 to 20 feet long and between 4 and 7 inches in diameter. Knock off the branches with a small axe (if you are using spruce, keep these branches – they'll come in useful later) before threading the ridgepole through the

HOW
TO TIE
POLES

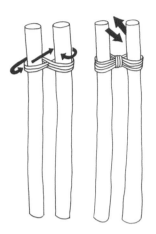

The key to making a good A-shape for your tent is to use strong flexible cordage. Wrap it round two poles as shown above.

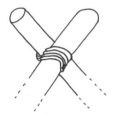

The cordage tightens without wearing down when the poles are twisted into position.

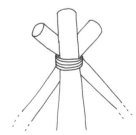

If you want to add a third pole, for example to make a tripod for a freestanding tent (see page 20), find a slightly shorter pole and tie this to the other two.

tent. The pole will need to be hoisted to around 7 feet. If you can't reach, quickly improvise a ladder. To do this is easy: simply harvest two lengths of pole and make them equal in length; then cut steps from the offcuts and hammer them on to the long poles, pointing the nails downwards so that when you climb the ladder your weight pushes them into the pole, not out.

Once the tent is hanging, it must be tied out. For this you will need to harvest six lighter poles, approximately 5 yards long. Don't cut the poles all from one spot – move about and thin selectively. Often young trees grow very closely together and competition is fierce, so look out for a slightly scrawny tree that might be hindering a better tree's chances. Lean two of these poles against the ridgepole, creating an A-shape at either end of the tent, and then two more along the ground running parallel to the ridgepole. Tie all the poles firmly together with rope (see left), bearing in mind that they may have to withstand strong winds, and then pull out the tent sides, attaching them to the frame using short lengths of rope, nylon, string or natural withies (e.g. honeysuckle, spruce roots or blackberry runners). Remember that the frame goes on the outside rather than the inside of the tent.

Now you need to find some heavy objects with which to weigh it down. I usually use river stones or lengths of fallen wood. Place them on the excess canvas hanging down the sides of the tent, and then roll the edges back in towards it. This will keep the wind from blowing the skirts of the tent about.

Your tent is now assembled, and the outside will be looking good. You have not finished yet, however, so now might be a good time to take a break. Set up your fire, not too close to the opening of your tent (see page 54), and put a kettle of water on to boil – remember that it is important not to get dehydrated. While the water is heating, you can get on with the job.

To make the tent perfect inside you need to create a floor. Now you can use that pile of fragrant spruce boughs that you trimmed from the tent poles. (If you weren't able to use spruce, find something similar – reeds, long grasses or heather make a good substitute. Avoid bracken, as it harbours ticks and can cut like a razor when dry.) Lay the boughs out all over the ground, starting at the back of the tent and herringboning them out about 2 feet deep, stopping around 4 feet from the door. If you have extra spruce boughs, you can take them right up to the door to prevent the ground from getting muddy, but beware of laying them too near to the stove, as resin is a great fire starter.

Lay a tarpaulin or groundsheet over this delightful springy mattress and you will have before you a comfortable area for sleeping and lounging around. The padding should be as dry as possible (spruce boughs are ideal, as they don't hold moisture), but even more important is that it is deep enough to provide effective insulation between you and the ground.

When your floor is complete it is time to set up your stove, if you are using one. I use a 'Two-Dog' stove, which is lightweight and easy to carry, and also great for cooking. It comes with sections of stovepipe that fit neatly inside each other for storage. When you've set up the stove, assemble the stovepipe, pushing it carefully through the stovejack and ensuring that it extends over the roof of the tent by at least 4 feet. (The good news with canvas, by the way, is that if it catches light it does not turn into a molten inferno but just singes quietly.)

Now go outside and make yourself a cup of tea – you deserve one! I recommend lapsang souchong, which seems to go uniquely well with camping. As you contentedly sip from a sturdy tin mug and look back at the tent, it will be clear that much space is lost at the sides where the canvas hangs down like the sides of a triangle. This will be fine for a night or so, but it will get tedious in the long term, so take your axe and head for the woods. Find some flexible lengths of hazel or willow, around 3 yards long, to further refine the frame of your tent. Feed the springy poles between the ridgepole and the canvas (at right angles to the ridgepole) and they will flex out against the canvas, creating a domed roof above your head. Now you will be able to walk upright in a pleasantly homely interior, instead of shuffling around like a chimp.

You will also have rafters, which create invaluable hanging space: Tommi used them to hang up herbs, drying-up cloths, clothes and even books. She quickly learnt that it is always better to hang things than lay them on the floor, where dampness and oblivion lurk. A wild floor is the camping equivalent of the Bermuda triangle: things can disappear within the spruce or heather, never to return.

Use young flexible lengths of wood that have just enough stiffness to push the canvas out. Coppiced hazel is perfect for the job.

Once that tripod is up, test it with your weight; if it holds you easily then it will hold the tent.

On the ground, thread the ridgepole through the tent, tie a timber hitch to it and then hoist it up. Do the same on the other side.

Tie the purlins to each side of the tripod then tie out the tent sides.

A freestanding wall tent

If there are no suitable trees to use as supports, you will need to make a freestanding frame. Here's how.

Cut nine poles, ideally spruce or fir, again putting aside all the fragrant boughs for flooring. The first pole, the ridgepole, should be about 18 to 20 feet long and all the rest around 18 feet (once again, these dimensions are for a tent approximately 16 x 14 feet). The tripod and side poles do not need to be very thick – just strong. Five inches at the butt and 3 at the tip will be sufficient. Drag them over to your camp. The easy way to carry lengths of wood in trackless country is to drag them by the tip or thin end of the pole – the rest will follow.

Set the ridgepole aside, and then lay out three of the shorter poles. Using your axe, sharpen the butts (the thicker ends) and then tie the poles firmly together about 3 feet from their tips (see page 18). Spread the poles out on the ground, digging the sharpened butts of the outer two into the ground before picking up the slightly shorter middle pole and walking it out, raising the whole tripod behind you. Dig this pole in when you feel the structure will stand. Then experiment with the position of the side poles until the tripod is sufficiently high to hold the ridgepole about 7 to 8 feet off the ground. To check it is secure, try hanging on it (see left). If the structure stands, the tripod is ready; if not, you will need to dig the poles in better.

Now lay the ridgepole on the ground along the line from the tripod where you expect it to be when the tent is up, and build a second tripod at the other end of the ridge. Once both tripods are in place, thread the ridgepole through the tent, ensuring that the tent is not inside out, and tie a length of rope on to one end. (A timber hitch is best for this – see pages 26 and 28.) Shimmy up one tripod with the free end of the rope in your hand, and then brace yourself firmly while you pull the ridgepole up off the ground towards the point where the poles cross (see left). Position the ridge between the poles and then drop off. For extra security you can tie the ridgepole to the tripod, but that shouldn't really be necessary if the ridgepole is correctly placed and there is sufficient length in the crossed-over poles to hold it snugly. Repeat the whole process at the other end.

If you have difficulty lifting the ridgepole, you may be able to pull it up one of the side poles; if need be, you can saw off one of the tripod tips if it is in the way. Take care when climbing on the tripods, and keep your head and neck clear of the tips – they will scissor if things collapse. Be agile: try to anticipate problems and be ready to move quickly out of harm's way. Living rough will help you to rediscover the agility that you once had as a child.

Once the ridgepole is up, follow the directions as before (see pages 18–19). The freestanding version is more vulnerable to wind, so as an extra precaution tie a rope to the apex of the poles on the windward side and anchor it to something heavy – ideally a tree. In the absence of a suitable tree, you can improvise a sturdy tent peg by cutting a stout 4-foot length of wood, sharpening one end and hammering it into the ground (the back of your chopping axe will make a good hammer).

The shape of a good camp

There is something depressing about a camp with no logic, where everything is haphazardly strewn about. And when things go wrong (as they always do), will you be able to find a length of rope or a vital tool in such a camp, most likely in the dark and pouring rain? Then again, I hate those camping busybodies who march around with their trousers tucked into their socks, nagging everybody about the 'right' way of doing things and getting militaristic about tidiness in camp. The trick is to view a camp from a different angle. I can be as lazy as the next person, but I know that order is necessary to create the space, time and relaxed frame of mind in which to laze about with delicious abandon. With this in mind, here is how I lay out my camp.

All seasoned outdoorsmen or women are strict about how their kit is transported (be it by sled, boat, horse, car or bush plane) and stored. Separation is the watchword. All fuels must be kept as far as possible from food and water. It is amazing how quickly petrol, for example, can imbue food and water with a chemical tang that renders them unusable. I usually store all my fuel in one set place, often designating a particular tree as my fuel depot. I use another tree to store tools, hanging them up on the lower branches, with the exception of axes, which can fall with Damoclean intent. An axe is best stored on the ground, with its blade between the roots of the tool tree and its handle resting on the trunk. On a third tree I hang food.

Although in Britain your food stocks are not going to come under threat from large predators such as bears, game should be hung out of reach of foxes, and in general it is good to keep fresh food off the ground. In a dry environment the shade of a spruce is ideal for hanging grub, but in a temperate zone I would advocate knocking up a game pole in a shady place and lighting a smoky fire to keep insects away if necessary.

The good shitter

When staying in the outdoors for any length of time, I am a firm believer in the importance of a good outhouse, a place where one can sit and ponder life's many questions while answering nature's inevitable call. Many people are unnerved by the prospect of having to settle their bowel-related issues without the comfort of a plastic loo seat, but I can assure you that it is possible to do so in a stress-free way. In the Interior of Alaska, I travelled with a portable loo seat with folding legs that became a prized possession, and together we stopped off in some of the most picturesque spots imaginable. When making long-term camp, however, it is not a good idea to pepper your environs with nature's equivalent of landmines, as they will encourage unwelcome visitors such as foxes, while discouraging more welcome guests. Hygiene is important, and the answer is to dig yourself what can only be described as a good shitter.

Find a private spot at least 50 feet from camp and downwind of it, and start digging. Your hole should be about 3 feet square and at least 4 feet deep; if you are staying for a very long time it will need to be even deeper. Carefully pile the excavated soil near the hole – it will be useful later. Now cut two stout poles about 3 to 4 feet long, sharpen the ends and hammer each one into the ground at a 45-degree angle, at two adjacent corners of the hole. Cut a further two poles, each around 4 feet long, and position them so that they rest against the ends of the shorter poles, hammering in a nail or two to keep them in place. Against this structure use some shorter lengths to create two steps: one to support your posterior, the other for your feet. You now have before you a hygienic scaffold which will be very comfortable to sit on, despite appearances, and which will position your tender parts precisely over the middle of the hole.

You can sit on this delightful facility comfortably for as long as it takes (unless of course it is midgy, and I can't recommend anything for that other than insect repellent or full body armour), until it is time to flush. Lift your shovel from where it has been resting politely against a nearby tree and carefully pour some of the excavated soil over your muddy statement. By doing this you will spare the next user the horrible vision of your ordure, and the soil will go a long way towards controlling its noxious scent.

THE GOOD SHITTER

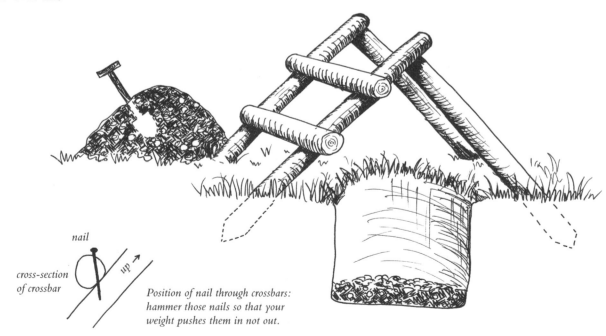

cross-section of crossbar

nail

up ↗

Position of nail through crossbars: hammer those nails so that your weight pushes them in not out.

Booze & company

We all know the effects of an excessive intake of alcohol, and even the best men and women can be transformed from mellow, well-adjusted individuals into antisocial misfits after a few too many. In the boonies, where there are no such conventional inhibitors as the police, bouncers or street lights, these effects can be multiplied a hundredfold. Overindulgence is a bad idea, as in the outdoors help is far away and you need to keep your wits about you. After all, accidents can easily happen, and I wouldn't want to be held responsible for people falling off cliffs when relieving themselves, stumbling into bogs or falling into their campfires. And hangovers under canvas are definitely to be avoided . . .

Generally a good rule of thumb is that certain 'types' will become even more exaggerated when given access to booze. Don't land up having to sit around a fire while some awful misfit swigs out of a bottle in between bouts of racist/misogynist/nationalistic/snobbish/know-it-all banter – this will introduce a thoroughly nasty atmosphere to your camp. My advice is to make camp with relaxed, easy-going people who are content to just sit back and enjoy time away from life's pressures. With such people, booze will work wonders, and only serve to enhance and lighten what is already good company. I have spent many nights comfortably slouched beside a fire, tin mug of whisky in hand, watching the sparks fly up into a starry sky while listening to a mysterious story or song.

All WGs will of course have their own preferences, but for what it's worth, I recommend two basic types of tipple. First, something soft and civilising – wine, for example – for sipping at leisure around the fire. This should be backed up by something strong enough to cut cleanly to the chase, as well as serving medicinal purposes if necessary. For this I recommend whisky – ideally Highland Park 18 Year Old, which is my personal favourite. I also carry Crabbie's Green Ginger Wine, which when mixed in equal parts with less refined whisky makes a wonderful drink called a whisky Mac, named after a Colonel Macdonald who nobly pioneered the mix. (No doubt Tommi will take a different approach to mixing her whisky Macs; ignore her advice! This is the authentic mix.)

Sometimes a good strong nip of booze can be useful when gutting and preparing game or fish, as the strong taste and smell serve to ward off any lingering whiff of offal. Brandy is best for this, and I suggest that all newcomers to field butchery carry a flask of good cognac.

There is nothing more demoralising than a corked bottle without a corkscrew, and this shabby state of affairs can lead to a range of botched opening attempts, frequently resulting in a loss of booze. Should this horrific possibility ever present itself, make your way to the nearest hazel tree and cut yourself a short osier the same width as the cork. Holding the bottle firmly, place the osier on top of the cork and knock it through with a few deft taps from the back of an axe or stone. Rejoice and pour double measures.

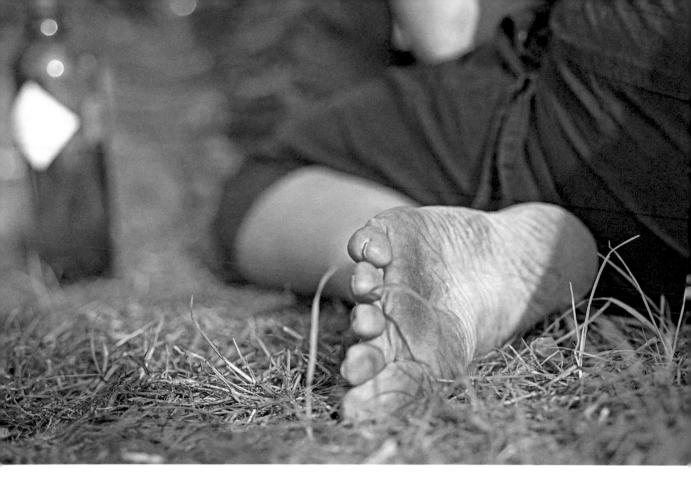

My best friends are knots & hitches

Mastering a good range of knots and hitches must become a passion for all WGs who wish to make camp, hunt, fish or travel in rough country. For as long as there has been cordage there have been knots and hitches, and many of the knots that we use today have existed unchanged for centuries. Every time I tie a knot I think of the hands that have traced the same pattern before me. Whose were they? Where were they? And who invented this useful knot in the first place?

Before I detail a few knotty classics, let us be clear about the basics. A knot is generally thought of as being permanent until undone, and — if tied correctly — should be failsafe. A knot will last as long as the rope. Bends are semi-permanent, and need to be checked and retied from time to time. Some of what we describe as knots are actually, strictly speaking, bends. The reef knot, for example, is more properly described as a bend, as it needs to be retied periodically and certainly can't be relied upon until the rope has worn away.

Hitches are extremely temporary, and exist to offer a bit of short-term assistance with lifting, pulling, carrying or tightening. However, as knot wisdom has been passed down to us from working men, whose knowledge is formed through action, we can be fairly loose about the definitions. In fact, the majority of our knots have their origins in the maritime trades – that is why Britain has been responsible for the invention of so many.

All knots, hitches and bends have one thing in common: they must be relatively easily undone, even after being subjected to great pressure. As with every section of this book, I must start with the proviso that I do not aim to provide a comprehensive knot guide – there are many excellent books if you wish to go into the subject in detail. In the meantime, here are a few of my personal favourites. If well learned, these should see you through most eventualities.

The bowline This is the king of knots, forming a useful loop that will not tighten or expand under any pressure, yet can still be undone easily. The bowline (pronounced 'bohlin') is a nautical knot that was first described by Sir Henry Mainwaring in *The Seaman's Dictionary*, although I am sure it has been around far longer. It was known as the 'bow line knot', and serves numerous purposes on boats, from the simplest (tying up alongside a quay) to the more complex (on square-rigged boats, tying to the weather leach of a sail and forwards to ensure that the sail could not be taken aback or blown in against itself). It has myriad uses in camp; I often use it to form a loop for towing, amongst other things, or to join two ropes together, by forming two loops, one inside the other. There are many variations on the bowline, but your best bet is to learn this first pattern.

The timber hitch This is a sublime hitch, so simple that it seems almost impossible that it could work so beautifully. Once again, its origins are nautical; a reference to it first appeared in *A Treatise on Rigging* in 1625. When I was living in the wilderness of Alaska, I used the timber hitch to lift and drag some very big logs for building a cabin, and I would have been truly stuck without it. The beauty of the timber hitch is that it cinches tight on an object and will not budge, yet is easy to untie when the pressure is released. It is ideal for dragging, towing and hoisting any object.

The clove hitch Also known as the 'builder's knot', this is a delightful hitch first written about in 1769 in William Falconer's *Universal Dictionary of the Marine*. It was used on square-riggers, where it was fastened to shrouds and ratlines to provide ladders for the sailors to reach high points in the rigging, and it still has many uses in sailing today. Recently I was anchored with my family off Norman Island, the setting for Robert Louis Stevenson's *Treasure Island*. I was reading the book to my two sons, and a ragged character called Ben Gunn said: 'You're a good lad, Jim . . . all of a clove hitch, ain't you?' The clove hitch will hold firm on a perfectly smooth pole if the pull is fairly steady and ideally from 90 degrees. It allows you to let out rope or pull it back in without having to undo anything. I use it to tie off guy lines and for many other odd jobs.

The figure of eight knot & figure of eight bend These
knots are first mentioned in *The Young Officer's Sheet Anchor* of 1808, though their
origins will be much older. The figure of eight is used as a stopper knot: it can be
tied in the end of a rope to stop it from coming out when pulled through a hole.
I drag a lot of kit about in a flat-bottomed sled, which is very useful in trackless
country. The two lines which I use for dragging a sled pass through holes in the
front of the sled, tied off in a figure of eight. A figure of eight can also be used to
put a stopper on the end of a length of rope or line so that it won't slip through
your hand, and of course there are many other uses, including joining two lengths
of rope of equal thickness. The result is a strong and rather pretty join.

Carter's hitch I use this to tighten a rope, be it over kit that I want tied down
or between two objects, such as trees. The beauty of this hitch is that once it has
done its job you need only give the rope a pull for it to untie itself in a second.
It can be tied and untied with one hand.

Sheet bend A sheet bend is a good quick way of joining two lengths of rope,
especially if one is thicker than the other. To make doubly sure of a good hold you
can thread through twice.

The slip knot I learnt this at around the age of twelve, when learning the
correct way to tie up a pony, as it is fast to tie and very quick to undo. For similar
reasons the slip knot has myriad uses around camp. I often use it when hanging up
game in a tree, and if I leave a long tail I can undo the knot even if it is high above
my head.

The round turn & two half hitches Another vintage and versatile
hitch used for hanging up kit or securely tying up items of any weight. It's as simple
and beautiful as that.

Coiling rope & hemming string There is always a use for spare
string or rope. In preference to biting my nails or picking my nose, when lazing
around camp I try to put my hands to good use and spend time coiling any spare
cordage, so that they don't lie around waiting to trip me up. If the rope is long and
could get easily tangled, I plait it so that it can be stored neatly and then uncoiled
quickly when needed.

I also hem all my bits of string, hemming being a method of wrapping the end
around the rope and keeping it from becoming a tangled and useless mess. My wife's
great-aunt, who lived in the Scilly Isles, owned a box that contained microscopic
lengths of string. It was labelled 'pieces of string too small to be of any use'. That
kind of attention to detail is what made Britain great!

KNOTS
& HITCHES

Bowline

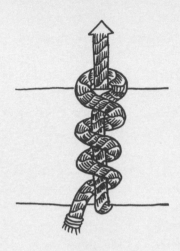

Timber hitch

Clove hitch

Figure of eight knot

Figure of eight bend

Carter's hitch

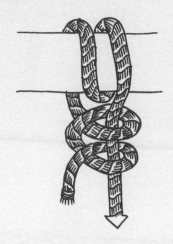

Sheet bend   *Slip knot*   *Round turn and two half hitches*

COILING ROPE

A good no-tangle method for storing rope.

HEMMING STRING

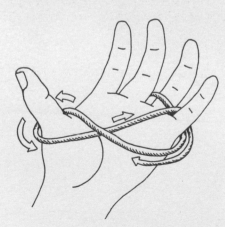

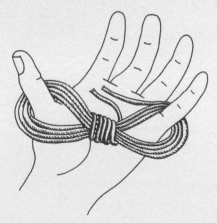

Your hand is made for bringing order to rebellious lengths of cordage.

Stores neatly, ready for use.

THE COOK'S CAMP

For me, the best part about camp was discovering how well you can live. Boiling hot water to wash my face in the morning was a ritual I grew to love; even if there was no river or lake to bathe in, I knew that my face would always be clean. Guy taught me about bush baths and tying knots so that we could always hang our clothes up to dry. Living in camp is not about letting your standards slide but more about rejoicing in getting back to the simple things in life. At night as I brushed my teeth before going to bed, the stars were the last things I saw, and the sounds of animals and insects lulled me to sleep. In the morning the crackling of the wood in the stove meant that my first cup of tea was not far away, and the world became a better place.

The wall tent had a shelf for my cookbooks, a cool area where we kept our provisions and a corner for muddy shoes. We had sticks on which we hung up our boots to dry by the fire and hazel sprigs across the ceiling where we hung up our clothes. I learned that you can go out and make a good camp and love living in it.

On our gastronomic journey, we hunted, foraged and fished, and sometimes we bartered our catch or exchanged labour for other ingredients. (A day harvesting turnips or weeding a field seemed light work when we got precious ingredients like lemons, oranges and eggs as a reward.) As a result we were able to feast our way around Britain. Our minds and bodies became tools of survival, so when hunting or foraging failed us, our wits and our muscle had to take over, and we survived by digging up fields for farmers, harvesting their crops or trying to preserve the food we had today to barter with tomorrow. I love the inventiveness of living outdoors: you look at what lies around you and see what it can get you – provided, of course, that you never take too much but instead always leave a little.

To enhance your enjoyment of such food and eat not as a survivalist but as a WG, every camp cook must travel with a few basic necessities. Depending on the cook, these basics can range from a tub of salt and pepper (mixed for ease of use) and a tin of coffee to a tuckbox packed with dry ingredients that will allow you to cook almost as you do in the luxury of your kitchen. Beware, though: the more ingredients you pack, the heavier the load you will have to carry. But this caveat must be tempered by the need to avoid the frustration of being in camp with a wonderful recipe in your head, only to find that you omitted from your 'must have' list a vital ingredient upon which the whole recipe hangs. Guy and I had the luxury of transport in the vegetable-oil-guzzling Santana and the haven of a large wall tent. This meant that I could carry a bountiful supply of ingredients with relative ease.

My larder ingredients

- **Extra virgin olive oil/sesame oil** (optional, for salad dressings and drizzling)
- **Olive oil/vegetable oil** (essential, for cooking)
- **Vinegar** – red wine, white wine, sherry, cider, balsamic; take at least two types
- **Butter** (for cooking and preserving)
- **Soy sauce or fish sauce**
- **Bouillon stock cubes**
- **Raisins/apricots/prunes** (these last for months and add a little *je ne sais quoi* to camp recipes)
- **Arrowroot/baking powder/citric acid** for the serious cooks
- **Capers**
- **Nuts** (if you are a good forager in the autumn you will have plentiful supplies of hazelnuts, walnuts and other nuts, but carry some bags of whatever nut takes your fancy to use at other times of the year and throw into recipes)
- **Coffee and tea**
- **Flour**
- **Soft brown sugar/icing sugar/caster sugar**
- **Honey/golden syrup/treacle**
- **Condensed milk**
- **Rolled oats**
- **Maldon salt/rock salt/pepper/peppercorns**
- **Rice/couscous/pasta**
- **Tinned plum tomatoes/dried lentils/dried pinto and butter beans** (if you can carry their weight, these will always come in useful)

- Tinned anchovies
- Dijon mustard/Tabasco
- Redcurrant jelly
- **Chocolate** (great for throwing into the odd recipe, as long as it's dark and full of cocoa. Guy would also add some hard Italian nougat into the box given half a chance, but you have to draw a line somewhere)
- **A packet of cornflakes** (see Rabbit Milanese, page 161)
- **Streaky bacon** (difficult to keep when travelling in the summer without a fridge, but invaluable in the winter for perking up scores of recipes)
- **A bottle of whisky** (or brandy or sherry, depending on your choice of tipple – and see page 24 for Guy's thoughts on this subject)
- **Cooking wine** (must be good enough to double up as a drink to have in the evening when the whisky runs out)
- **A bottle of ginger wine/port/cider**

Spice rack

Spices can be kept in small tiffin tins or, best of all, those portable trays for different screws that you can find in good hardware shops. The trays are easy to carry and great for housing lots of different spices, keeping them safe and well separated.
My favourite spices are:

- **Allspice** (whole, not powdered)
- **Bay leaves**
- **Cardamom seeds**
- **Cayenne**
- **Cinnamon sticks**
- **Cloves**
- **Coriander seeds**
- **Cumin seeds**
- **Dried red chillies**
- **Fennel seeds**
- **Juniper berries**
- **Mace or nutmeg**
- **Mustard seeds**
- **Powdered ginger**
- **Star anise**

Consider also making your own spice mix before you set out. Warm a few tablespoons of fennel, coriander and cumin seeds in a dry frying pan over a gentle heat for 5 minutes, together with peppercorns, a cinnamon stick and maybe some cardamom seeds. Blitz them all together in a spice grinder or grind using a pestle and mortar and store in a small pot to take with you on your travels.

Herb garden

I find cooking without fresh herbs tricky. I think keeping a little herb garden not only provides the distraction of watering and talking to the plants but also brings out one's lovely nurturing side, which might otherwise be buried in the bid for survival. I keep my herbs in a long rectangular tub that can take bunches of different herbs and which you can carry around easily. My favourite herbs are:

- Basil
- Chives
- Mint
- Parsley
- Rosemary
- Sage
- Tarragon
- Thyme

As you make your way around the country you will also be able to pick a large variety of wild herbs. Stay on the lookout and you may find yourself pleasantly rewarded with river mint, wild thyme, wild garlic, sage or wild fennel, to name but a few.

Kitchen kit

- **Large, heavy-bottomed frying pan** and matching lid
- **Casserole/Dutch oven** (see page 66)
- **A couple of small saucepans and lids** (to keep in heat and keep out insects and ash)
- **Small frying pan**
- **Sieve or colander**
- **Kettle** (absolutely essential for keeping spirits up)
- **A couple of wooden spoons** and spatulas
- **A set of teaspoons, spoons, forks and knives**
- **Bottle opener and tin opener**
- **Pestle and mortar** (for grinding spices and squishing garlic cloves and herbs)
- **Bin bags for rubbish** (Keep Britain Tidy)
- **Two kitchen basins** (for washing up and washing)
- **Good coffee pot**
- **Chopping board**
- **Large roll of aluminium foil**
- **Matches** (never forget these; for us they were for use in the unlikely event of Guy's flint failing him)
- **Kilner jars** (for preserving)
- **Muslin for protecting meat from flies, straining fruit etc.**

Rosemary, one of my essential herbs. It will grow even in the worst conditions.

- **Large chopping knife** (for almost everything)
- **Small knife** (for almost everything else)
- **Filleting knife** (for that beautiful bit of fish/meat you just got for supper)
- **Drying-up cloths, kitchen paper, washing-up cloths/brushes and an apron** (you'll be living in it, so make it a good-quality one, whether it's camouflage or Cath Kidston)
- **A small collection of plates, bowls and mugs** (these will be indispensable, so try to always keep them washed and safely packed away, ready for the next time you'll need them)
- **Tupperware/containers/old jam jars for storage**
- **Slotted spoon**
- **Rubber gloves**
- **Grater** (for horseradish)
- **Measuring jug** (although our trusty mugs came in very handy as measuring tools on most occasions. One mug is about equivalent to 200ml, and 1ml is approximately 1g in weight, which is useful when measuring things like flour and sugar)

And the most vital piece of kit . . .

A partner in crime

The beauty of having a partner in crime in this sort of caper is that it not only cuts down the workload (in our case that meant Guy chopping wood and doing the heavy carrying, amongst other jobs) but also means you have someone to share the good times with. A tiring day out hunting or foraging is never more enjoyable than in the evening when you are sitting by the fire, reminiscing with your friend about the day's events. Never leave home without one.

*'In the woods we
return to reason
and faith'
Ralph Waldo Emerson*

GETTING WOOD

If the WG can't get wood, he (or, of course, she) should give up even thinking of
sleeping rough. A true outdoorsman must learn to look into the woods in a different
way to the casual passer-by – the woodland is a potential storehouse of tools, and
fuel for your campfire. Therefore, a fundamental skill must be to acquaint yourself
with trees, and to have the ability to select good firewood.

Wood for fuel

One of your first jobs once you have set up camp is to build up a decent woodpile.
It is important to collect a sufficient supply to keep you going for a while, and to
keep topping the pile up to make sure you always have some in reserve.

Before setting out to gather it, have a think about the various stages of your
fire's life and the fuel it will need at each stage. When it is young, you will need
tender shavings, light dry twigs and maybe even feather sticks. As it progresses
through adolescence, it will need heavy dry logs to establish its character and build

certainty and conviction. As it reaches adulthood, it will continue to burn bright and hot, but will have the confidence to slow down a bit. At this stage you could add some green 'sappy' wood to make it burn more sedately, giving off a satisfying heat but using less fuel. A combination of green and standing dead wood makes the best fire, and, as I said earlier, if banked properly will burn for hours. It is important not to add the green wood too soon, however, or else the fire will go out.

To start the fire you will need plenty of light tinder such as strips of bark (the best is birch) and light flammable twigs (see also page 56). The best fire-starting twigs are to be found around the base of coniferous trees, where the twigs are dead, dry and resinous. On top of this, you will need kindling. I cut kindling from dry logs in various thicknesses, ranging from the width of a feather to that of a paperback book.

It is amazing how many people don't realise how important it is that the wood you collect for burning is dry; many times I have been presented with an armful of wood so wet that it might have been collected under water. It is worth restating that wood for burning should never be gathered from the ground, as it will always be damp. Instead, select dead wood that is still standing, which means finding dead branches or, if you are very lucky, a whole dead tree. Dead trees provide good habitat for wildlife, so be wary of taking them, but coniferous plantations often have many standing dead trees that can be taken without any ecological fallout.

The bulk of your woodpile should be made up of dry wood, and only when you have collected plenty should you set out in search of some green or live timber, which, wet with sap, burns slower and balances out the faster-burning stuff. Cut the wood carefully, so as not to cause damage to the woodland: find a dense overcrowded thicket which will yield good slow-burning round logs that can either be split or burned whole, and thin it lightly. If burning wood in a stove, you will need to make sure you cut the logs at the right length – I measure them up along my forearm. Below I describe some favourites.

Birch *Betula spp*

In Britain there are two types of birch: the silver and the downy birch. Generally the silver birch has a more pendulous, drooping set to its branches while the downy – sometimes known as hairy – birch has more upright branches. The silver has sharper-looking leaves and twigs, which have a kind of warty texture, while the downy has twigs with a 'fuzz' of hairs. There has been much crossbreeding between the two, however, so sometimes it is hard to identify exactly.

In the north the birch was associated with good luck and with Freya, the mother goddess of Scandinavian mythology. If I were a pagan (and I am considering a conversion), I would become a disciple of birch. You will be lucky if you come across a stand of birch trees, as the wood can fulfil all sorts of functions around camp. Birch bark makes a superb fire starter, which burns better than paper, and its wood makes good green logs. As an added bonus it has a captivating scent, like the kind of incense made of frankincense and myrrh that priests swing about in Catholic churches.

Birch wood can also be carved into all sorts of useful objects. Although the timber is not noted for its quality, it has a high strength-to-weight ratio (for this reason birch was often used to make aeroplane frames), and you can get surprising endurance from a birch-carved spoon or fork. The very blood of the tree is also useful: some seasoned bush-dwellers start each day with a cup of birch sap in the spring, swearing that the stuff is manna from heaven. Birch sap is beautifully clear, and can make a good water substitute when brewing bush tea. In the spring the trees are flush with gallons upon gallons of sap, and it is simple and harmless to the tree to tap a little. A friend in the Hebrides makes delicious birch wine by combining the sap with honey, cloves, lemon peel and yeast. The result is a golden-coloured drink that tastes like medium dry sherry, but beware: it is considerably more potent!

Ash *Fraxinus spp*   When I think of ash I think of strength and power. The Viking gods Odin and Thor both carried spears with handles made of ash, and for a long time the wood was used as a metal substitute, for instance as the outer edge of carriage wheels and as handles for all sorts of hard-usage tools. Its strength is still put to use in objects such as oars, polo sticks and even wooden truncheons. It can be viewed as mean-spirited – it is the last tree to get its leaves in spring and the first to lose them in autumn – but despite this cosmetic hang-up I am an admirer. For burning, ash is really the best wood around, as it has a very low water content, and even when green and unseasoned it will burn nicely.

Ash coppices well. (Coppicing is the age-old practice of pruning back growth on a tree in order to harvest young strong branches. Over time this activity increases the vitality and productivity of a woodland.) When correctly coppiced, a single ash tree will go on growing for many hundreds of years. Coppiced ash provides excellent poles for all sorts of uses around camp. I don't use ash wood for making eating tools, however, as the green wood has a smell that is off-putting.

Hazel *Corylus avellana*   For thousands of years the hazel tree has been a staunch ally of man, and it occupies a very special place in every woodsman's heart. It comes from a good family – it is related to the birch – and is known as the common hazel, hazelnut, cobnut or sometimes a filbert. The great joy of hazel is that it has perfectly straight, strong osiers of varying widths and length, which have a multitude of uses around camp. If coppiced every seven years or so hazel will replenish itself over and over again, lasting far longer than its usual lifespan of 50 to 70 years. Green hazel osiers make first-class fishing rods and cooking tripods, and can also be used to set up a long net, as well as standing in for all sorts of other odd but essential tasks, such as opening a bottle of wine (see page 24). Hazel can also be used in the making of coracle frames, wattle and daub frames, hurdles, fencing panels, bender poles for shelters, walking sticks, sadomasochist crops and much, much more. Hazelnuts, of course, are highly edible – see page 261.

To keep your fingers steady when cutting kindling, hold the wood from the side. Do not place a finger on top of the block.

Find the best cutting angle.

Let gentle rhythm and controlled force do the job.

Spruce and other coniferous friends There will be times when the WG will be far away from shelter, perhaps hunting for deer or seeking out mushrooms in some distant glen or valley, and may be caught out by darkness or bad weather. For this reason you should learn to siwash, which means making an overnight shelter using materials found in the surrounding environment or sleeping outdoors using only natural resources. (Siwashing is a Native American practice. The word was formerly used by white men as a term of abuse, as it was seen as lowly and animal-like to exist without a house. Now the term is back, and used in terms of admiration and respect.)

Coniferous plantations provide good refuge from wind and rain, as well as useful lengths of strong, straight wood for creating a shelter. The boughs can also be used as flooring, although you need to cover them with a tough tarpaulin or blanket, as some species have very sharp, rigid needles that can feel as if you are sleeping on a nail bed. I have spent some perfect nights within spruce A-frames, lulled to sleep by the sighing of wind in the branches and surrounded by the sophisticated scent of spruce sap.

Coniferous sap can also be used to plug cuts, and it forms a hard, antiseptic layer that stays in place for days. Pine needles can be used to make tea, but that is best reserved, in my view, for extreme situations, or for torturing your guests – there are plenty of alternatives that are far nicer (see pages 74–8). The only deciduous conifer that grows in Britain is larch, and while it doesn't provide shelter or bedding in winter, it makes very good poles, which are stiff and less prone to sag than other types.

Cutting wood

An axe and saw will be your main allies when carrying out these tasks, and it pays to know how to use them properly. All axes are potentially deadly, and many a hapless tenderfoot has done terrible personal damage with one of these awesome tools.

A saw will be necessary for cutting down trees and thick branches. When cutting wood from live trees, take care to cut low and ensure that you make the cut at an angle. Cutting low means that you and subsequent users of the woods will be safer, as there will be less chance of poking an eye out if you are moving around in darkness; cutting at an angle is important as a flat stump gathers rain, which leads to rot.

The trick to using an axe to cut logs is to understand that the game is all about angles, not brute force. Firstly, make sure that your axe will not catch on anything around you. Once this has been done, work steadily and deftly: bring the axe down on to the wood at an angle of about 45 degrees. By bringing the axe down firmly, though not with excessive power, it is possible to 'clink' perfect stove-sized logs from an otherwise unwieldy lump of wood. You cannot hope to master the axe purely through reading; find an old pro' who you can watch and learn from. In order to cut kindling from a log, there are a few useful tricks to bear in mind (see left).

*'If there is magic
on this planet, it is
contained in water'*
Loren Eisley

GETTING WATER

Any WG who embarks on a great adventure must stop from time to time to refuel. Like an engine without petrol, man without water is nothing. Water is needed not only to survive but also to maintain your fitness and awareness. A dehydrated WG is both a risk to himself and a danger to those around him: with a desiccated mind you may forget to handle a rifle or shotgun carefully, for example, or injure yourself when chopping wood or negotiating difficult country. Dehydration leads people to take the easy way, not necessarily the right way. When you are camping for a night or two, drinking bottled water is fine; however, if you are living outdoors for a sustained period you will need a clean source of water near to camp, and you will need to take measures to ensure that it is safe for drinking.

Clear streams and fast-flowing rivers are always good for water; however, in this crowded island you have to be careful, as the water may harbour sewage or other invisible nasties. If you are high up a river's course, and if there is no habitation, intensive farming or industry upstream, you can be pretty confident that the water will be clean. Whether or not you are prepared to risk drinking untreated water is of course up to you: I probably err on the side of risk taking, and so far I have come away unscathed. It is nevertheless sensible to take precautions, as there are serious water-borne diseases. One thing is definite: you must never, ever take water from a still or unmoving source, and if you are forced to do so you must rigorously sterilise it. Water purifiers are available from any outdoor store, and they work on various different principles. Mine works by filtering the water through three ceramic-based filters which catch any pollutants, but you can do the same job the old-fashioned way simply by boiling it. I am happy if water is boiled for a couple of minutes, as this will kill pretty much everything, but some hysterical people advise boiling for anything from five to 20 minutes. For good measure, you could use a few drops of iodine, which will kill bacteria but leave the water tasting nasty. As an alternative, you can also use water purification tablets. Some claim to leave the taste unaffected, but I have never used them and so cannot vouch for this assertion.

If you are unable to set up camp near a source of fresh water, in this rain-sodden country you can usually rely upon collecting some rainwater. I use a special plastic

COLLECTING WATER WITH TARPAULIN

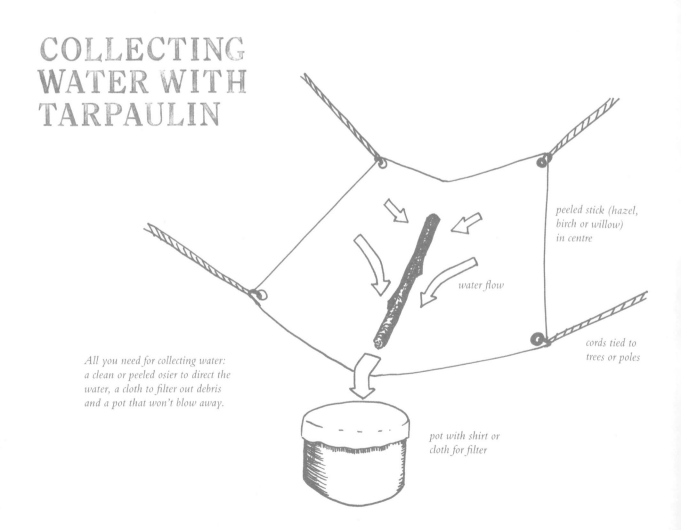

peeled stick (hazel, birch or willow) in centre

water flow

cords tied to trees or poles

All you need for collecting water: a clean or peeled osier to direct the water, a cloth to filter out debris and a pot that won't blow away.

pot with shirt or cloth for filter

flysheet that I keep solely for this purpose to avoid it becoming contaminated. I tie up the four corners of the sheet to trees or poles with the two rear corners slightly higher than the front two corners. I then cut a nice straight bit of hazel or birch and peel off the bark before laying it in the middle of the sheet to create a track from back to front. All the water runs dutifully down this track before flowing off the edge of the sheet. Below it I place a clean water storage jug, with a piece of clean cloth over its lid to collect any leaves or insects. The water is thus filtered as it runs into the container. If everything has been kept scrupulously clean there should be no need to purify the water.

In the unlikely event that you find yourself camping out in snow, you can fill a clean cloth or sheet with snow and hang it near but downwind of your fire above a water container. The snow will melt and drip through the sheet, which will filter it as it melts. If you collect water from a sedimentary river, it pays to leave the water to stand overnight to allow the sediment to settle.

With all these methods of collection, you can improve the taste of the water by re-aerating it – it is loss of air in the water that leads to that unpalatable stale taste. I do this simply by pouring the collected water from one jug to another from a height. It seems like a small detail, but if you have nothing to drink but water this will make an enormous difference. Probably, however, you will have other beverages at your disposal, such as wine, whisky, beer or cider for non-essential merry-making.

Hygiene

Hygiene is important at all times, but even more so in the field. Too many people believe that living in the outdoors means letting standards drop and having to put up with odious personal grime. Not so in my camp, where, if people become intolerably dirty, I take them to the nearest pond and wash them by force if necessary. I also remind my partners in the bush that if my standards ever drop, I am perfectly happy to be dealt with in the same manner.

It's not hard to keep squeaky clean in the sticks, and it's about feeling happy and comfortable in one's own skin. Being grubby leads to poor morale and gets in the way of making friends and helpful contacts while moving through the country. If the appearance and/or smell of a WG is off-putting, people will be reluctant to venture too close, and unlikely to be forthcoming with suggestions regarding, for example, the best sources of mushrooms, fish and game.

The ceremony of washing can become a joyful meditation at the start or end of the day, giving you a chance to reset your personal co-ordinates and feel that all is well with the world. I always travel with an indestructible bar of carbolic soap that never fails to generate a good lather for washing and has a scent that is reminiscent of simpler times. If you are lucky enough to be near fresh running water or a good lake or pond, you will have no problems: all you have to do is jump in and wash.

If not, you will have to carry water to camp in containers (I have a number of these, which hold 10 and 25 litres respectively), and conserve it carefully.

At a discreet location in camp I lay down a length of wood to serve as a washing block, and in the morning I strip off and stand on the block with my water container near to hand. After a brief dousing, I soap myself thoroughly from head to toe, and then rinse off. An invigorating wash is complete, and my feet have been kept clean by the block (which could be anything from a length of wood to a large stone). When water is very scarce, I stand in a tin tub, hold the jug up as briefly as possible for the first wetting and then pour the water collected in the tub over myself for the final rinse.

A sturdy bar of soap is easily packed: I use carbolic. Tommi introduced the sponge. I don't approve.

If you have forgotten your soap, or if you have become incurably rustic, there are some superb natural stand-ins. Horse chestnut leaves make a good soap substitute and are also mildly antiseptic: soak the leaves in a can of warm water before scrunching them up and rubbing them between your hands to form a lather. The best washing plant of all is soapwort (often found growing near the sites of Roman baths). Used for centuries for washing fabrics, it was even reputedly used to wash the Turin Shroud. It has also been – and continues to be – used to treat a vast range of health problems, ranging from venereal disease to eczema, bronchitis and liver complaints, and also acts as a fungicide. The plant grows in a straggly, tall shape with large pale pink flowers that have a distinctive clove-like smell, and can be found in damp places, beside rivers and in hedgerows, where it is referred to as hedge pink, amongst many other names.

You can of course heat water for washing, but this means using up more wood, as well as considerably more effort – unless you have a stove, in which case you can put on a pot of water to warm any time. In my view it is best to become acclimatised to cold water, and to learn to enjoy it. Do this by washing in cold water at home as often as you can. I have not washed in hot water for years, and only have the odd hot bath as a treat from time to time. Better yet, sample the joys of cold water swimming. Tommi was very good at dealing with cold water and I was deeply impressed by her readiness to (literally) take the plunge. In her last life I think she must have been an otter.

*'The fire had died down
to a great coal pinned
like a crimson rose to
the dark earth'*
Laurens van der Post

MAKING FIRE

I worship fire. Watching wood burn and savouring the sublime scent of wood smoke never fails to make me feel happy and in tune with the elements. Many times I have found myself alone and very far from people, dwarfed by the land around me and sometimes a little bit nervous about the creatures that I know surround me in the thick bush. In these circumstances fire has always made me feel safe and content, and I have sat within its orbit like a planet, comforted by the scent of coffee on a slow rolling boil and watching with childlike joy as white smoke curls up between the swaying trees.

Without a good fire your camp will be a sad and bereft place. Where there should be a womb-like point of warmth and security there will be only a dark and empty space. You will miss the merry hiss and crackle of burning logs and the whistle of the kettle as water comes to the boil for morale-boosting mugs of tea; and even the most effective camp stove is no substitute for cooking over charcoal.

During our gastronomic tour of Britain, Tommi and I depended entirely on an open fire and my stove, and it was good to see that Tommi shared my love of fire.

I learned to create fires that ministered to her every need, be it for a slow-burner, a hot flame or even an oven.

To be worth the title, the WG must be able to make fire pretty much anytime, anywhere. As a beginner there will be times when you feel humbled by it, and when your fire brings tears to your eyes as it wraps your face in sharp smoke. Sometimes you will create an inferno that burns out quickly and leaves you with nothing; at other times you will create a damp, mean-spirited fire that takes all your effort to keep going, and even then refuses to give out heat and warmth.

Once you engage in the art of making fire, it will become a guiding passion, and in the early days of the love affair you will find yourself scrabbling through the woods in darkness, crossing rivers and ravines and ignoring all risk to life and limb in your determination to sustain your fiery relationship. As time goes on, however, you will learn from these itchy lessons and find that you have at last become the master; you can take things more slowly.

As with almost everything else in life, the key to a successful fire is being organised. Start by thinking carefully about where to site your fire pit. You want it to be in the heart of your camp, with plenty of space around it for sitting and cooking, probably about 10 feet from the opening of your tent. If you need a fire for warmth – if the weather is very cold or if you are siwashing – the fire needs to be close to, but obviously not directly outside, the opening of your shelter.

If you have been clever and positioned your doorway at 90 degrees to the prevailing wind, the tent will not fill with smoke, but you will still benefit from the fire's warmth. On the other hand, if you are in midgy country, you may choose to place the fire upwind of your tent opening. The smoke will deter the little monsters from entering your tent, and it will also make all your clothing and kit smell heavily of smoke, acting as a further deterrent; and I'd choose smoke over midges every time.

Next make your fire pit. If there is turf, carefully dig out a square of a suitable size for your purposes, roll it up and put it to one side. (This is so that you can replace the turf when you move on. I usually water it and then wrap it up in a plastic sheet and store it in the shade, ready to be re-applied over the fire site when I break camp.) As you dig the pit, have a careful look at the ground. If it is pure peat, be aware that you could start a ground fire, so use a metal container to contain your fire. Dig the pit a foot or so down and line it with stone if there is some. Surround your fire pit with stones, heaped earth or even large green logs. These can be used to stand cooking pots on or to shelter the fire from the elements.

Now you need to gather fuel. As you will have thought carefully about where to site your camp, there will be plenty of wood about. Go out while there is still good light. First find a good-sized block for chopping (I usually find chopping blocks in devastated areas of former forestry, and I carry a small one with me in case I can't locate one near camp) and then stockpile a stash of proper wood. For more on all matters relating to gathering or cutting wood, see pages 39–42. If you can't find standing dead wood and have to use green wood at the early stages of the fire

HOW TO BUILD A FIRE

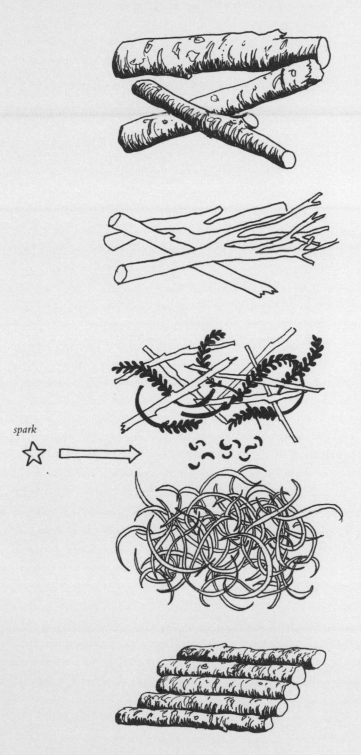

That first bit of thicker wood is now ready to be gently placed. Standing dead wood is always best; never gather from the ground.

Add good bone-dry tinder about the thickness of a thumb.

Over this nest place very fine kindling mixed with good flammable stuff like dry bracken and birch bark.

Make a little nest in this ball that is sheltered from wind/rain etc. and fill with something to catch the spark. I often file in some magnesium if my tinder is damp.

Make up a ball (bowling ball or bigger in size) of very light, very dry tinder. I love using roughed-up dry grass.

If the ground is wet make a platform from green wood.

spark

(it will burn more successfully once your fire is burning hot), use split lengths. As you gather fuel, take the opportunity to look around for mushrooms, edible plants and signs of animals – constantly keep an eye open for opportunities.

As well as collecting good-sized lumber for burning, collect what you will need to start the fire (see below) and anything that will catch quickly once the tinder is making heat. If there is nothing suitable, you will have to cut kindling or feather sticks back at camp (see page 40).

Fire starter

Before lighting your fire, make sure of two things: firstly, that there is nothing on the ground that might catch light, and secondly, that there is no danger of burning down a tree. Think about the wind's direction, and the consequences if it were to change. Be sure that you can control the fire, and that you have materials to hand, such as earth or water, to put it out quickly if need be. Sometimes just having a shovel near by is all you need to be sure you can control a runaway blaze.

Think also about what you want the fire to do, as this will determine its size, as well as the amount and type of wood that you need. If you simply want to boil some water up for a quick brew, you will need hardly anything; in fact a kettle of water will happily boil over a twig fire, which can be made very quickly anywhere. All you need to do is keep feeding the fire with twigs until the water boils.

Sometimes it is best not to build your fire too big, as a smaller fire consumes less fuel and requires less work to keep it going. A small fire can be very good for cooking, and will keep you nice and warm – you just need to sit a bit nearer to it than you would a larger one. A classic mistake is to light a blazing fire that you have to sit miles away from, wasting hard-earned fuel and heat. A small fire has the added benefit of creating less smoke and leaving little trace.

Most of the 'art' in starting a fire comes at the beginning, and if you build your fire correctly from the start you will usually have no problems. First you need to create a 'nest' of tinder, which is light, highly flammable material that will flare up immediately at the touch of a spark or match. Suitable tinder can be found almost anywhere – I fill my pockets with anything good that I come across during my travels, even if I am not planning to have a fire for a while. In fact, the longer that tinder stays curled up in a warm pocket the better.

One of the best kinds of tinder is dry grass. I often collect clumps of this, and when I have a good amount I rub it between my hands before storing it away. The rubbing breaks the grass down and softens it considerably, making it much more responsive to a spark. If I come across a birch tree, I gently peel off the dry outer layers of bark, and store this amazingly flammable material with the grass; birch bark burns better than paper. Fluffy seeds of rosebay willow herb and thistle are also good, as are cotton grass tops. In fact almost anything will do, as long as it is light and thoroughly dry.

Put the tinder nest into your fire pit, and then over it place more highly flammable grasses and fine twigs, kindling or feather sticks. Make sure that you keep the structure light and loose so that air can circulate freely through it. Now light the fire, either with a match or by putting a spark into the tinder using whatever method you choose. I usually use a magnesium flint, which is easy to carry and doesn't have to be kept dry as matches do. In damp conditions, you can scrape a little pile of magnesium on to the tinder, making it easy to light.

I am always armed with fire-lighting materials, including wind- and wet-proof matches, normal matches and a magnesium flint. Unless you are unlucky enough to find yourself lighting a fire for survival, you should never need to use chemicals or plastic. Don't ever be tempted to use petrol, which does nothing except create a massive whooshing explosion that singes hair, damages morale and leaves the fire structure stinking, blackened and impotent. Mother Nature has supplied all that you need to start a fire and keep it going – you just need to supply the spark.

(Left) Cut and place some thin lengths of bone-dry kindling.

(Middle) Make a nest and place your tinder in it, then use the back of your knife to make the spark. In this case, I am aiming the spark for some magnesium filings, as the tinder was damp.

(Right) If you have been mean with the tinder, you may have to help: blow steadily for a while.

Once you are experienced at making fires you can set yourself the challenge of friction fire starting, a skill that should be learned by all true devotees of flame. There is not space here to explain fully this delicate art, but there are sources that are devoted to this most ancient method of generating a fire-starting ember. It takes some time, however, so it is best to have some matches in your pocket as a back-up.

When you light the fire, white smoke will rise as the flames seethe through the waiting fuel: this is a sign that the fire is starting nicely. Enjoy the perfect scent of grass and twigs catching light, and get ready to gently place light lengths of wood on to the little inferno. As the fire grows in confidence, you can trust it with heavier lengths that will sustain it for longer, and add some green wood when you feel it is ready to slow down a bit. Now you can relax – the fire is ready to serve.

Tips for cooking on the fire

- Make sure that you have cut a great pile of thin lengths of wood for your cooking fire, or have a large stash of bone-dry branches and twigs cached nearby.
- When you need to be able to bring a section of your fire up to a frying heat (remember other parts of the fire might be providing a slow heat), simply lay light lengths of wood on to the embers. Blow for a bit to get them burning, and in a moment your fire will be hot enough to fry. It is a common mistake to think a hot fire needs big logs. The reality is light dry lengths and lots of them will create a ferocious heat. Keep adding as long as the frying heat is needed.
- To simmer or boil, put pans over charcoals that have a fair amount of white ash resting over the embers or use a slow-burning log.
- If cooking with the pot hung from a tripod, temperature can be controlled by either raising or lowering the pot. This is done by shortening or lengthening the rope, wire or branch pot-holder.

Extinguishing the flames

It is a sad moment when you come to kill your campfire, but nevertheless it is important to make sure that it is properly, thoroughly dead. Plenty of people have left their camp confident that they have put out their fire, only for it to come back to life and rage out of control. By the time you come to put it out, your fire should have burnt down nicely, and you will be able to crush it with the back of your shovel. I pour over a large quantity of water as well, before turning the whole thing over with my shovel and covering it with earth. I then stamp it all down, and pour over some more water until the fire is dead. If I am leaving camp for the last time, I replace the turf that I removed earlier, tread it well in and water it. The site will now look more or less as it did when I arrived.

A clove hitch is good for hanging a kettle or pot from a tripod. In this case the kettle can be lowered or raised without the hassle of the knot being untied.

A wonderful way to end a fire's life is to create an impromptu sauna. This works best if you have made your fire on a pebbly or boulder beach. Cover the fire with stones and pebbles until it is completely buried, and then build a tripod over the top (see page 18 for how to tie a tripod), using lengths of hazel, birch or whatever is to hand. Cover it with tarpaulin to create a tent, leaving enough room for sitting space around the stones. Bring a bucket of water in and use a tin mug to pour water occasionally on to the hot rocks. Soak up the steam and relax. Like all good things, this is best done in company, naked, and ideally with a gloriously cold river or waterfall near by to plunge into afterwards.

COOKING IN CAMP

I have always thought that simple cooking is the best. Of course it is a treat to eat at Michelin-starred restaurants, where hours of thought have gone into the presentation and flavour of every mouthful, jus, foam or demi-glace, but the kind of food that really gets my pulse racing is honest, unfussy good food.

There is a frisson to cooking outdoors. For a start, the food tastes so much better, probably because you appreciate it more. Also, the fact that you have to cook far from your own kitchen limits the ingredients and utensils you can physically lug around and thus cuts down your options, so you have to rely more on your wits and creativity than you do when in the comfort of your kitchen and its gadgets.

This also heightens the fun. Cooking outdoors isn't necessarily easy, once you factor in tasks such as transporting the equipment, setting up the camp and chopping wood for the fire. The labour can be back-breaking, but the funny thing is that the enjoyment of the food you prepare on an open fire is in direct proportion to the amount of work that has gone into producing that food. Once you've got the basics organised, you can get on and enjoy it.

Here are the bare essentials you'll need for the true freedom of cooking and eating outdoors.

Water

When cooking, you need water. You never appreciate the ease with which water gushes from a tap more than you do when you are far from one. Lugging a jerrycan of water up half a mile of steep woodland track to your clearing is no joke. And the speed at which you get through it can be both depressing and enlightening if you are someone who is starting to worry about rising sea levels, erratic weather patterns and plunging water tables.

Water is essential at a campsite for several reasons. When preparing game for cooking – a job best done well away from the cooking area – you need a basin of water for cleaning down. Salad leaves and foraged herbs should all be washed in clean water, which you can re-use as long as you boil it thoroughly.

There are myriad things for which you need boiling water: poaching game, boiling or steaming vegetables, boiling an egg for breakfast, etc., quite apart from the essential cup of tea to keep you chipper. Washing your face and brushing your teeth are vital to get you going and feeling civilised in the morning. Possibly the most important use for water is for putting out the fire after you've finished with it. Never, ever leave a fire still going: that is the easiest way to start a bush or forest fire. It is crucial always to ensure that you have enough water left over at the end of cooking to put the fire out, especially if you are breaking camp and moving out of the area (see also page 58).

Wood

Guy knows far more about wood than I will ever pretend to – for information on collecting wood for a fire, see pages 39–40 – but I am learning. Some split birch on a fire burns with a beautiful smell and hazel makes ideal spears for spit roasting. Give me some hard wood for a long burn and I'm in camp heaven.

Fire

There is a knack to cooking on fire, but once you know a few basic points it becomes an exhilarating and rewarding process, with more heat control than cooking in an oven at home. First you need to get the fire ready for cooking. (For making a fire, see pages 53–7.) When the fire is first burning, you can use it to quickly fry an egg, sear a pigeon breast or get some water on the go, but it is not until the wood burns to charcoal that you get a proper cooking heat. Before then, the flames are wild and will blacken meat on the outside, leaving it raw in the middle. Once the fire has burnt into coals, hold your hand a hand's length away from the fire. If you can keep it there for five seconds, it is ready for you to cook over. Alternatively, just wait until the coals have gone grey.

There are generally three heats you will need in cooking: a low heat for gently sweating vegetables or making egg-based sauces; a medium heat for frying onions or bacon or simmering stews; and a high heat for browning meat, frying fish or steaks or making omelettes. The fire will give you all these heats depending on the amount of wood you use and the time you give the wood to reach its core temperature, the optimum burn.

If you rule your fire calmly, it will work hard for you. Always have a tin of water by the fire, and if the flames flare up and get out of control, dip your hand into the water and flick water on the fire to temper it. Equally, if your fire is dying down you will need to build it up again. Shovel all the hot coals to one side of the fire and start building a new fire next to it with thinly cut lengths of wood. You will be able to carry on cooking on the old coals while new ones are being made next door. And while the new charcoal is being made you will have a fast frying heat. Guy, the arsonist, had a few cardinal rules which are worth remembering (see page 58). Fires are also wonderful for keeping cooked food warm. Just place a large, flat stone next to the fire where you can rest your pots and pans, waiting for when you are ready to eat.

Cooking methods in the bush

Anyone passionate about food and cooking will get carried away occasionally, but the outdoors is perhaps not the best place for it. Or is it? With the right fire and wood knowledge (see above), you'll be amazed at what you can do.

These recipes will also work well cooked in the comfort of your own home, so I have given adapted methods if you wish to try them indoors.

Pan-frying/sautéing
Armed with a large, heavy-bottomed frying pan and some wooden spoons and spatulas you will be all set to get pan-frying. This is the easiest and quickest way to cook outside. Get the pan piping hot, add oil or butter and get that sizzling before adding your ingredients. It is easy to burn things when pan-frying, so check the heat of the fire and if it looks too hot stir the embers with a piece of wood. See Guy's advice on the various ways to keep your fire at the right temperature for different cooking methods on page 58.

Good dishes to sauté include:
- Chargrilled pumpkin wedges with mixed wild mushrooms and sage beurre noir (see page 298)
- 'Devils on horseback' pheasant (see page 145)
- Warm beetroot and pigeon salad (see page 153)
- Rabbit Milanese (see page 161)
- Pan-fried eels with rosemary oil (see page 238)

Braising/one-pot cooking One-pot cooking is extremely satisfying. Layer your ingredients and leave them to cook slowly in a Dutch oven (see below) buried in the ground, or casserole dish on top of the stove, where the dish will cook away. There will be no more work to do until the washing up, so you can get on with whatever you want while the smells become richer and more enticing, minute by minute. When you are ready to eat, all you need do is lift the lid from the pot and tuck in.

Great one-pot wonders include:
- Rabbit, apple and cider stew (see page 159)
- Slow-braised rabbit with olive oil, sage and lemon (see page 160)
- Venison braised with chilli and chocolate (see page 167)
- Chestnut, thyme and potato soup (see page 274)

In-the-fire cooking The easiest way to cook food when your fire is glowing is to bake it in the embers. Root vegetables lend themselves particularly well to this type of cooking. Scrub the vegetables clean and either bake them whole or, if you are pressed for time, chop them into smaller chunks. Rub them in oil and some sea salt (and herbs, if you like) and wrap them in aluminium foil. Find a corner of the fire that you can access easily and tuck the parcels in the embers. Cover them evenly with the charcoal so that they will all be ready at the same time. Different vegetables take varying times to cook, so start testing them after half an hour.

Sweet potatoes, normal potatoes, parsnips and celeriac are particularly delicious baked in the fire. Make sure you have plenty of butter, salt and pepper ready for when they come out.

Spit roasting Spit roasting is my favourite type of outdoor cooking. Armed with some hazel spears or skewers, a simple marinade of olive oil and herbs and the meat for cooking, you can have a feast fit for a king. Spit roasting works beautifully with whole birds such as grouse or pigeon, with larger birds such as pheasant, chicken or guinea fowl, cut into joints, and with animals such as beef, lamb or venison, cut into hunks. All taste better the longer they are left in the marinade, but without a fridge hot weather may prevent you from marinating for too long.

Lovely recipes to spit roast include:
- Mixed game spit-roast feast (see page 142)
- Flash-fried Sicilian venison steaks with pine nuts and raisins (see page 168)
- Barbecued leg of lamb with laver salsa verde (see page 171)

Dutch ovens Before my first foray into cooking outdoors I had heard the term 'Dutch oven' but I had no idea that the world of Dutch ovens was so large and so complex. The original model is a cast-iron job that can roast a chicken or a joint

Venison meat is delicious spit roasted; the charcoals bring out the rich complex flavour of the meat.

of meat or bake a loaf of bread in a fire outdoors just as an oven would in your home. The idea is that you put the rimmed lid on the casserole-shaped pot and put the charcoals from your fire on top to create an oven-like effect. The pot (or sometimes kettle) normally has a flat bottom, three legs to hold the oven above the coals and a steel handle for carrying it. The name apparently originates from the casting process, which came from Holland in the 1700s. The Dutch oven is a wonder of design.

The original cast-iron oven may prove too heavy, unless you are staying in one spot for months. I always think the less you pack the better; otherwise you will be lugging around huge amounts of equipment. Instead you could look for a cast aluminium oven, which will be heavy enough when it is full of food. You can get a couple of different sizes: a shallow one for baking bread or biscuits and a deeper one for roasts. What you choose will depend on how important the gourmet experience is to you. We had only a deep one, as in times of need we had Guy's bannock bread to feed us (see page 72), which didn't require an oven.

As with a Dutch oven, when cooking in an aluminium oven you will need a large fire that will burn down and give you enough charcoal. Alternatively you can cheat and buy charcoal/briquettes from a garage, and then light these and use them to surround the oven. To get the perfect oven effect I recommend putting about

A Dutch oven, perfect for cooking stews and casseroles, not to mention roasts and even cakes and bread.

two-thirds of your charcoal on the lid of the oven and about one-third underneath (just inside the outer edge in a circle works well), but make sure your oven comes with instructions and follow them. The most important thing is to experiment with it a couple of times before an important cook-off. The last thing you want to be doing is messing around with temperatures when you've asked some friends to your camp for supper. Make sure you protect the fire from wind or else you will race through the charcoal and run out of heat.

Never use soap to clean your oven, as it will damage the non-stick casting. All you need is a stiff brush, some warm water from the kettle and a bit of elbow grease.

Good recipes for cooking in the Dutch oven include:
- Rabbit, apple and cider stew (see page 159)
- Slow-braised rabbit with olive oil, sage and lemon (see page 160)
- Venison braised with chilli and chocolate (see page 167)

Cooking in the ground
Cooking food in the ground is a wonderful way to slow cook a joint of meat, bake a whole fish or cook a stew. Essentially you need to dig a hole that is large enough to house the coals/wood that you are cooking with and the food that you are cooking. You can wrap food up in plenty of aluminium foil and place it directly on to the coals, before covering the whole lot with earth; or you can suspend the food over the fire before covering it, either in a Dutch oven or in parcels wrapped in banana or other leaves. Whichever way you cook, the most important thing to do is to seal the food totally in its container so that no moisture can escape and you have a juicy, succulent dish at the end of the cook.

Preserving
I once spent an unforgettable four days in a beach hut in Anglesey, living entirely without electricity, fishing and foraging for food. It made me appreciate the cook's most under-appreciated and valuable item, the fridge. So when Guy and I set off on our journey, we went armed with equipment to help us keep our food in eating condition for as long as possible: wine, rock salt, muslin and Kilner jars.

The very nature of living outdoors means that there will be periods of glut and periods of famine. Often when out shooting, for instance, you bag more birds than you can possibly eat. In times of glut, preserving food for a rainy day is the most precious skill a cook can master. In our case it ensured our survival in leaner times, when we could either eat it or barter it for something we could not get hold of, such as carbohydrate. Basic preserving techniques include: hot and cold smoking; dry curing; kippering (see recipe on page 240); pickling; and salting.

Kilner jars in different sizes are a great thing to carry around with you for storing the food you want to preserve; they have an all-important airtight seal. I used them constantly during our journey for potted pigeon, jellied eels, and fish rillettes, for example.

A word of caution

Unless you are camping in sub-zero temperatures, where there is always a chilled place to store food, when storing and preparing food outdoors where you cannot easily chill it you risk contracting the bacterium *Clostridium botulinum*, better known as botulism. Once ingested, the bacterium reacts to create a toxin in the body that is potentially fatal. In the summertime nature has no freezer, so go by a few golden rules to make sure you don't give up the ghost in such a silly way.

- Be aware that bacteria are massively sensitive to temperature. Cooling things down only delays the growth of bacteria; heating food to a high temperature for a good ten minutes will destroy them.
- Bacteria need moisture to grow. Storing meat in a pickling solution, brine or under fat, or smoking it for long enough to dry it out completely, will eradicate the growth of bacteria (hence the popularity of beef jerky in the bush).
- Be careful when storing any kind of food, and always err on the side of caution by keeping food in a cool place, e.g. in a container in a stream, or hanging in the shade of some trees.
- Eat any shellfish you catch immediately. They are a classic way to contract food poisoning.

Camp snacks

WGs will know that the most disheartening part of any journey is making camp after a long, weary day, only to find that there is nothing for supper. More importantly, there may be times when you feel physically weakened by the scarcity of food, just as you may be overwhelmed by glut when the hunting is good. When morale and energy levels are low, you are most at risk from the elements. Eating and drinking are great boosts to morale. The best tonic for flagging camp spirits is a cup of reviving tea, or perhaps something more sustaining. Within seconds the mood miraculously lifts, the sun comes out (metaphorically speaking) and the world is right again.

Over the centuries even the most hardened travellers have learned always to carry a few provisions tucked away in case food runs out. Guy would never dream of starting out on a journey without some bacon stashed in his belongings, while I am a huge fan of nuts for a sure-fire energy boost. Here are some easy-to-make snacks and refreshments: some that you could prepare prior to setting off and some that you can rustle up once camp is built in the evening.

Hazelnut butter

Makes about 300g
300g hazelnuts
½ teaspoon salt
¼ teaspoon soft brown sugar
½ tablespoon vegetable oil

This butter is a great way to harness and store the incredibly nutritious hazelnut. If you find hazelnuts, get picking at once. They are packed with protein, carbohydrate and fat and so provide bundles of energy for the WG. Get on with the fiddly business of shelling the nuts and make the butter to keep in your store. It is tasty on bread or crackers and provides the basis for a delicious satay sauce for pigeon, rabbit or squirrel with the addition of stock, chilli and spices.

Shell the nuts and lay them out in a single layer in a large, heavy-bottomed dry frying pan. Toast them over a medium heat for 5–10 minutes, shaking continuously, until lightly golden on all sides. Remove from the heat and pour the nuts into a tea towel. Rub them together in the towel to get rid of the skins.

Using a pestle and mortar, grind the nuts in batches to a coarse texture. Add the salt and sugar and keep on grinding. To make a smooth butter, add the oil little by little and grind until the mixture becomes a fine paste. Store in jars. This keeps for at least one month.

Fruit and nut bars

Makes 16–20 bars
100g blanched almonds
4 tablespoons golden syrup
2 tablespoons treacle
200g butter, and some for
  greasing the tin
200g demerara sugar
½ teaspoon powdered
  ginger
½ teaspoon ground
  cinnamon
300g rolled oats
100g dates, chopped
  into tiny pieces
100g apricots, chopped
  into tiny pieces

These delicious squares of chewy, nutty oats are a delicious, energy-packed snack to have with you on your travels. Make a batch at home, cut into small squares and wrap them up to take on the road, and you will know that you will not be short on energy.

Preheat an oven to 190°C/gas 5.

Toast the nuts in the preheated oven for 4 to 5 minutes until they turn a pale golden colour (or alternatively you can use a dry frying pan). This will release their flavour. Roughly chop them. In a saucepan over a low heat, melt the golden syrup, treacle, butter and sugar together. Grate in the spices and stir in the oats, fruit and nuts.

Butter two 23cm cake tins, preferably with loose bottoms, and press the mixture into them. Flatten the top with a spatula. Bake in the oven for 15–20 minutes until golden brown and bubbling. Set aside to cool for 15 minutes before cutting up. These will keep for at least 10 days.

Fruit and nut mix

Makes 400g
200g mixed nuts (e.g.
walnuts, cobnuts, seeds,
almonds)
200g dried fruit (e.g. raisins,
cherries, prunes, apricots)

An easy, fail-safe food to travel with. Carry this mix around in your backpack and you'll never be short of energy.

Toast the nuts in a dry frying pan over a medium heat until golden brown. Chop the fruit into small pieces. Mix together in a plastic bag. (You can throw in chocolate or sweets for good measure.)

Guy's bannock bread

Feeds 6–8
650g flour
2 tablespoons baking powder
20g sugar
a large pinch of salt
250ml water
1 tablespoon vegetable oil
2 tablespoons butter or
animal fat, melted

Carbohydrates are often the scarcest of foodstuff outdoors. Preserved meat after a big hunt can last for ages, but if you are unable to find a friendly farmer to barter with, you may find that those taken-for-granted vegetables such as potatoes, celeriac or carrots are hard to come by. Keeping a pack of flour in the camp kit can get the WG out of some culinary fixes. Bread is not only a vital, energy-packed carbohydrate but is also delicious with stews and soups for supper, or toasted and munched with a wild fruit syrup (see page 290) for breakfast.

Guy seems to have spent considerable time in Alaska living on this bread. Traditionally the dough is wrapped around a stick and cooked in the campfire like a kebab. You can add dried fruit, nuts or oats, eggs or honey to the basic dough to make all sorts of versions.

Sieve the flour, baking powder, sugar and salt into a large bowl and make a well in the centre. Pour the water and fat into the well and gradually beat into the dry ingredients.

Knead the dough in the bowl for about 5 minutes. It should be soft and pliable; add more water or flour if the mixture is either too dry or too sticky. Let the dough rest for 5 minutes, and then knead for another few minutes.

Roll it into balls the size of a small egg, and then flatten these on your hand, or roll them flat with a rolling pin, until they are ½cm thick. Wrap the breads around a stick or lightly oil a heavy-bottomed pan and cook over the fire for 25–30 minutes, until toasted on the outside and cooked in the middle. Eat at once, warm and delicious, or allow it to cool and wrap it up to take onwards on your journey. It will keep for a couple of days.

Chestnuts by the fire

chestnuts

whisky

ginger wine

This is the best camp food known to man. The combination of freshly toasted chestnuts, still hot from the fire, and a glass of whisky Mac has to be experienced to be truly appreciated. I urge you to go camping in the autumn for an opportunity to taste this treat. If it is a clear night, so much the better – you will be able to gaze at the stars while you enjoy them.

Mix the whisky and ginger wine in proportions that please you. I like two parts whisky to one part wine, with a generous splash of water to release the whisky's flavour. (Guy frequently scoffs at me for this, saying I am watering down the drink; see page 24. Of course he's the type who would be happier drinking moonshine, so I advise sticking to my more civilised mix.) Lay the chestnuts out on a stone or in a pan over the fire. Toast on all sides until they are lightly charred and cracking – this will take about 15 minutes.

Rub the chestnuts between your hands with some pressure to shell them (they will be quite hot, so be careful). As they cook, replace the toasted ones with fresh ones so that you have a constant cycle of hot, toasted chestnuts to munch.

Essential drinks

On our travels we honed some recipes for drinks using common wild flowers and leaves (many of which contain medicinal properties). At the end of a long day there is nothing more calming than the soothing sound of the kettle hissing and a mug of reviving wild tea between the hands. (Though you must be absolutely sure you know what you are picking before you make infusions so you don't poison yourself.) All of the teas listed here are best drunk without milk.

Delicious teas can be made with wild river mint, chamomile flower heads, lime flowers and borage, to name a few. Just steep them in boiled water when ready to drink. Here are some other good ones.

Yarrow tea Yarrow leaves have ancient therapeutic properties, purportedly used by Achilles to stem the flow of blood from his warriors' wounds; they are said to be a powerful astringent, so they are indeed used to heal open wounds. The leaves were mixed with elderflowers, wild fennel and peppermint as a remedy for colds and flu. Yarrow tea is supposed to stimulate the appetite and help poor circulation. For the WG, it provides a welcome respite from plain, boiled water when the coffee runs out. It has a curious side effect too: if the hardened adventurer drinks too much yarrow tea, he or she may find himself becoming unusually sensitive to light. Artists used to drink cups of it so as to equip themselves with a supernatural light perception.

Pick only young, fresh-looking leaves. Old leaves tend to have rather a bitter after-taste, although they can be eaten as a vegetable if you are really hungry – just sweat the leaves in butter.

Infuse the yarrow leaves in hot water for 5 minutes and sweeten with honey or sharpen with lemon juice if you like – I prefer the tea without either.

Heather infusion Make as you would yarrow tea (see page 74), using the heather tips. This tea is a mild sedative and is good for regular bowel movement.

Hawthorn tea Hawthorn berries are amongst the most widely found in Britain and were widely used by herbalists for their ability to strengthen the heart and cardiovascular system and lower blood pressure. If you come across a hawthorn bush resplendent in berries in the autumn, do try them this way: take 1 teaspoon of berries, pour over a cup of hot water and allow them to stand for 10 minutes before drinking.

I also like to mix hawthorn berries with yarrow and fennel leaves and infuse in hot water to make another delicious and relaxing drink.

If you find a bumper crop of berries, lay them out in the sun to dry so that you can take them with you for future tea making.

Elderflower cordial

Makes 1 litre
12 heads of elderflower
zest and juice of 2 oranges
zest and juice of 1 lemon
600g sugar
½ packet citric acid
*   (about 30g)*

If you find yourself on a journey in June you will most likely come across the elder bush in full flower. The flowers have a delicate smell and make a delicious and refreshing cordial. In ancient times the elder was supposed to ward off evil influences – see if it works for you. A dash of it is a great addition to a gooseberry or elderflower pudding, or you can even make an old-fashioned posset with it, the wonderful syllabub-type pudding our grandmothers used to make and which has made such a comeback.

Omit the acid and sugar and you will have elderflower water with which you can wash your face every morning. It is said to be a wonderful skin cleanser. We also found it good for bartering.

Pick over the elderflowers, removing the stems and getting rid of any insects. Do not wash them, or you will lose the precious scent. Combine the fruit juices and zest, sugar and citric acid in a large bowl. Bring 1 litre of water up to the boil and pour into the same bowl, stirring to dissolve the sugar. Stir in the flowers and leave for 24 hours. Pour through a sieve and keep in thoroughly cleaned containers. The cordial will keep for at least six months.

Dandelion and burdock

Makes 1 litre
200g nettles
50g dandelion leaves
50g burdock root, finely sliced
2cm piece of fresh ginger,
*   peeled and finely sliced*
juice and zest of 1 lemon
300g sugar

Dandelion and burdock was a soft drink my parents used to rave about when we were growing up. It tastes a little like ginger beer and was our equivalent of Coca-Cola. I was delighted when we discovered some burdock root in a field in the West Country. It is surprisingly good for you, with the roots providing essential vitamins and minerals.

Burdock root can also be boiled and treated as other root vegetables. See also the recipe for Potato and burdock root scones (page 273) – I can't recommend them highly enough.

Put the nettles, dandelion, burdock root, ginger and lemon zest in a large saucepan with 1.5 litres of water. Bring to the boil and simmer for 30 minutes.

Put the lemon juice and sugar into a large bowl and strain the hot liquid on to them, pressing down on the solids to extract all the flavour and stirring the liquid to dissolve the sugar.

Cool and store in a cool, running stream if possible, so as to enjoy lightly chilled. It will keep for up to one week.

Coffee in camp

If, like us, you are more hooked on coffee than you would like to admit, it is as well to keep an eye out for coffee substitutes on your travels. Although we wouldn't dream of setting off on a journey without a pack of precious ground coffee beans, they do inevitably run out. At this point a little plant knowledge comes in handy.

Dandelion coffee Dandelion roots have long been used as a coffee substitute, though they will never be a match for the real thing. If you are desperate, collect a quantity of the roots (single, long roots are the best) and dry them out in the sun for a day. When they are bone dry, remove the hairs, and using a pestle and mortar grind them up and add hot water, as you would for coffee (see below).

Acorn coffee Although at a stretch acorns can be used for food, they are pretty unpleasant to eat, as they are incredibly bitter. Instead roast them and turn them into a perfectly passable coffee substitute. Crack open the shells and roast the nuts in a heavy-bottomed pan over a medium heat for 15–20 minutes, until they are toasted on all sides. Using a pestle and mortar, grind them before toasting again. Grind to an even finer powder and add hot water (see below).

Making the coffee Without a cafetière you will find the old bush way of settling the coffee grounds an essential piece of know-how. Place the coffee or substitute into a jug. Boil the water and pour it over the coffee. Stir it around to create a whirlpool effect and allow the grains to steep. Then dip your hand into cold water and flick water over the surface of the coffee a few times. The action of the cold water on the surface of the hot coffee will make the grains sink to the bottom of the jug. Tap the jug sharply and then slowly pour the coffee, leaving the grains behind. Ingenious.

PART II

LIVING OFF
THE LAND

> *'Even the dumbest creatures in the slaughterhouse know what is in store for them'*
> Lewis Mumford

THE MILITANT GOURMET

In an ideal world, I would hunt for all the meat that I put on my family's table. Wild meat is healthy, as animals living in the wild tend to be leaner and are not pumped full of growth hormones. Killing animals by traditional hunting methods is also more humane: one minute the animal is happy and free, grazing calmly without a care in the world, and the next it is stone dead. It has been spared the horror of being herded out of its field, forced into a lorry and then corralled into the slaughterhouse, where its keen senses are singed by the smell of death. Pigs, which are regularly shown to be particularly sensitive and intelligent animals, have been known to faint from fear, so terrifying is the experience of their final hours. The animal has also been spared the terror of seeing people up close – and we are frightening creatures to look at. On the simplest level, the fact that we move about permanently on two legs is profoundly spooky.

Then, of course, there's the whole subject of an animal's living conditions before it reaches the point of slaughter: let's not even talk about thousands of turkeys stuffed into an intensive rearing shed, for instance. There's no doubt in my mind that if I had to be killed and eaten (and maybe Tommi and I deserve to be in our next lives) I would far prefer to be knocked off immediately and without warning, preferably at or just after dawn, when all I am thinking about is breakfast.

Subsistence hunters are amongst the happiest, most respectful and knowledgeable people that I have met. Needing nothing but their skills and their senses to score a good meal, they are happy because – in this respect at least – they are truly free. Clocks, timetables and cash are not needed in the simple economy that exists within communities who are able to hunt for most of their food. During our gastronomic tour of Britain, Tommi and I were lucky enough to experience this ancient and happy rhythm of life, and we found it liberating.

This chapter offers advice and tactics for the militant gourmet (or MG, as I will call him or her) when hunting for the pot in Britain. Even here, on this crowded island, wonderful meat can find its way to your table thanks to the careful application of a bullet or shot. I will also describe several well-tried, ancient and less explosive methods of taking responsibility for your meat, some of which – namely long and purse nets – are immensely effective and provide meat in grade-A condition.

There will not, however, be any advice on snaring. I don't approve of snaring in this country, or indeed anywhere where the living is easy: snaring may lead to a very painful, terrifying and drawn-out death. In my view, snaring can only be justified in survival situations, when because of extreme conditions people are unable to risk embarking on long hunts. In this country we have the luxury of being able to make the welfare of the quarry a top priority, and we should do so in every situation. All the hunting methods that I recommend kill the animal very quickly.

I must point out that book after book could be, and has been, devoted to each hunting method that I describe here. Take reading this as a first step. As I write, I imagine a worn pair of hands turning these pages, and the occasional snort emanating from a silvery height as age and experience come to bear on my youthful advice. Thus it is also with humility that I pass on, for what it is worth, what little I have learned so far. Hunting is a vast subject, and no matter how experienced I become I expect I will always find plenty of opportunities to marvel at my own stupidity. Nevertheless, I have caught good meat through each of the methods described here. I have also come home, many times, with nothing but mud on my boots. An empty game bag is as important as a full one, in my view, as failure in the field breeds respect. We must keep learning from experience as well as continually debriefing those who know better, in the hope that, next time, there will be meat.

I must mention a personal itch, which is bragging about hunting: generally I feel that killing is a subject for modesty and restraint. However, even I wouldn't deny the hunter-gatherer, at the end of a successful day, the satisfaction of sharing the highs and lows of his day. When the quarry has been beautifully plucked, gutted and prepared for the pot, and the smell of cooking is wafting through the air – that is the time to laugh, rejoice and tell inflated tales. The plate before you shows that you have killed for the only reason that can be defended: you killed for food.

The most effective way of getting wild meat for the pot is through the skilled use of a shotgun or rifle. The shotgun is an absolutely superb tool for the devotee of wild meat, and the MG must become adept at handling one. The rifle involves more complication, in terms of both licensing and use, but is necessary if you wish to kill larger animals such as deer. The design of each weapon is completely different, as is their method of use. I hardly need say that both are lethal if misused, and thus must be approached with great care and attention.

The shotgun

Nothing beats the shotgun as a means of killing a fast-moving animal for the pot.

There are five basic types: single-barrel, double-barrel, pump-action, semi-automatic and bolt-action. In some parts of the world shotguns are used for hunting quarry as large as deer and wild boar; in Britain, however, the shotgun is used mainly for bringing birds and small four-legged animals to the table. At appropriate ranges a shotgun is an exceptionally effective and humane weapon that kills instantly. (The range of a shotgun can extend to a maximum of 60 yards, but the weapon is at its most effective at 40 yards and below.)

The theory behind its design is that whereas a single projectile or bullet can seldom be relied upon to intercept a fast-moving target, the shotgun's wide pattern of shot increases the chances of success by covering an area through which the quarry passes. If a hunter locks on to the flight pattern of a pheasant, for example,

SWING THROUGH

A shotgun is about movement: find the line of flight, pull through it and fire, then follow on.

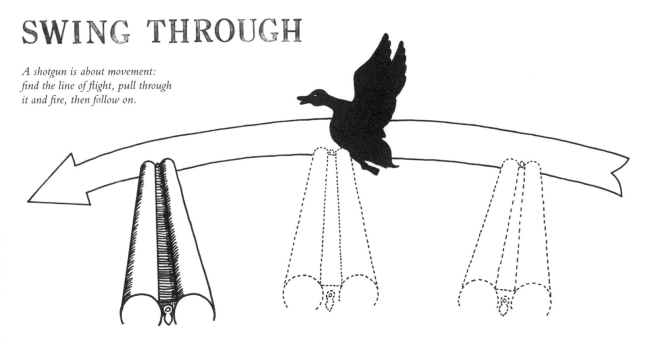

he can swing the muzzle along the arc of flight, aim ahead of the bird and then fire. The hope is that a fatal mid-air collision will occur between the bird and one of the pellets that make up the cone of shot.

CONE OF SHOT

As the shot leaves the barrel it widens out, becoming less densely packed. The art is to hit a bird with just enough shot to kill it but not enough to badly damage the flesh or to wound. To do this the MG must learn about range, as well as the best shot size for the quarry.

The beauty of a shotgun is that the type of shot used can vary. Shotgun cartridges may contain as many as 395 pellets. These spread out as they leave the gun in an elongated cone shape. For a light quarry, you might use a dainty shot, so as to maximise the chances of keeping the meat in good shape as well as sending more pellets out to reach a smaller target. For faster, larger quarry, a heavier shot can be used, to ensure a good clean kill.

To be a capable gunner you must make quick judgements about the range of the quarry in relation to your position. Shotgun pellets lose their velocity very quickly (unlike the ballistically efficient rifle bullet) and if the animal is too far away they may not strike it with sufficient force for a clean kill. Thus the MG must never take a chance on a long bird, as this will lead, more often than not, to injury and shame. Yet here is the rub: if you get overexcited and shoot too soon, the bird will be hit with outrageous force and often rendered inedible. It will die instantly but pointlessly, as you will be left with nothing more than a mass of shattered bone and pulped flesh. Thus the MG must practise restraint: if a bird lifts at or near your feet you must prepare yourself for the shot, but delay until it is distant enough for it not to be pulped.

With sufficient practice, the use of the shotgun becomes instinctive, and as with everything in life, success or otherwise is all about timing. Once you have started the swing, you must finish it: to stop halfway is to render the whole act useless; to stop and think is to miss a chance. The shotgunner does not aim at the quarry. Instead, you must recognise it, point, swing and fire, all in a single movement.

Types of shotgun
Shotguns come in a number of different bore sizes or gauges. For most of the world's hunters three bore sizes dominate: 12, 16 and 20 bore. In Europe the dainty 28 bore is also used, as well as the .410. Without delving into it too deeply, the 'bore' refers to the opening at the end of the shotgun barrel, from which the shot is fired. The number of the bore is a very old-fashioned way of defining the power of the shotgun. This is calculated by the number of lead bullets that together weigh one imperial pound; so the higher the bore number, the smaller the lead balls, thus the smaller the diameter of the cartridge case. In most countries hunting with a bore heavier than 12 is forbidden; in Britain and the United States, however, heavier bores are permitted. I once shot a 10 bore and it felt as though I had shouldered one of Nelson's cannons. I shudder at the thought of a 2 bore.

Amongst standard-sized shotguns the 12 bore is the dominant size, as it can use a wide-diameter cartridge and thus propel a good amount of pellets. The recoil (or kickback) is quite heavy (around 40 pounds), however, and thus MGs of a slight build or shape might do well to use a lighter bore such as a 20 or even a 28. For grace and lightness, I recommend the use of a classic side-by-side shotgun.

Here, for those considering the idea of converting the pantry to a gunroom, a quick note on types of shotgun might be useful. The side by side (s/s) is a double-barrel shotgun where the barrels are aligned beside each other. Traditionally this design was the standard. Another type of double barrel is that called an over and under (o/u), where one barrel sits on top of another. Both the s/s and o/u rely on the gunner manually reloading each barrel after firing two rounds. The gun is broken or opened and two cartridges are slipped in after the empty cases have been either automatically ejected or manually pulled out.

Some shotguns only have one barrel and only fire one round. Of these, a pump-action shotgun allows the gunner to pull cartridges from a magazine into the breach by pumping the forestock back and then forward. As the forestock moves back, the empty case is ejected and a new round chambered. This system is rugged and very reliable.

In bear country I carried a pump-action shotgun with eight rounds in the magazine just in case I disturbed a grizzly. The pump design was also very good in arctic temperatures, as it unjammed quickly when frozen. In the UK it is illegal to carry a pump that fires more than three rounds. The only word of caution on these guns is that they might not suit a short-armed person, as they jam if the pump action is not fully extended.

Semi-automatic shotguns feed a new round in automatically and need no manual reloading between shots. This type of gun can be unreliable and hard to mend in the field. It also needs very thorough cleaning in order to avoid jamming.

Bolt-action shotguns are heavy, cumbersome and slow to reload, as the bolt action has to be larger than usual to handle the shot cartridge. They exist only because they are cheaper than most other types of shotgun.

The rifle

Unlike the short-range shotgun, which is designed to send a spreading pattern of shot towards a moving target, the rifle is loaded with single bullets and designed to kill a stationary or slow-moving animal at a considerable distance. Whereas a shotgun is superbly useful at 40 yards, with a rifle an MG could bag a red deer at 200 yards, or even further if experienced. In open country a rifle can kill at over a mile, the bullet sometimes leaving the muzzle of the rifle at over 30,000 feet per second – and bringing a whole new meaning to the term 'fast food'. Experiments conducted by boffins with a penchant for explosions have shown that the whole event, from deciding to fire until the moment of the bullet's impact, can be over in less than one second.

There are some riflemen who are completely inept with a shotgun, and vice versa. This is because the use of a shotgun is very different from that of a rifle. A shotgun is a weapon of movement and estimation, requiring the hunter to make quick calculations before pointing at a quarry on the move. The rifle, on the other hand, is a precision instrument which demands absolute stillness as the user aims directly at a point on the animal's body.

Pointing a shotgun is rather like hitting a tennis ball with a racket: it is about hand–eye co-ordination and follow through. Aiming a rifle is about lining up a target through sights or looking through crosshairs. A shotgun has a smooth bore, which does not direct the pellets, whereas a rifle has a barrel that is spiralled internally with grooves that direct a single bullet by sending it into a tight spin as it leaves the barrel.

Both weapons kill instantly, but in quite different ways. The shotgun often kills through sheer shock as much as by any internal damage, whereas the rifle bullet singles out a vital organ – usually the heart or brain – and destroys it. When the bullet strikes the animal, the impact flattens the soft metal, thus widening its diameter and making it even more destructive. If used well, the rifle is very humane as the animal has been taken by surprise; thus when killed the creature will be in a completely relaxed state. It will provide superb meat for the table, as you can aim at a part of the animal that is inedible, which means that nothing is wasted; using a shotgun may lead to spoiled meat, as the shot that peppers the animal's body may rupture the intestines. A rifle is not just useful for large animals, either: a rabbit, for example, can be killed with a rifle as well as a shotgun.

Types of rifle
There are six main types of rifle: lever action, pump action, semi-automatic repeaters, double barrel, single barrel and finally the repeater with bolt action. The most common is that with the bolt-action mechanism, patterned on the Mauser action developed in Germany. The bolt-action design is simple and reliable, and no other design has ever improved upon it. Rifle strength is measured in calibre, which indicates how large a bullet can be handled by that particular weapon. There is a large variation: some rifles have a calibre sufficient to fell a dinosaur, while others are better suited to dealing with rabbits.

Ideally the MG would have two rifles. The first would be light calibre, for killing small game effectively without destroying the meat. The ideal calibre for this job is the .22 rimfire, loaded with hollow-point rounds. These rounds are designed to deform quickly on impact, leading to massive damage and thus a very quick, humane kill; also, as they deform easily, they are less likely to ricochet than a harder bullet.

The second rifle in the MG's cabinet should be a heavier centrefire rifle, suited to the job of quickly killing larger game such as deer or wild boar. Here a .308 calibre offers considerable flexibility, as it can handle bullets of various weights. (Bullet weights are measured in grains, a British weight measurement originally based on a grain of barley.) A .308 calibre rifle will be able to fire bullets as light as 130 grains as well as heavier rounds up to 180 grains.

TYPES OF RETICLE

*There are many types of aiming
reticle. Here are three classics.*

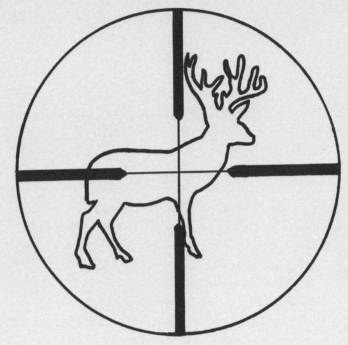

Single crosshairs: very simple to use,
but slightly less effective at bringing the
point of aim quickly into focus.

Dual thickness crosshairs (above and
below): the gap between the thick outer
lines guides the rifleman's eye swiftly to
a point of aim. Good for most hunting.

Post and crosshair reticle: the thick-
bottomed post is easier to see in poor
light and the single crosswire helps to
avoid tilting the rifle off the aim.

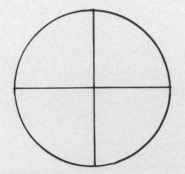

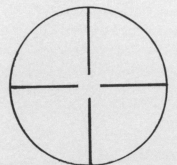

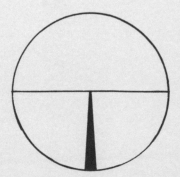

Optics & sights A rifle needs to be aimed with great accuracy in order to ensure that the bullet ends up in precisely the right place. Thus you must be fully conversant with the sighting apparatus of your weapon and its use. Rifles can have either telescopic sights, or mechanical or steel sights, but telescopic sights or scopes are used most widely for hunting. Scopes magnify the target and assist the hunter by gently lining up his aim with the help of an aiming reticle. The three main types used for hunting are crosshairs, the dot and the post.

Scopes are highly effective, but they can be problematic in rain or snow and add weight and expense to your hunting trip. They can also lead to overconfidence, tempting people to take unduly long shots. In close-up scenarios they are not helpful, as instead of seeing the whole animal you simply see a blur of hair and colour, which makes it difficult to aim accurately. Nevertheless, if you are setting out to hunt large animals at a distance, there is no substitute.

Mechanical sights come in two kinds: open sights and peep or aperture sights. The open sight allows the hunter to fix the target over a V- or square-shaped rear notch and a front post at the end of the barrel. Aperture sights have the hunter looking through a rear ring. Mechanical sights are rugged and less vulnerable to being damaged than a scope. With mechanical sights the hunter might also use more fieldcraft to get nearer to his quarry, and thus only shoot when feeling close enough, which can only be a good thing.

What is essential with both types of aiming system is that they are properly 'sighted in' and regularly checked. Simply put, a hunter must ensure that his aiming sights will send a bullet exactly where he wants it to go at a given range. A rifle can be sighted in to hit the bullseye at 25, 100 or 200 yards, for example. The only way to sight in a rifle properly is to spend some time shooting at a target at the desired range and make adjustments to the windage and the elevation of the scope or sight.

Safety & the law

Britain is a crowded country and thus, quite rightly, has strict firearms laws. You cannot legally purchase a shotgun or rifle unless you have a certificate granted by your local Chief Constable of Police. You must demonstrate that you have legitimate reasons for owning a weapon, and that it will be stored in a secure place, such as a steel locker bolted to the floor and walls. In order to get these permissions your background will be rigorously checked, and if your past resembles that of one of the Corleones you might have to forgo the cordite and skip to the section on nets and ferrets.

Where firearms are concerned, safety is paramount. Shotguns and rifles are deadly at the point where the breach is loaded with a live round. Here are some golden rules:

- No gun, loaded or unloaded, should ever be pointed at anyone.
- A shotgun should always be carried broken and unloaded over the forearm, so that it cannot fire under any circumstances and this can be seen by all the world.
- Never trust the safety catch – many experiments have shown that a dropped firearm will go off even if the safety catch is on.
- Never, ever carry a round in the breach. This is the only way to be absolutely safe – if there is nothing there, the gun cannot fire.
- Shotguns should be unloaded before crossing a ditch or climbing a fence, and all guns should be unloaded before being placed in a car or brought home. Many an 'unloaded' gun has killed and maimed.
- When closing a loaded shotgun, keep the barrels pointing down, and bring the stock up gently but firmly.
- Only when you are settled in position to fire, when the weapon is pointed away from people and at your quarry, should you chamber a round. Then the safety catch will be in action, but with the added safety of a backstop behind it to stop the bullet from dangerously continuing on in its trajectory. When ready to fire, you can release the safety catch.
- It is illegal to shoot one hour before sunrise and one hour after sunset.

Before loading a gun, you must look through the barrels to check that they are clear of any detritus, and you must be very careful to keep them from getting clogged up, as they do by prodding the muzzle into the ground, for example. If a bullet travelling at over 900 metres per second or a load of shot hits a clod of earth, the barrel will blow up, causing death or severe injury.

With a rifle, a backstop is very important, so that whether or not you hit your target you can see where the bullet will land up. One can all too easily imagine a scenario where an inexperienced marksman takes a shot at a deer on the skyline and misses, while a fraction of a second later, nearly a mile away, Mrs McGill hesitates while hanging up her washing, wondering what flying insect made that odd noise. Little does she know that a lethal piece of metal has just singed through the air, missing the top of her head by centimetres.

Finally, before using a gun on live quarry you must get to know it, so that you are completely familiar with how it shoots. In my view it is irresponsible to attempt to shoot wild game until you have reached a certain level of skill. For shotguns, use a clay pigeon shooting school for practice, and for rifles a range. Never allow your understandable desire to be seen as a good shot or stalker to cloud your judgement. If you are a beginner, make this clear to those around you so that they can be extra vigilant on your behalf – this will afford you much more respect, as well as giving you the opportunity to learn. Even if you are experienced, make a habit of reminding yourself that you do not know it all, and that you must keep learning. This way you can enjoy many fascinating and fulfilling days' hunting without the unfortunate downside of killing yourself or an innocent stranger.

Hunting with a shotgun

Here is a general shotgun hunter's principle: when hunting small game, particularly birds such as pheasant or partridge, you must first flush the creature from whatever cover it is hiding within. Pheasants resist flying if possible, and only take their chances on the wing if they cannot run any more. Many a hunter has set out hopefully after whole coveys of birds, only to watch them 'disappear', seemingly melting away like a platoon of Viet Cong insurgents. What has actually happened is that the birds have been running from him into thick cover, ducking and weaving through the undergrowth, or simply curled up very quietly, allowing their perfect camouflage to take effect. The lone hunter might be lucky enough to unseat a sitting bird by walking close enough to scare it into the air, but the chances will be decidedly slim.

Generally speaking, there are two methods of hunting effectively for pheasant, partridge and grouse. The first uses people and dogs to drive and flush the birds over a line of waiting guns; this is known as driven shooting. The second entails simply walking out alone with a gun and a dog, known as walked up or rough shooting.

Driven shooting This is a relatively complicated affair, utilising the skills of a number of people, usually headed up by a gamekeeper, who is responsible for ensuring that the shoot operates with military efficiency. He plays the role of general, organising beaters, who move noisily through thick cover, beating the vegetation with sticks so as to flush sitting pheasants into the air towards the line of waiting guns. The keeper also uses dogs to help lift the birds, and to retrieve shot birds that have fallen into deep vegetation or even begun to float mournfully down picturesque yet inaccessible streams.

All driven shooting places great emphasis on marksmanship. In a classic driven pheasant shoot, eight guns or armed people will spend a day moving from one drive to the next. At each drive the guns will each be assigned a peg or place to stand, usually within clear sight of their neighbours. The gun then waits for a pheasant to be driven over or near to his position. He will hear the distant line of beaters advancing, and at last the rusty wheel-turning call of a cock pheasant may precede the sight of the first bird, powering up high into the air in search of safety. Soon the air will be full of birds, soaring up and across the line of guns.

The shooters need to keep calm and level headed. On fixing on their quarry, they must assess whether a bird is too low, and thus dangerous to shoot, or too high, when a shot might wound without killing. They must also avoid shooting the bird at too close range, as this will destroy the meat, and of course they must keep a watchful eye out for the position of their neighbours. It is crucial that all these observations and judgements are made very quickly, and only when satisfied on all counts should the shooter line up with the quarry and take the shot. If the circumstances are not right, he must let the bird fly past, but if he decides to shoot he must do so confidently and decisively.

Generally pheasants present themselves singly, allowing the shooter a degree of space in which to think. Driven grouse and partridge, on the other hand, often fly in good-sized coveys or groups. This can be confusing for an inexperienced gun, who might be tempted to just fire 'into the brown', which almost invariably leads to a miss. In this situation the gun must carefully pick out a single bird within the group and lock on to its line of flight before taking the shot.

Driven shoots are very successful, and will often result in well over 100 birds being killed within the day. Their carcasses are carefully hung in a game larder, where they are kept for the game dealer, who will have the creatures plucked, gutted, butchered and packed for market.

It is a fact that many people do not approve of driven shooting, as it is perceived as wasteful to shoot so many birds on one day. In fact, it is very rare for shot birds' lives to be wasted, and driven shooting supplies the bulk of game birds to our dining tables, as a game dealer is linked to every driven shoot. The system is not intensive, as shooting is kept within strict seasonal rules, to ensure that the birds have peace and space to breed (for dates of shooting seasons for different species, see page 307).

Unlike much of the other meat that we buy, these creatures live within a superb natural environment, with additional bonuses such as extra winter feeding thrown in as well as the luxury of an armed guard to deal with such predators as the rapacious fox. They are free to wander about happily. One crisp morning they hear movement in their thick cover and decide to get out of the way. They scurry in the opposite direction and then decide to make a flight for it. Up they go — and then they are dead. Next stop the bird arrives at the game dealer or butcher, ready for eating. What's to object to? More difficult to justify is shooting's role as a sport. This is a complex debate and one I don't wish to go into. However, my instinct tells me that since man first walked the earth, he has enjoyed his most fundamental role in life: the need to find food for himself and his family.

Rough shooting
Rough shooting is a much less organised affair, simply involving a lone person going out into the countryside in search of game. There is a great sense of freedom in this method of hunting, as the shooter is free to roam (within agreed limits) wherever he chooses, taking advantage of any opportunity that presents itself.

The rough shooter must enter the world of his quarry: he must stray from the path and work hard for his meat. When a chance comes, he must act with speed and accuracy, as he may not get lucky again. As a method of food gathering, rough shooting is about as far away from convenience food as you can get, as you must commit to many hours of searching, with a strong possibility that there will be no result. When the rough shooter gets lucky, however, it is a great feeling: the carcass weighs heavily in your game bag, and there's the sense of a battle won fair and square. Unlike driven shooting, where it is possible to become quite abstracted from what you are doing, with rough shooting there is no hiding from the fact that you have killed a living creature. And with this reality comes great responsibility – you are responsible for everything: finding the quarry, flushing it into range, killing it and then carrying and preparing the carcass. Nothing is done for you.

A dog is a great asset to the rough shooter – in fact I would go so far as to say it is essential (see page 98). However, an uncontrolled or poorly trained dog may scupper your chances altogether. If the dog charges ahead, you will be subject to a particularly enraging scenario in which you find yourself watching bird after bird flushed well out of range of your shotgun.

An effective dog will work closely with the hunter, carefully quartering the ground ahead and never straying outside the truly effective shotgun range of 35 to 40 yards. As the shooter you must also move stealthily, learning the kind of terrain favoured by different game species and hunting as much with your mind as the gun. To be a successful rough shooter, you must carefully survey the land and hunt it from the perspective of the animal that you wish to kill.

One of the rewarding aspects of rough shooting is that you frequently return home with a varied game bag. You may be expecting all your shots to be at birds but instead find yourself shooting rabbits. Either way, setting out on a day's rough shooting can be the start of a great gastronomic adventure, which may lead to a wonderful range of wild seasonal meat for the table, or nothing at all.

The difficulty with rough shooting is deciding where to go. Obviously you can't simply set out into an unknown patch of countryside with your gun on your shoulder – you need to have permission from the landowner, and, for safety reasons, to let people know that you will be shooting in the area on that day. Unless you are lucky enough to own your own patch of land, or to have a good friend who does, you will have to rent your day's shooting, and certain estates and farms around the country will allow you to rough shoot by the day.

Make sure you have the right shot size for your quarry. An ideal shot size for pheasant, for example, is a number 6, and for duck, a 4 or 5.

The MG's best friend

Whether or not you are a dog lover, it is difficult to deny dogs' usefulness as hunting partners. In fact, I would almost go so far as to say that when shooting you can't succeed without one. Rough shooting (see page 96) without a dog is virtually hopeless, as without a powerful nose and pair of ears on one's side the game will hide or scurry away long before you come within range. On the rare occasion that you get the chance to take a shot, you may well be unable to find your quarry once it has fallen to the ground – this is the ultimate hunter's frustration. A well-trained dog will solve both these problems, firstly by flushing the game within range, and then by retrieving it once it has been shot, wherever it has fallen.

Dogs are also useful for that sombre moment when an animal has not been killed immediately and, though wounded, manages to get out of sight. Without a dog the hunter will often be unable to find the creature and have no choice but to leave it to a slow and painful death.

Dogs have done a lot for me over the years, from the sled dogs that provided transport for me in Alaska to my present retriever, Juno. As a former cat person (sadly there is no such thing as a gun cat), initially I found it difficult to work with a dog, and throughout Juno's training there were many highs and lows. It is a tribute to her breeding and character that she now works so well for me, as well as being an important member of the family. Training a gun dog is a long and exacting process, and not something I can go into here (for some good books on this subject, see page 310).

Specific breeds are often best suited to specific jobs. Spaniels often excel at working very rough cover, for example, while retrievers are renowned for working in water, ideal when hunting duck and wildfowl. Setters and pointers are thought of as best for walking up grouse, as they will stop and 'point' at the quarry, allowing the hunter time to prepare before flushing these fast-flying birds. There are no hard and fast rules, however, and often a retriever has been taught to work rough cover almost as well as a spaniel, while many spaniels make very good water dogs. Much depends on the trainer.

Once your dog is working well, you will feel great joy when his tail starts wagging wildly as he locks on to the scent of something that may soon land on your table, or as you see him emerging from thick cover carrying a shot bird gently within his jaws. He will also make a great partner and add considerably to the pleasure of your day's hunting, whether or not you return victorious.

Juno is a good dog, and when she fails in the job it is usually my fault. I trained her, which makes it doubly my responsibility.

Shotgun quarry

Again, this is intended not as a comprehensive guide but rather as an introduction to and rough overview of the subject. I will describe different types of game and their cover, as well as detailing techniques for hunting on various kinds of terrain.

It is worth remembering that all of these techniques come best to one through practice and experience. Mistakes are going to have to be made and there will be times when you'll find the going very steep; thus, the best thing to do is to not only read everything you can, but spend time watching and learning from other hunters. Try to approach the whole thing with the humility of a monk and don't ever hesitate to ask a question; remember that he who is afraid to ask is afraid of learning.

As for what to do once you have your kill in the kitchen, see pages 130–4.

Pheasant *Phasianus colchicus* The pheasant is not a wise bird – in fact, in the world of game birds, he's the sixth-form dropout. Yet he has a certain wariness, combined with good eyesight and hearing, that will challenge the rough shot. In order to catch a pheasant unawares, the MG must step lightly yet swiftly. Your dog must move with great control too, and set out to scramble a pheasant only on command.

Carefully approach the area that you suspect holds a pheasant (usually low-lying ground vegetation, such as bracken, rushes or the edges of woodland), using whatever cover is available and watching out for dry twigs, which will crack and give the game away. The aim is to force the bird to make a rushed strategic decision, which usually happens only if you can get to within, say, 15 yards of it unnoticed. Ideally approach downwind of the bird, as the breeze will mask your scent and any sound of approach. Then make your signal and send the dog in. If the dog is good, it will zero in on the pheasant even if it is hiding and exuding little scent. If you are downwind the dog will be able to follow a line of scent that leads straight to the quarry. Once disturbed, the bird will lift into the air in a panicky blur of plumage and flapping wings, complete with alarm call.

Your pulse will quicken, but stay calm, raise the shotgun and flip off the safety switch. Line the muzzles up with the bird, but do not yet put the stock to your cheek; allow him to lift into his flight, following his course with the muzzles until he is the right distance away. Then fully mount the gun, swing through and pull the trigger at the bird's head, following through so that the barrels obscure him completely. If your concentration is complete, you will not even hear the bang, such is the power of the focused mind – in fact, the moments when I have noticed the sound of the gun have been the times that I've missed. Of course, every shotgunner has his own technique. The only way to find your own way of working is to start doing it, and there is no substitute for practice. Sometimes the pheasant will opt to stay still and quiet instead of taking to the air, hoping to remain undiscovered. In this game of hide and seek, if you don't have a dog, the pheasant will often win out.

Techniques for hunting pheasant vary according to the type of terrain. Generally during daylight hours the birds will be in fairly open ground, searching for food, but near cover should danger appear. Hunting a hedgerow can be difficult, as the pheasant will often flush from the quiet side, away from the sound of your approach. Hunting as a twosome and placing an armed friend on the other side can overcome this: walk together, one on either side of the hedge, with the dog working the vegetation. In this way you should be covered whichever side the bird flushes from.

If you are alone, there are a few techniques for hunting hedgerows that are worth mentioning. Birds generally take off into the wind, so place yourself upwind of the hedge, putting the dog on the other side. As being downwind will help your dog to scent the bird, this will suit your dog too. If the hedge has more vegetation on one side than the other (for instance, if it is on an overgrown hill), put your dog on that side, as birds are more likely to be gathered there. Finally, assess which way the pheasant is most likely to fly – he will almost always go towards the woods where he roosts or was released in. Considering all these factors before you begin will help you to be prepared, and thus much more likely to have a successful shot.

Woodland can also afford a rich day's hunting. Expect to find our tasty friends along the fringes or in cover beside clearings and water, as well as along trails cut within. In bad weather pheasants can often be found around blocks of conifer first thing in the morning when they have just hopped down from their roosts. Approach the woods at sunrise and with luck you may catch a few late-risers who are still lingering about before heading off into the fields and hedgerows for the day. Bad weather may help you to surprise the birds, whose ears will be full of the sound of wind through the creaking trees.

Grey partridge

Grey partridge & red-legged partridge
Perdix perdix, Alectoris rufa

There are two different types of partridge to be found in Britain: the indigenous grey partridge and the introduced French or red-legged partridge. The hunter should not lump these two types together; to do so would be to make a big mistake, as their habits are not similar. Our indigenous grey partridge is truly happy in open rolling grassland, just like his relatives on the great Hungarian steppe. With the advent of arable farming he adapted to this new kind of habitat, and thus is now mainly found on arable land. The red-leg is much less a creature of open land and prefers scrubby, rougher country. In southern Europe, where the red-leg is native, he happily hangs out in orchards and olive groves. In Britain, where there are few such civilised retreats, he has to be content with hills and valleys that are not intensively farmed.

Partridge are harder to shoot than pheasant, being smaller, less plentiful and faster. Like pheasants, they prefer to stay on the ground than to take their chances on the wing, and when pursued by a hunter and dog will run away, if they spot the danger soon enough. Red-legged partridges, introduced for sport in 1673 by Charles II, are particularly good at outrunning pursuers, and make good use of cover. Many a hunter has lost out as red-legs run for a hedgerow as he enters the field and then flush out from the other side, well out of range.

The greys prefer to sit tight as long as possible before flushing. Usually their first flush will be out of range of the gun, but if the gun pursues they might sit for longer, allowing him to get close enough to shoot. Grey partridge have suffered badly as a result of intensification of agriculture, and at one time were in danger of extinction. Now there are strategies in place to help restore the species, such as areas of set-aside unfarmed land. Nevertheless, my advice is to shoot the red-legs and leave the greys. Be sure that you know how to spot the difference between them. A good time to catch partridge is at the end of the summer, when arable fields have been cut and the birds feed in the stubble. When hunting red-legs, the best bet is to find a few friends who can handle a shotgun and approach en masse, as these agile little birds will run rings around the lone gunner. A few guns walking in line will do well, as the sight of several people seems to inhibit the bird, encouraging it to sit tight for longer.

Another technique that is sometimes successful for a group of hunters is to drive the partridge from their field towards nearby cover. The tactic is simply to walk an area of open ground, such as barley or wheat stubble, towards a patch of thick cover, ideally sugar beet or some other crop with good leaf spread. Although partridge are not keen on sugar beet in times of peace, they certainly seem to appreciate it as a refuge in times of trouble: the thickness of the beet growth encourages them to sit tight for longer, believing that they will remain unseen.

The guns can approach the cover and work it very carefully, using dogs, while getting ready for the 'return drive'. Unlike pheasants, the partridge can be driven back to where he came from almost immediately. If the gun moves off to another area, the partridges will simply walk home. If the hunters then immediately mount a drive in the reverse direction, they may well have a chance to shoot it.

Learn all you can about this superb little bird, and if you fail the first time, try and try again, as the culinary rewards are immense.

Red-legged partridge

(Following pages) A successful day's hunting for red-legged partridge. Partridge yields the most delicate, tender meat of almost any game bird in Britain.

Red grouse *Lagopus lagopus* The red grouse is the king of all game birds, and the highest prize for any MG. Grouse habitat is heather moorland, and in Britain vast areas are maintained for the benefit of red grouse stocks. All grouse are wild, and it takes great skill to manage the population so that there are sufficient grouse for shooting while also ensuring healthy regeneration year after year. A key element in managing grouse moorland is fire, which gamekeepers use as a way of clearing away old, tough heather and making space for fresh growth, which encourages grouse to settle on the moor. Some areas of heather are deliberately left for the birds to nest and shelter in, and as someone who has often bedded down amongst the thick, springy plants, I can confirm that there is no better place to spend the night.

Driven grouse shooting is similar to driven pheasant, as described on pages 95–6, but it is not for those on a tight budget. Sadly, as I have been on one for most of my life, my experience is limited. Grouse can fly at speeds of up to 80mph and require a high level of skill to shoot. Upwards of 30 keen and effective beaters are needed to move the birds into a position where they can be shot. Early in the season grouse are relaxed and less alert, and when they pass over the guns they invariably do so in small, fast-moving coveys that fly into range at intervals as they are flushed by the advancing beaters. Later in the season they will be far more canny, and when airborne frequently mass into one giant covey that passes over in one. When this happens, fewer birds can be shot and the landowner and gamekeeper will start thinking carefully about when to call a halt to that season's shooting.

Rough shooting for grouse is rarely done, as they are found almost entirely on privately owned moorland, where only driven shooting is permitted. However, if you are lucky enough to find yourself rough shooting for grouse, the method is to set out as a line of guns, with good 'pointing' dogs quartering the ground ahead. As with all flushed birds, the hunter must be controlled and allow the bird to reach sufficient distance before taking the shot. It is always a sin to destroy meat by shredding a bird at close range, but I cannot even imagine the horror of rendering a grouse, as the meat is sublime.

Woodcock *Scolopax rusticola* These birds are so well camouflaged that you might imagine the forest has painted their feathers. If you manage to flush one, the chances are that you will not be able to shoot it, such are the bird's strange, lilting patterns of flight. Woodcock inhabit the kind of country that farmers hate: wet, acidic and downright boggy land, all set about with scrub birch, alder, willow, sessile oak and ash. Holly bushes are also common spots for woodcock to make their day beds. They like hilly country, with a preference for milder weather affected by marine weather patterns. Thus the west coast of Scotland and its islands enjoy good numbers of these birds, as do western Cornwall and Pembrokeshire.

Those who go in search of woodcock must prepare themselves for tough walking through the kind of vegetation that hurts. Many a time I have sampled the uniquely painful slap in the face of a bent branch whipping back as I shoulder my way through a thicket. If the hunter's dog is very disciplined he will be an asset, lifting the bird at good close range and giving the hunter the chance to shoot fast. As the birds disappear so quickly, they have to be shot close, and this means using a light shot cartridge such as a number 7. Clearings and fringes of woodland are good spots to hunt woodcock, as the birds often make their day beds along the periphery.

The cunning rough shooter searches for woodcock at dusk or dawn. Unlike duck, woodcock take flight in better light – a blessing, as they are hard enough to see in broad daylight. I don't like the idea of hunting a flightline, as greedy people often overshoot these mysterious routes; often, too, the woodcock will not return to the flightline for some time after being shot at. However, do remember that it is illegal to shoot the hour before sunrise and the hour after sunset.

Mallard

Greylag goose

Wildfowl Tommi and I were lucky enough to be invited to join a highly experienced father and son who have been shooting wildfowl for a long time on the Alde estuary in Suffolk. Wildfowling is one of the most demanding forms of hunting, as ducks and geese are not only very canny but frequently best hunted when the weather is mean and light is low.

We set up a hide on a high spot beside the water and hunkered down to watch a Homeric dawn spread gently across the eastern skyline. It was a clear day – not good news, as the birds would be able to fly high and see and hear clearly. We had to cover our faces to ensure that we didn't give the game away, as a white face can be seen for miles when set against the drabness of a muddy foreshore.

Two perfect widgeon arrived not far from the hide, and the boy beside us skilfully whistled their call, demonstrating a knowledge of their language that comes only from years of practice. Despite a number of opportunities the fowl outsmarted us and the day ended with nothing. Still, we felt privileged to have had the chance to sit in peace, watching a new day settle over the land. This is the beauty of wildfowling.

There are nine species of duck (mallard, teal, widgeon, pintail, shoveler, gadwall, tufted duck, pochard and goldeneye) and four of goose (pink-footed, greylag, white-fronted and Canada) that can be shot in the UK. Unlike any other quarry, wildfowl are completely dependent on weather conditions, and if you do not pay careful attention to their habits you will return home with nothing. Although many geese breed here in Britain, things only really get going when the winter migrants arrive; September is usually spent hunting for the succulent, home-bred mallard duck. It is difficult to pin down where geese and duck can be found, as frost, flooding, heavy rain and even the phases of the moon all have a great effect. What is definite is that each species has a unique pattern to their migratory lives, which often varies dramatically. The teal, for example, is a most elusive character, sometimes filling a particular marsh and at other times leaving it deserted.

The difference between the goose and the duck, both wonderfully tasty species of bird, is all about lifestyle, and the MG must become darkly familiar with the nuances of each species' life.

The goose lives according to a very civilised and disciplined life plan. He spends his evenings at roost in large open spaces, so as to minimise the risk of being ambushed. A large open field, estuary or lake suits him perfectly. If the moon is full, however, he may choose to graze at night, taking advantage of the increased visibility; a full moon can therefore make his pattern more erratic and harder for the hunter to predict. On a normal day, he will lift majestically and head off for breakfast around sunrise.

All geese are grazers, and many a Sunday league football referee will have witnessed the peaceful sight of Canada geese grazing across the playing fields as he sets up for the day. As well as grass, many species of geese will happily graze stubble fields, nibbling leftovers of wheat and barley and even the relics of the potato harvest. Often geese will fly over perfectly acceptable feeding grounds in favour of an old haunt. Their reasons for this are enigmatic, but my guess is that the old bird who leads each skein simply behaves like many an old bird within our own species: conservative and mildly stubborn, she prefers to stick with what she knows rather than innovate. Thus over time special goose fields develop, where every year these mysterious birds gather. Many times I have narrowly avoided driving off the road while surveying sumptuous-looking geese in a particular field near my home in the Hebrides.

The duck's way of life is more akin to that of a night worker. During the day, ducks hang around on large expanses of water where it is safe for them to rest. From this point of safety they head off to feed through the night, returning to base at first light. Ducks move at the very first stirrings of dawn and right at the latest margins of dusk. Like geese, they will also graze happily over stubble, and if there are any puddles about, so much the better. Ducks' ideal scenario is a river flowing through arable land, as this allows them to land on water and then waddle ashore for dinner, like rotund yachtsmen stepping ashore for a night at the yacht club. As with geese, a full moon will set things awry, so always be aware of this and be flexible in your tactics.

The best time to shoot wildfowl is during morning or evening flight, when the birds are either arriving at or leaving their base. You are more likely to have success in bad weather, as the birds will be preoccupied with keeping in the air and less likely to look around with complete attention; also rough weather will force the birds to fly lower, bringing them into better range for a quick and humane kill.

If hunting in the morning, you must set out in darkness in order to be well positioned by the time the first streaks of dawn are colouring the sky. Ideally you will be dressed in camouflage gear that would put the SAS to shame, as wildfowl have very keen vision and will spot and avoid anything below or ahead of them that looks out of place. A white face will stand out, and thus is best covered with a dark scarf or at least a good-sized hat.

Weather permitting, the dawn will be busy with duck returning to safe daytime haunts after their night's feeding. The duck are the first to flit through the air, often in near total darkness. Mallard and wigeon move first, followed by teal and pintails. Decoys are useful if placed within a pond or gravel pit that might look good enough for their daylight refuge. You can equip yourself with light shot for duck and then, if you have chosen your position cleverly, when most of the duck have passed you can sit back and wait for the geese, which will give you time to switch over to heavier shot.

Pink-footed geese generally move first, followed by greylags and then Canada geese, which often move well after sun-up. Generally it is a good idea to leave the lead bird in a formation, as he will be old and wise and thus the meat will be tough – better to try for a youngster towards the back. If you are still unsuccessful one hour after sunrise, stop. Leave the creatures in peace and come back another day.

Evening flight is the best time to hunt mallard and teal. Find a spot near the water, where you know duck are likely to land. Most of them will arrive when the light is really poor, so camouflage is not so important, but you need something in front of you to conceal you from the water – if there is some good natural cover like a ditch or bushes, use it. You will need to be controlled, as duck frequently circle the water for a while before landing and popping up too early could spoil your chances. Dallying for too long could lead to danger, however, as you may shoot the duck too low, or you could scare off the next group of arrivals. A good idea is to find a pond and 'feed' it by regularly scattering barley or other feed about its edges from late August onwards, thus persuading the ducks to include the pond on their flight plan.

The trick with feeding a pond is to start with it in late summer and to keep on feeding regularly. This ensures that you are able to establish a good routine early on in the year, before the winter's icy grip starts forcing the ducks in your region to start heading off in pursuit of other feeding opportunities. When the ducks have begun to associate your pond with easy living, you will be able to ambush them from time to time in search of grub for your own table.

Hunting in near darkness is also possible. A time that works particularly well is when the moon is full but there is an even spread of cloud. Hides need not be so elaborate, and if you hit upon a goose field you can be very lucky. Here, once again, restraint must prevail, and remember the rule about hunting after sunset. Take enough for the meal, then break your gun and go home.

Woodpigeon *Columba palumbus* 'Time spent in reconnaissance is seldom wasted' is an old military adage, appropriated by the legendary pigeon decoyer Archie Coats in his book *Pigeon Shooting*, which was written before I was born. This maxim applies to everything in life but especially to hunting pigeon. The woodpigeon is one of the wiliest birds around, and to hunt him successfully you need to spend some time just watching his movements, as well as talking to people who live and work on the land over which you might hunt him.

There are an estimated 18 million of these outrageously tasty birds in Britain, and they are officially classified as pests. Personally I believe that the greatest pest on the planet is man, but I am keenly aware that if I were a farmer who had suffered the anguish of watching hordes of pigeon laying waste to my newly sown crops, my opinion might be different.

The woodpigeon is constantly eating, because he has a rather inefficient digestive system that does not process food very effectively. Like duck and goose, he is very social. This combination of greed and gregariousness is the pigeon's undoing and can be exploited by the MG to lethal effect. Whenever a pigeon finds some good grub (and pigeon will eat anything from seeds to greens) others will quickly follow, and soon a large flock will have gathered to enjoy whatever bounty has been discovered.

Woodpigeons' feeding patterns are much less rigid than those of other birds, and the versatile woody can dot about at whim, sometimes leaving the hopeful but ill-informed shot staring at an empty field for hours on end. Thus it is worth reiterating that to do well the MG must seek out local knowledge, as well as spending plenty of time just watching, in the hope of spotting a local pattern.

During the spring when farmers are drilling seed, pigeon will often flock on to fields to pick up any seed that has been left undrilled. They most commonly hit crops that have a hefty seed, such as beans or peas, and farmers have often told me of fields looking 'blue' with pigeon. In the following months as new growth breaks the soil the birds will dot about in search of tasty wayside morsels. I have often found clover and dandelion in pigeons' crops. (The crop is a holding sack at the base of the neck where food is held before entering the stomach.)

Once summer is in full swing, pigeon will happily graze any crop that has been flattened by wind or heavy rain. As with all other birds, the stubble of late summer and early autumn are also good spots for feeding, as there are rich pickings of spilt grain to be had. It is a profound joy to find a pigeon's crop full of wheat, barley or corn – perfect feed for sweet meat. In autumn, the pigeon also feeds on fallen beech mast, chestnuts and acorns, as well as sunflower crops. During the long, dark winter months, they exist on mean little rape seeds and whatever other bits and pieces they can scavenge, gradually losing condition in the process.

The woodpigeon is a real gentleman of leisure, and his daily routine is so relaxed that it almost seems ill mannered to intrude with a shotgun. At first light pigeon flit from their roosts, motivated by the desire for a quick bite to eat. After breakfast they head off in a leisurely fashion to rest up in some trees or hedgerows, or amble along the edges of fields and woods like Edwardian gentlemen taking a stroll before lunch. Around midday they feed again, but gently, with no real show of intent. As the day wears on things change, however, and by afternoon they are striking hard, feeding with serious intent. As the day comes to a close, they head for their roosts high in the trees, finally descending to more sheltered levels as it draws dark, when they feel safe from predators.

DECOY PATTERN

This is the classic decoy pattern, and although there are many variations the rules are always the same: place the decoys facing into the wind and within ideal killing range of your shotgun. Pigeons land into the wind, so if the wind shifts, move the decoys.

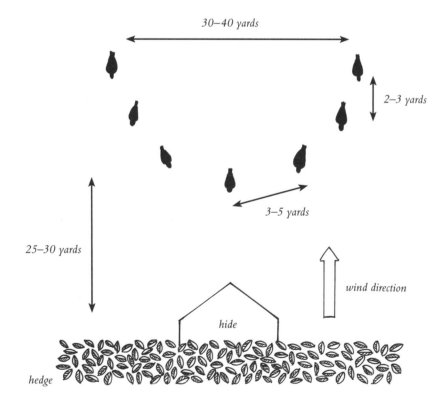

30–40 yards

2–3 yards

3–5 yards

25–30 yards

wind direction

hide

hedge

Setting up a decoy The most reliable and effective method of killing pigeon is by using decoys. In theory this is simple. False or dead birds are laid out in a likely spot, in a convincing pattern. The hunter conceals himself within good range, and waits for his false animals to attract real ones. As most birds are social, a lone pigeon will rarely pass a friendly-looking group without at least saying hello.

It is not quite as simple as it seems, however, and a number of factors need to be taken into consideration. The pigeon is blessed with the kind of eyesight that would shame the good people at Zeiss. Thus camouflage is essential, in the form of a good hide, clothing that blends into the backdrop, a camouflage hat or suitably drab head covering and a face cover made from breathable material. Some perfectionists even cover the barrels of their gun with material so that there is no chance of a glint or reflection. (From my own experience I can pass on a note of caution: do not travel to your pigeon hot-spot dressed in this manner – in these tense times the sight of a man dressed for ambush can cause considerable alarm.)

Once you have found a spot that looks good for decoying, you can build your hide. A hide is a temporary shelter designed to offer a place to lie up while you and your dog wait to ambush a curious bird. As with using decoys, there is an art to building a hide. The aim is to build a structure that conceals the hunter but also allows him to do three things: to see effectively; to remain stationary and in comfort for a long time; and to be able to quickly shoot when an opportunity presents itself.

There are many ways to build a hide, but most use a long camouflage net suited to the colour of their backdrop and situation. If, for example, you are shooting in the height of summer, when most of the greenery is light and burnt out, a dark green net would stand out like honesty in government. Always think about blending in.

Arrange the net so that there is a good backdrop and you can remain relatively concealed even when ready to shoot. Sometimes you can appropriate natural shelter and conceal yourself within a handy tree or even a field where the crops, such as maize, are high enough to hide you. Tommi and I had a very good day shooting pigeons over a wheat field in Hampshire. For a hide we used straw bales, rolling the great wheels towards the edge of the field and making face screens from clippings of elderflower. The pigeons were used to the sight of those big bales and thus the hide worked very well.

A hide is nothing without decoys, which should be laid out in ground no more than 40 yards from the gun and in a pattern that will look convincing to passing pigeon (see illustration, opposite). Pace the range out from your hide and lay the decoys accordingly. As you do so, remember that woodpigeon are terribly polite and, unlike their grubby urban cousins, keenly aware of personal space. Lay the false birds out with enough space between them for a pigeon to feel that he can land without crowding a fellow grazer or even having to fly over him. The decoys must all face into the wind. Pigeon always graze in this direction because, like most birds, they use the wind to lift up quickly into flight, like kites; thus placing the decoys in any other direction is a dead giveaway.

Always unload your gun when crossing an obstacle. If you trip or become tangled, it could go off, and many a gun, even with the safety on, has failed.

Once you have set up the decoys, you can retire to your lair and wait. In the hide a few useful rules apply. The first is to never raise your head above the netting or screen of vegetation but always to look through it. This will ensure that you do not 'skyline' or show a pallid face like a white flag of warning. Next you must have your gun ready to shoot quickly, and make sure that you can move swiftly and safely into a shooting position. Have a few dry runs at bringing the gun up to aim, to make sure no tangles lie ahead. As the pigeon flies in to investigate the decoys or even to land, you must remain very still, as sharp-eyed *Columba palumbus* will be constantly scanning the ground beneath him and the cover all around.

If the decoys are set out right, there will come a very clear point at which you should rise and shoot. Watch the pigeon as he alternately beats his wings and glides in your direction. Keep your face lowered and try to look up just below the rim of your hat as he comes in.

The pigeon should land in the spot that you have designed as your killing ground. For a moment he will have to stop scanning about to examine his landing zone. As he looks down, he will bring his wings into a flutter. Now is the time to strike. Rise silently or raise the gun over the net, point just below the hovering bird and then fire and pull up. If you have shot well, a little cloud of feathers will drift in the wind just above the plump carcass of a perfect meal.

If the bird is lying on his back, you will have to exit the hide and turn him on to his stomach, as any passing bird will not be too keen on the idea of settling beside an ex-pigeon. It also pays to use a twig to raise his head a bit, so that he looks as though he is alive and contentedly sitting with a group of grazing pals. Gradually, if you are lucky, you can remove all your false decoys and use dead pigeons instead. Nothing does better than the real thing. If shooting in hot weather, bring all pigeons not being used as decoys into the shade to prevent the meat becoming fly ridden.

Ageing a bird

This is not as difficult as you might imagine, and only takes a few seconds. The age of young partridge and grouse can be judged by their primary wing feathers. Stretch the wing out fully and look at the outer feathers furthest from the body – the primary feathers. If the bird is young, these will be neatly pointed and trim. With an older bird they will be more rounded. A young red-legged or French partridge will have a gentle white tip on its outer primary feather which only lasts for its first season.

Pheasants are slightly more complex. Spurs can be an indicator of age, and a big old cock will often have large, pointed, sharp spurs. However, this will only give you a rough indication. To be more exact apply the bursa test. The 'bursa' is a little hole just above the anal vent which has no known purpose, and seems to be a kind of biological cul de sac. Nevertheless it can give a reasonably accurate indication of age, as if the bird is young, a tooth-pick, match or even a feather can be gently pushed up into this hole to a depth of about 2 inches. An old bird will not have a bursa.

Hunting with a rifle

Armed with a rifle, as an MG you must empty your mind of all shotgunning thoughts and principles. The rifle is a weapon of stealth and stillness, and to use it effectively the hunter must exercise a complete mental and physical change of approach, as explained on page 90.

When using a rifle (and the same applies with a shotgun), you must become very familiar with range. You must be able to make reasonably accurate estimates about the range over which you wish to shoot. Ideally all shots with a rifle should take place at or well below 200 yards from the target. There are some very capable people who will shoot at greater range; however, I am not experienced enough to attempt those kinds of shots and believe it would be irresponsible to do so.

My logic is that once the animal is hit you need to be able to keep it in aim, ready to take a second shot in case it has not been a clean kill. If you shoot the creature at 100 yards, the chances are high that, should it not be dead, you will still be well within range to finish the job quickly. If, however, you shoot the beast at 300 yards and wound it, you may not be able to cover it effectively for the second shot, as it might limp out of good striking range relatively quickly. The trick is to use good field craft to get as near as possible to the target. Remind yourself that this is about killing and nothing else. You must kill that creature fast and effectively, and if you cannot get within appropriate range, do not take the shot.

When learning to judge range, in order to figure out what 100 yards looks like just pace it out and mark off the distance. Put a peg or rock down on some level ground – ideally a quiet road or straight path – and wrap or tie some string to it. With a measuring tape, walk out 25 yards from the peg, holding the string and keeping it fairly taut as you go. Fasten the string to a peg at the end. You now have 25 yards, so you need to repeat the process only three times to get up to 100 yards. Place a good visible marker at the 100-yard point (I always carry a red rag – or you could use a spare friend) and go back to where you started. Stand for a while and just look at the distance.

Now it is time to employ a method of measuring distance that was pioneered by the Romans. Walk at your usual speed along the 100 yards, using a normal stride, and count double paces. Sounds complex, but it is not: just count left foot to left foot or right to right, not both at the same time. Repeat three times and calculate the mean amount. You will now know how many steps you take to cover 100 yards.

Try the same on rough country and you will see that you use more steps. Get in the habit of asking yourself odd questions such as: 'How far off is that pole?' In the end that clever grey mass of yours will become tediously fanatical about range. A word of social warning: keep this subject to yourself, as it will drive friends and loved ones to the brink of conversational despair. Do not, ever, ask them to help with pegs and measuring tape – the result will be sudden loneliness and a deserted home.

Rifle quarry

Every type of animal that can be hunted with a shotgun can also be killed effectively with a rifle. What follows, however, is the quarry most often hunted with rifles in Britain.

Rabbit *Oryctolagus cuniculus* Some say it was the Normans who introduced the rabbit to Britain; others say it was the Romans. Whoever it was, I thank the lords of culinary luck that it got here, as Britain would be a much less gastronomically rich island without it. People don't eat enough rabbits in Britain: their meat is healthy, tasty and plentiful, and can be put to good use in any number of ways. Each time I see a bunny I can't help but imagine its delicate meat being applied to an endless list of sublime gastronomic inventions.

The rabbit is essentially a grazing animal, and does much of its work at night. Generally rabbits live in burrows; but they are also quite happy to settle for above-ground living, and will set up home in hedgerows and other types of dense cover such as gorse thickets. When the living is good, rabbits breed . . . like rabbits. When times are hard, or if the population becomes too high in a particular area, they stop breeding, and embryonic rabbits can actually be reabsorbed into the womb by the doe. Thus rabbit populations can rise and fall quite dramatically.

Rabbits can cause great harm to crops and trees, and are pests to farmers. In the 1950s rabbits were infected with a virus called myxomatosis. It killed nearly every rabbit in Britain, using the rabbit flea as a vector. The signs of a rabbit infected with this virus are very clear: swollen eyes, unnatural stillness and lesions around the head. It looks like a terrible way to go; anyone coming across an infected rabbit should kill it immediately. On one occasion I was driving through the Lammermuir Hills in Scotland when I came across a hunched rabbit, sitting in the middle of the road and clearly suffering awfully from myxomatosis. I got out of the car and quickly broke its neck, wanting to end its suffering, but then I heard a little shout of horror coming from a nearby garden. A family who had been fondly observing the animal were aghast at my action, but I looked at them with equal dismay: how could they fail to take action when the animal was clearly dying such a terrible, drawn-out death?

A .22 rifle with a sound moderator is ideal for bringing rabbit back to the kitchen. It allows the possibility of killing more than one rabbit when a group is out.

Fortunately many rabbits are now immune to the virus and, although it re-emerges in a new form from time to time, the population is alive and thriving. Myxomatosis cannot affect humans, but a rabbit with the condition will not be in a suitable condition for eating – the earliest signs are found internally, with a pale, swollen liver. The kidneys and spleen may also appear darkened and enlarged.

The ideal tool for catching rabbit is the highly accurate .22 calibre rimfire rifle, loaded with hollow point rounds. Below are some rabbit-hunting techniques.

Sitting up Dress warmly and inconspicuously, and find a spot within range of a warren that is comfortable, well hidden and downwind. Take up a position lying prone or leaning against a tree, and wait for rabbits to emerge from their warren to commence the evening's grazing. Ideally your rifle will have a sound moderator, which silences each shot considerably. Extreme accuracy is required, as you must kill the rabbit immediately – a wounded rabbit will return to the warren and then nothing else will come out. In the open you will be able to get a second shot, but not beside a warren. The range should not exceed 80 yards.

Stalking If the land has good cover, you can stalk a rabbit. Using binoculars, spy the rabbits from a distance, and then keeping the cover between yourself and the quarry, stalk to within good range. A high degree of field craft is needed for this approach, as rabbits have superb sight, hearing and scenting capabilities. Generally this method and the one above will not yield high quantities of meat – you will be lucky to go home with one or two rabbits.

Lamping This technique involves going out at night in a vehicle, ideally a pickup, with a powerful spotlight. From the back of the vehicle, you and your partner search for rabbits by scanning the spotlight across the ground, looking for the glint of a rabbit's eye and hoping that it might become confused enough to remain motionless for a few seconds. A rabbit's response to danger is to freeze in the hope that it won't be seen. A tap on the roof will tell the driver to stop and turn the engine off, so that you can shoot from a still shooting platform.

Some advocate walking beside the vehicle and shooting with a stick to lean on, as there will be less vibration than there is when shooting from within or on a vehicle. I can't help but feel that this is dangerous, particularly at night, when confusion about a backstop could occur. If you shoot downwards from a pickup, a backstop is more dependable, as the bullet is heading downwards whether it hits a rabbit or not. Do not lamp over country that you have not seen during the day, as deadly confusion can occur.

Complete caution must be exercised at all times when lamping. The person shining the spotlight must be sure to keep the spot ahead of the shooter's scopes, as any light coming from behind will distort the optics. Lamping can yield large numbers of rabbits, and if you are after a lot of meat this can be a very good method.

Grey squirrel *Sciurus carolinensis* The grey squirrel is another tasty rodent worth sampling, with the added bonus that by knocking off a few of these bully boys for the pot you are doing the countryside a favour. Grey squirrels came to Britain from North America in the early part of the last century and have driven our native red squirrels to the brink of extinction. The grey squirrel is universally hated by farmers, environmentalists and foresters because, as well as its crimes against the red, it is destructive to trees and the habitats of other species. However, the MG should learn to love this nutty-flavoured tree rat and long for the sound of its heavy carcass thudding on to the forest floor. Although small, grey squirrels are plentiful, and if well prepared their meat can be very tasty.

The best time to catch squirrels is very early in the morning or in early evening. Do not use a .22 for this job, as the shots will be at an upward angle, and in this crowded country one cannot be too careful. A shotgun is better, as its pellets will rapidly lose lethality; however, it is very loud, and will scare off other squirrels as well as disturbing all the wildlife in the area. The ideal weapon for this job is a powerful air rifle with a scope, which is both silent and accurate.

The MG must be very, very patient and extremely quiet when approaching this crafty überpest. Stalk quietly through the woods, constantly scanning from right to left; when hunting, it is best to use this method as it helps you to pick up the slightest movement or disturbance in the undergrowth. We have been conditioned to look at the world from left to right, and this habitual approach allows our brain to be lazy and to take short cuts. Move silently from tree to tree, stopping from time to time beside a suitable tree on which you could lean and shoot if necessary.

Sometimes a squirrel will not see you and you will be able to shoot him from his vantage point on a tree, or even on the ground. At other times he will run up a tree and hide. Then you will have little chance of catching him, so return a little later and scan that tree with total accuracy, leaving no part unexamined. Often you will see a squirrel cross the path ahead of you. In this case move fast to where it crossed and search the likely trees. Keep your ears open, too, as a squirrel's sharp little claws will make rapid scratching sounds as he climbs. Squirrels also chirrup from time to time when playing or chasing off other squirrels.

As with rabbit, always aim for a squirrel's head, as the meat can be easily spoiled by body shots. It is also more humane to aim for the head, as there is less danger of wounding the animal – if you hit you will kill, but if you miss it will invariably be a clean miss.

Last word of warning: whatever you do, do not shoot a red squirrel!

Keep your game cool to avoid meat spoilage, and carry it in the outer netting of a bag or, even better, loose in your hand.

Deer When Tommi and I reached Scotland, I was offered the opportunity to stalk red deer on a 38,000-acre estate in the Highlands. Armed with a solid Ruger rifle firing a .308 round, I set out across very rough country on a wet stormy day in the company of Craig, the estate gamekeeper. We walked half the day before coming within range of a trio of hinds that would make suitable quarry.

The deer were totally unaware of our presence and sat contentedly in their beds in the heather. Craig and I crouched together watching them – I had identified what I thought was the best hind, and waited for her to stand up so that I could take aim. Ten minutes passed, then 20, and after half an hour the deer still hadn't figured out that we were there. 'Guy,' Craig whispered, 'I think we may have found the only blind deer in the parish.'

I peered through my scope, breathing slowly and working to empty my mind of every thought except that fatal zone a little behind and above the hind's foreleg. Craig whispered that sometimes he waited a very long time for the right moment, and if that moment did not come he would go home rather than take a bad shot. Craig killed most of his deer with headshots, as he was a vastly experienced and accurate hunter. We lay on the ground and waited. And then, just as we were considering going home, the hind stood up, turning side on and giving me the perfect opportunity. I brought the reticle over the point of aim, took a deep breath and slowly breathed out again, while at the same time smoothly squeezing the trigger towards me with the end of my finger. The rifle fired and the hind ran fast across the hill.

'She's dead,' Craig said, and a moment later the animal's legs gave way and it fell to the ground. I covered it with my rifle, levered in another round and watched in case it got up again, but it did not. I waited for a few moments, and then made the rifle safe and walked over to where the hind had fallen, feeling a tremendous surge of responsibility and determination that not one centimetre of that animal's life must be wasted.

I was happy to discover that it was a 'yeld hind' (a deer that has not had a calf that year and thus has not had to feed anything beside herself.) The tail was thick and fleshy, and I could not feel the spine across its rump because of a nice covering of fat. This meant that it was in perfect condition for eating. I gralloched the animal. ('Gralloch' is a wonderfully onomatopoeic Gaelic word that describes the process of gutting.) Later, when we had brought the carcass down from the hill, I skinned and hung it in the deer larder. When I examined the heart, I was relieved to find that it had been completely destroyed by the bullet, which meant that the deer had died quickly and with the minimum of suffering.

I cut out a portion of tenderloin from the carcass and took it back to camp, which was set below a venerable Scots pine in the shadow of some great cliffs, over which a series of waterfalls thundered. A storm was coming in from the Atlantic, and strong gusts blew the waterfalls back up their courses, the white spray reminding me of the raised tails of Arab horses. I got the stove burning and Tommi cooked venison steaks accompanied by a hawthorn sauce made from berries that she had collected that day (see page 291). We ate in silence, enjoying a meal that had come from a great adventure and feeling profoundly humbled and lucky to be alive. All around the wind roared, surging over our little hollow and singing in the needles of the pine.

Deer are the largest wild animal that can be hunted in Britain. Unlike many of this country's other former residents, such as lynx, wolf and bear, our two largest breeds of deer – the red and fallow – have both had the benefit of some powerful friends. The Normans set aside areas of woodland as royal deer forest, where the resident herds were protected from overhunting: anyone caught killing a deer without permission was subjected to severe punishment. Today deer are thriving all over Britain, benefiting from new 'parks' in the form of the many blocks of soft wood forestry throughout the country. In Scotland the land mass is thought to be sufficient to sustain 150,000 red deer, but there are estimated to be over 300,000.

There are six species of deer in this country: red, fallow, Japanese sika, roe, Chinese water and muntjac. The smallest is the muntjac and the largest is the red. Red and roe deer are indigenous, and reached this island 18,000 years ago by means of the land bridge that then existed between Britain and Europe. Numerous excavations show their importance to our Neolithic ancestors as a source of food. The fallow deer has also been around for a long time; it was probably introduced by the Normans at the end of the eleventh century, though there is evidence of their presence earlier. All other species were brought over in the nineteenth century by enthusiasts, and proceeded to escape equally enthusiastically from their enclosures and set up happily within the many blocks of woodland that exist around the country.

The huge abundance of deer presents the MG with an enthralling panorama of carnivorous opportunities. Yet the job of killing one of these animals is challenging,

Dainty hinds relax beside an ash tree in spring sunshine. Perfect, free, happy, free-range meat.

as they are large, and thus need to be hit very hard. The big red, roe and fallow require extremely powerful rounds fired from centrefire rifles. The smaller muntjac, Chinese water and sika also need to be hunted with centrefire rifles, firing slightly less heavy rounds. At least as important as the size of bullet and weapon is accurate shot placement – you must ensure your shot hits a vital organ, thus causing a quick and relatively painless death. If you fail in this, you will wound a large animal and have to live with this terrible shame for life.

The best places to hit a deer are either in the 'engine room', which contains the heart and lungs, or the head. A shot to the head is more difficult, as it is a smaller target and the slightest movement of the animal can lead to terrible wounding; unless you are very experienced, therefore, I do not recommend it. In the unfortunate event that the deer is not killed instantly (sadly it does happen), you should fire a second shot.

When assessing whether to take a shot at a particular deer, you must make judgements about the animal's age, sex and condition, and consider whether its death will have a negative impact on the herd (for example, if it has a young calf) as well as whether it will be good eating. It is not a good idea to take the biggest stags, as their meat is likely to be tough. Best to go for a youngish animal, or the ideal for the table, which I was lucky enough to shoot, a yeld hind.

Stalking The largest population of red deer can be found in Scotland, but a significant number are spread throughout other parts of the country – for example, the New Forest, Exmoor, the Quantocks, Suffolk and the Lake District. Their selection of habitat is mostly linked to the availability of food, but other factors such as weather and fly infestation can also influence movement.

Red deer will retreat to higher ground or deeper woodland during the height of summer to avoid flies, returning to lower or more open ground when food becomes scarce and the weather inclement. Their daily movement pattern will lead them from the lower, more sheltered areas, where they spend the nights, back to higher sunny slopes, where they spend the day feeding, resting and chewing the cud. These daytime areas will normally be good vantage points from which they can easily see approaching danger. Red deer have got amazing eyesight – possibly the best of all deer. They also have superb scenting abilities and blend perfectly into their surroundings.

To get within range of one of these beasts, you must become very good friends with the land and learn to keep the ground between yourself and your quarry until it is time to shoot. The trick is to carry a good pair of binoculars and constantly stop and scan the surrounding country. Sometimes just a twitch of an ear will give one animal away, and you will then find many more near by, utterly hidden in the bracken or long grass. Once you have spotted a small group, you must assess your best route of approach and be sure to never find yourself upwind of your target. You must be fit enough to be able to carry a heavy rifle and move through country that is usually steep, boggy and hummocky, especially in Scotland, where the terrain is the toughest in Britain. The last part of a stalk can often involve a long crawl until a suitable point is reached to take a shot.

Unlike the stalking of red deer, which normally takes place in high, open country, most other deer hunting takes place in woodland. This involves more strategic planning but less hard graft. In the woods you must try to intercept the deer's routine. You need to be up early or out last thing to hunt in the woods, as these are the times when the deer, like most animals, are on the move. The art to hunting deer in the woods lies in being in the right place, and stalking in woodland means spending most of your time seated on a branch or leaning very still against a tree. Silence and stealth are much more difficult to achieve in the woods, where every twig is a potential giveaway. The shooting is also potentially more dangerous, as there may well be obstacles between yourself and the target, and it is difficult to be absolutely sure that there are no people around. With any stalking, once again, you must get permission from the landowner, and unless you are very experienced it is advisable to be accompanied by a gillie or gamekeeper.

The unarmed gourmet: hunting with nets

If you are keen to avoid firearms and the inevitable complications that come with them, then there are other methods of catching game, though it will all be of the furred rather than feathered variety. In fact, in this country, the only creature you can realistically (and legally) catch without using a gun is a rabbit.

The silent and lethal long net There are many ways in which long nets can be used to catch rabbits, and I cannot hope to cover the whole spectrum here. Once again, take this as an introduction. Generally long nets come in three sizes: 25, 50 and 100 yards. With skill and practice, over time the MG will learn to use the net effectively, intercepting running rabbits by night or sometimes even during the day when he or she has sufficient experience.

The knack with a long net is learning to deploy it quickly without tangles and chaos, and then to take it down in a manner that will ensure easy deployment at a later date. The MG must also, to use a terrible golfing phrase, 'be' the rabbit, and start looking at the land with a number of questions in mind, such as: 'If I was a rabbit grazing in this field where would I run if I got scared?' Or: 'If I was a rabbit in that meadow, would I feel safe enough to crouch and hide, or would I run straight away?' Success or otherwise with a long net is largely strategic, and the placing of the net is of the greatest importance in making one's plan of attack.

The long net is best used at night, and some preplanning is required for successful deployment over the course of a few days. Let me paint an ideal picture. Happening upon some rabbits grazing a field at dusk, the MG should spend some time just watching them and assessing the ground. It should be clear where they have come from, as they always start grazing near to their burrows – this is where they will try to run back to if under threat. Look at the ground closely: if the field is large and lumpy with rough growth such as long grass, nettles and docks it will be ideal.

Gradually the rabbits will venture further out into the field as darkness falls, and armed with this intelligence the MG can return home with a mind full of possibilities. The next day he should return to the field, setting out his net in a long line between where the rabbits first appeared the evening before and where they went off to graze. There are a few differing ways of setting up the net, but here a 'straight set' will work fine. Once correctly laid out, the MG should tie the net up so that the rabbits can run beneath it and grow accustomed to its presence. The MG must ensure that there is a good 'bag' or area of slackness in the net about halfway up from the ground. If the net is too tight the rabbits will bounce off it like tennis balls, giving them a chance to escape. Some slack is needed so that the rabbits become irreversibly tangled when they hit the net.

The next night will be perfect, moonless with a light breeze blowing across the fields. At home, the restless MG sits in the kitchen, watching the clock ticking. He knows that he must allow time for the rabbits to get well out into the field – far enough that if they see him they will feel safer crouching in light cover than risking a run for their burrows. With a couple of friends, he sets out when it is fully dark, deftly lowering the net before placing himself well out of sight in a corner of the field. At the far end of the field, approaching by a roundabout route, his helpers have

LONG NET

Two MGs 'wump' the field with a length of rope. This flushes crouching rabbits into the waiting long net that lies between the rabbits and their holes in the hedgerow.

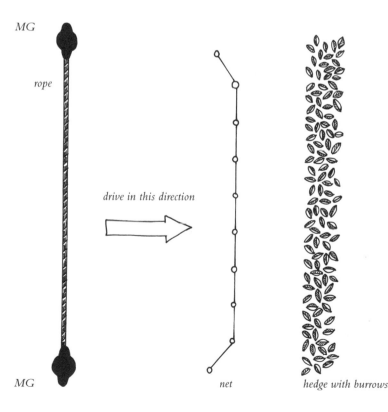

MG

rope

drive in this direction

MG

net

hedge with burrows

127

stretched a rope out between them, and now walk towards the net, keeping the line taut whilst also letting it drag across the ground between them. The running cord will 'wump' the ground, touching any rabbits that are trying to crouch out of sight and forcing them to bolt for their burrows.

Gradually rabbits will hit the net and become quickly entangled. The MG now approaches the net and, after a quick assessment, swiftly breaks the necks of any rabbits that are suitable for eating – any rabbits that are surplus to requirements are let go. This is an advantage of netting, as it allows for careful selection of meat, also producing a carcass that has not been touched by a bullet or shot. The down side of course is the animal's fear whilst caught in the net, exacerbated by the human's approach. For this reason quick action must be taken. If adept the whole exercise of net retrieval and killing can take place in well under one minute.

During the day, long nets can also be set out to catch rabbits flushed from crops or from thick cover. There are myriad methods of daytime long netting, but a classic is to set the net up between a hedgerow and field of crops that is about to be combine harvested. As the combine harvester moves through the crop rabbits dart out for the safety of hedgerow burrows, only to be caught in the net.

Ferrets and purse nets

Ferrets are nature's equivalent to a guided missile, except instead of seeking heat they follow a line of scent. For centuries ferrets have been used to drive rabbits from their burrows into cleverly placed nets. Poachers throughout the ages have favoured this method, and the alliance that has developed between the ferret and this motley bag of scoundrels has earned these clever and determined animals dark associations as well as a deserved reputation for being smelly and vicious creatures. In reality, however, if properly managed ferrets can be great allies.

Ferrets belong to the *Mustelidae* family, which includes other sharp-toothed and quick-witted assassins such as the wolverine, stoat and mink. Typically the animals in this group have long bodies, short legs and outrageously sharp teeth. These teeth are, of course, the warhead within each furry missile, and with proper control they can be a very useful part of the MG's armoury.

The ideal method for using ferrets is with purse nets. These are individual round nets that are placed around the exit holes of a warren before the ferret enters. The ferret is then released into the warren, while the MG stands quietly out of sight so that bolting rabbits will not be inhibited from running out. When the rabbits detect the ferret and his musky and terrifying odour, they bolt for the nearest exit. As they explode from the holes, they become caught in the purse nets, which quickly close around them. Long nets can also be used, and here the tactic is to set the net up either around the perimeter of the warren or on the opposite side to the waiting MGs.

Tommi and I joined a highly effective ferreter in Yorkshire, who used his ferret and long net to catch six superb rabbits for the pot. In exchange for helping him he gave us three perfect parcels of meat, which we took back to a bivouac made of spruce in nearby sheltered woodland. Over glowing charcoals Tommi made a subtle rabbit stew that warmed to the bone, all brought to us through the skilful use of a ferret.

I have often hunted successfully using a combination of ferrets and purse nets; however, the ferrets have always belonged to someone else, as I have an instinctive dislike of any animal that finds it so easy and instinctive to bite the hand that feeds it. I also find ferrets' honeyed, musky smell unpleasant and their murderous characters off-putting. Yet it is this very aspect that makes ferrets so profoundly effective as a hunter's assistant. They can flush almost anything from a dark place for the simple reason that ferrets are the last thing you would ever want to meet in a dark alley. In fact, if I were a rabbit, I would happily run into any net, or face any number of shotguns, in preference to coming up against one of these weasly marauders.

Find the warren, cover all the holes with purse nets and then apply the assassin – the rabbits will smell a ferret's musky scent and quickly run to the nearest hole.

Unless well trained, they can be difficult to control: once inside the warren, for example, rather than flushing rabbits out sometimes the ferret will catch one and 'lay up' to eat it before falling contentedly asleep. If this happens, the MG will have the tedious job of digging out the ferret and excavating him from his ghastly lair. Making sure that the ferret has eaten well before he starts work can usually prevent this problem.

Preparing an animal for the table

Any self-respecting MG will relish the moment of putting their gun aside and preparing the kill for its joyful entry into the kitchen or deer larder. Here are a few starters for those wishing to play a full part in the circle that starts with the hunt and ends with a sublime meal born of true culinary adventure.

Immediately after you have shot your game, if you don't plan to eat it straight away, give it a chance to cool down in the open air. Don't throw several carcasses into a tight space. Try to carry them either in a breathable sack or in the netting section of a game bag. I often tie them to a pole and place this in a shaded bit of a hedge or woodland until I am ready to make for home.

Hanging game Most game needs to be hung for a while before it is eaten, to give the meat time to tenderise. Chemical actions in meat carry on even after an animal has died, but since the blood has stopped flowing, any by-products of those actions will no longer be carried away in the bloodstream and will build up in the muscle instead. One such product is lactic acid, which is crucial to the hanging process. In freshly slaughtered meat it imparts an unpalatable metallic taste; however, given time it tenderises the meat and develops its flavour.

There are no fixed rules regarding the length of time to hang meat: the temperature at which the animal is hung has a bearing, as do its age, size and condition. Personal preference also plays a part: some people like their meat more 'gamey' than others. In cold weather I would probably hang a mature cock pheasant for as much as a week before plucking and butchering. If it is warm and the pheasant is young, two to three days would suffice. (With experience you will be able to approximately judge game birds' ages just by looking at them. For more accurate measurement, you can use the bursa test on page 114.) Hen pheasants generally need less hanging than cocks, as their lives involve less physical activity. Some animals are fine to eat without hanging: I find rabbits and partridge perfectly palatable.

When Tommi and I were shooting pigeon in Hampshire, we needed to find a good cool place to hang the birds, as with the weather being hot there was a risk that the meat might become fly blown. Walking through some woods near by, I came across a Second World War pillbox, which gave me an idea. Inside, the temperature was markedly cooler and the flies couldn't get in, so I hung the pigeon there. A few days later, I returned to find them in a perfectly refrigerated state, despite the very hot weather. It is usually possible to appropriate something in this way as a poor man's game larder – just hang the game in such a way that foxes cannot get there first.

When it comes to hanging, make sure that the carcass hangs freely, without leaning against or touching anything, as a point of pressure will create an area vulnerable to rotting. Hang game birds by the neck. With rabbits, I make an incision between the ankle bone and the Achilles tendon of one leg, and then push the foot of the other leg through this hole and make a small nick behind the heel of that foot with a knife to create a natural loop for hanging.

Paunched rabbits about to be butchered for Tommi.

Preparing feathered game Far too many people think that gutting and butchery are unpleasant jobs to be got over as soon as possible. I completely disagree. To do the animal justice, I want to ensure that it is perfectly prepared for cooking, and to do a perfect job you cannot be a machine. Recently I was in a kitchen belonging to friends in the north of England, preparing some partridge and a woodcock for supper.

It was cold and drizzly outside and the stove quietly purred behind me. Between my legs I had placed a bin to catch the bits and pieces. (For newcomer MGs about to embark on their first gutting session, I would always recommend having a glass of brandy. This powerful spirit not only gives courage but also very effectively clears the nose.) The house was silent and I was utterly content.

All birds are plucked and gutted in more or less the same way, and you will find out for yourself about the subtle differences between them. The first thing I do is to cut off the bird's legs at the elbow, leaving the familiar drumstick joints exposed, before cutting off the wings as close to the body as possible. With larger birds such as pheasant I leave on the wings and pluck them – even though these are the hardest feathers to pull it is worth it, as the wings make good eating. Then I angle the bird over a bin and begin to pluck.

Light, quick movements are best for plucking, using your forefinger and thumb, and you must always take care not to tear the skin, especially over the breast of the bird (pheasant, above all other birds, have the thinnest skin over this area, whereas pigeon and duck have good, tough skin which does not tear easily). Moving faster over the tough-skinned legs and back, I carefully pluck the entire bird. I always pluck a little way up the neck, too, as I want to cut this section off through skin, not feathers. Once the bird is clear of feathers, I cut the neck section off by placing the bird on a board and very firmly cutting with a heavy knife. Then I carefully pull some of the skin down from the remains of the neck to reveal the crop, which I ease away neatly from the meat with my thumbs. Often the crop will tell me a happy tale about what the bird has been feeding on – wheat or barley, for instance, or even little niblets of clover.

After the crop is out, I cut carefully around the vent or anus, being careful not to rupture the small intestines, as this will allow gastric juices to seep into the meat. With two fingers, I then draw the innards out of the bird: when the intestines are out I insert two fingers right into the body cavity, following the breastbone until I can feel the internal organs with the pads of my fingers. I then curl my fingers down and scoop everything out neatly. Finally I wash the carcass out with cold water and pat dry with kitchen paper. The job is done. A few almost transparent hairs will remain on the bird – don't worry about these, as they will burn off in seconds during cooking.

Sometimes when the skin is not needed you may choose to skin the carcass instead of plucking. This takes a fraction of the time, and is ideal if you are going to be jointing the bird. Here's how I skin a pheasant: first I cut off the legs and wings as

(Below) There is a knack to plucking any bird, and practice always makes perfect. Swift, deft movement is essential; always watch for accidental tearing of the skin.

(Opposite) Woodpigeon's best meat is from the breast. This pigeon had been feasting on delicate spring growth before it was shot. The crop was also full of little nibbles of clover.

Skinning a rabbit: hold the stumps of its rear legs and roll the pelt away, keeping fur on fur and never on flesh.

above, but then I gut the bird while it is still feathered, although I remove the feathers around the vent in order to make the incision cleanly. I make a small incision below the crop of the bird and ease the skin open until I have two fingers underneath the skin and can clearly see the dark meat below. Then I steadily pull the skin back and over the bird's shoulders, stopping to cut off the neck before pulling the skin off in one.

Preparing furred game With most furred animals with a pelt the process of preparation starts in the field, as their innards are larger and contain gases that will lead to expansion unless they are removed shortly after the animal is killed.

Rabbit Pick the rabbit up and hold it with its head upwards, sliding your thumbs down its undersides and squeezing any urine out of the carcass as you do so. Now you need to paunch it; this is the same as gralloching a deer – essentially removing the intestines. There are many ways of doing this. My method is to make a cut below the last rib and then place the gut hook of my knife in the cut and slice down towards the anal vent. If I haven't got a gut hook, I use the knife with the blade pointing up and my fingers beneath it, to make sure that I don't rupture the intestines. Then I turn the underside away, bending the animal's back legs back on themselves until they touch the ears. Holding the two together, I use the knife to cut and scrape out the intestines. Some people leave in the 'lights' (or kidneys, liver and heart), but I prefer to clear them all out. Now the animal is ready for the game bag.

Back in camp I cut the legs off at the first joints (ankles and wrists); then I ease the skin over each hind leg, rolling the fur in on itself over my fist, being careful not to allow it to touch the meat to avoid contamination. Once the skin is clear of the hind legs, I carefully pull the whole pelt towards the head, easing out the forelegs before pulling it up to reveal the neck, which I cut off.

Laying the animal on its back, I now cut through the pelvic bridge, so that the hind legs fall back and the anal canal is revealed. With my finger I clear out this canal and then carefully cut out the anal glands on either side. Many people forget to do this, and then wonder at the odd musky taste of the meat. I finish by washing the whole carcass through with clean water and drying it with kitchen paper. The animal is now ready for the table, and can be neatly jointed or cooked whole.

Grey squirrel Gutting and butchering a squirrel is just like getting a rabbit ready for the pot, except that the animal is smaller. Also, just as with rabbits, skinning an older animal is always toughest as that pelt will have been there for a while, so be prepared for some hard pulling if you have bagged a veteran.

Of course there are many ways to skin an animal, but here's how I get a squirrel ready: first, chop off fore- and rear legs at the first joint. Make a shallow cut through the pelt at the base of the ribcage, being careful not to cut into the white gut lining. Aiming the knife blade upwards, cut down the length of the belly towards the vent.

Ease the pelt off each rear leg, rolling and pulling so that the fur does not touch the exposed meat. Once the legs are clear, grab the saddle and pull the pelt upwards, popping the forelegs out on the way. Pull the pelt up over the shoulders until it has hooded the head and exposed the neck neatly.

With one hand hold the pelt and head, and with the other cut or chop through the neck with a cleaver, knife or axe. Next open up the stomach lining, being very careful to not puncture the internal organs. Keep the knife blade pointing upwards or use the gut hook on the end of your knife. Use two fingers to clear the internal cavity of intestines and organs and immediately discard. Be quick, as if there is a cook around they will want to do something ghastly with the liver or kidneys.

Finally wash the whole carcass inside and out in clean cold water and pat it dry using kitchen paper. If storing, tightly wrap it in cling-film and refrigerate or freeze for later use.

Deer After shooting one of these majestic animals, you must gralloch it straight away. Take the beast's forelegs and drag it round so that the carcass is lying with its head pointing downhill. Using a good long-bladed knife, stick the blade in just above the brisket (the lower part of the animal's front end, effectively the chest), waggling it around until a gush of blood comes out. You might even push down a bit on the sides to assist in this process of bleeding.

Now make a long cut up the lower side of the deer's neck, and expose the windpipe and attached oesophagus. Make a cut high up towards the head between the windpipe and the oesophagus. Carefully separate the oesophagus from the windpipe, so that you can cut away the reddish tissue that makes up the outer layer of the oesophagus, until you reach a white under-layer. Ease the red tissue back until you can see about 3 inches of this white under-layer, tie a knot in the oesophagus below the white band and then slide the knot up until it holds neatly over the exposed area. This will prevent the stomach contents from flooding out of the oesophagus when the stomach is removed: the knot will hold the bile in and the oesophagus will simply bulge like a water balloon.

Once this is done, it is time to pull the intestines out, leaving the 'pluck' (the organs within the chest cavity) inside. Make a cut just below the last rib and then either using a gut hook or guiding the knife with your fingers to avoid cutting into the intestines, open the beast up fully. Then take the uppermost hind leg and heave the deer over to its side with a strong flicking motion. The innards will flop out. Reach in and pull everything out apart from the heart, lungs, liver and kidneys.

Back at base, when you have achieved the difficult job of transporting the heavy carcass over what will doubtless be several miles of rugged terrain, it is time to skin the beast. Normally you would either use a skinning chair or skin the beast from a hanging position. The sooner you can skin the deer after it has been killed, the better, as the hide always comes off a warm body easily; a grisly but nevertheless important point. First, find a good branch or branches from which to hang the animal, and get some good strong rope together. Now, drag the animal on its back over to the hanging branch.

Stand between its rear legs and grip them, with your thumbs on the inside of the legs. Slide your hand down each leg until your thumb finds a faint depression in the bone before the first joint. Uncannily, you will find that this depression seems made to fit the outline of a man's thumb. Keeping your thumb in the depression, cut immediately above it with a sharp knife. If done correctly you will neatly remove the leg, leaving a clean joint exposed.

Up over the joint, towards the thigh, you will find a strong tendon reminiscent of our Achilles tendon. Slide a stout pole through this natural hitching point on each leg, thereby joining the two legs together. The deer will hang from this one pole (a thick length of hazel is best). Now tie a rope to the centre of this pole, and throw the rest of the rope over the branch and hoist the deer up to a height that is workable.

Carefully cut down the inside of each thigh towards the anal cavity and then, keeping the knife blade pointing up, away from the meat, cut up to the open body cavity. Do the same with the forelegs.

Now ease the hide off the rear legs and carefully use your very sharp knife to cut away at any tissue that adheres between the hide and the meat. Don't ever cut into the meat. Use light, deft strokes of the knife.

Once you have got the hide peeled off the hind legs, down and past the tail of the deer, you can get a good grip on the hanging curtain of hide. Keep the fur folded away from the meat and use your weight to pull it down the back and off the forelegs, and finally the neck. To help the process, you can push your fist down between the meat and hide, right up to your shoulder, and then push out the hide with your whole arm. Although this all sounds horribly gruesome, it isn't – it is the basis of respect, because you are taking responsibility for every stage of getting meat ready for the pot.

Once it has been skinned, the animal should be hung in a cool larder until ready for consumption.

(Following pages) A succulent and tender roe deer. It is kept off the ground on a cool bed of rhododendron leaves in preparation for being slowly and lovingly cooked over a fire.

Recipes

I subscribe wholeheartedly to the old-fashioned view (neatly coined by Fergus Henderson in the title of his lovely cookbook Nose to Tail Eating*) that if you have to kill an animal for food, you can at least do it the justice of eating every last bit. There are, therefore, a few brilliantly quick recipes here that you can whistle up in no time at all, using the underrated body parts such as the liver, kidneys and heart. Please do try them in your outdoor home. They will fill your body with protein, iron and minerals and put a smile on your face with their taste. How will you know how much you love offal until you've tried it?*

Aside from the livers, hearts and kidneys of the animals you hunt, their fat is also a precious resource for the adventurer. Avoid pheasant fat, which has a distinctively bitter flavour, but try to collect fat from other meat. Render the fat down in a pan over a low heat and sieve it to remove unwanted detritus. Keep the fat in a Kilner jar and use it to make bread, preserve pâté or fry onions. It will add flavour and goodness to your cooking.

It is also worth making a stock from the bones of animals every now and then, especially if you already have a fire going. Simmer the bones with onions, garlic and herbs, or whatever aromatics you can lay your hands on. Once you are satisfied that you have extracted sufficient flavour, drain the stock and reduce it right down for easy storing. Keep it in a bottle or pot in a cold stream or shady spot (or fridge, if you are at home). If the weather is warm, use it up quickly, making sure you bring it to the boil before you use it.

Mixed game spit-roast feast

Feeds 6

3 grouse or partridge

1 pheasant

1 mallard

120ml extra virgin olive oil

2 tablespoons red wine
  vinegar

For the rosemary salt:

leaves from 2 large sprigs of
  rosemary, shredded

2 tablespoons Maldon
  sea salt

1 teaspoon peppercorns

2 teaspoons soft brown sugar

In exchange for a wonderful day's rough shooting on a beautiful red grouse moor in Yorkshire we agreed to cook lunch for the laird, Anthony Milbank, and his wife, Belinda. Anthony had warned us that he was a dab hand at cooking grouse, so the pressure was on to prove that we could cook a mean lunch with our catch without the luxury of an oven.

We had lunch in one of their old outbuildings to shelter us from the icy cold wind and torrential rain. Luckily there was an old grill where we could build a fire. The spit roast was a feast – marinated meat cooked directly on to flame has the most delicious taste. Guy chopped down some green hazel for our barbecue spears, but metal skewers with handles would do. Try it on Bonfire Night, when game is in season.

We ate the grouse with Celeriac chips (see page 277) and braised red cabbage. My mouth waters at the memory.

First joint the pheasant and mallard. With a pair of game scissors, cut out the backbone of the grouse or partridge and cut each bird down the middle into two halves.

To make the rosemary salt, using a pestle and mortar grind all the ingredients into into powder. Put the birds on to a large plate and rub all over with the salt. Drizzle over the olive oil and vinegar and leave to marinate for at least an hour.

When you are ready to eat, spear or thread each piece of meat on to a hazel spear or skewer. Cook over a direct flame (or, if indoors, under a hot grill) for 10–15 minutes, depending on how you like your game. I think the only way is pink but some like it better done, although flavour and a tender texture are sacrificed.

Grouse pâté

Feeds 2
hearts and livers from
3 grouse or partridge
(about 50g)
an equal quantity of butter
a scattering of thyme or
rosemary leaves
salt and pepper to taste
a splash of whisky, brandy
or sherry (depending on
your tipple)

Having gone to the trouble of shooting, plucking and gutting a beautiful bird such as grouse, it would be a terrible pity to waste any part of it. Here is a quick and easy way to use up the heart and liver, which will preserve them for a short while. It is delicious on some of Guy's bannock bread (see page 72), preferably toasted on an open fire.

Trim any gristle and outside membrane from the livers. Melt the butter in a frying pan over a medium heat and when it is sizzling, add the hearts, livers and herbs. Cook them in the butter for 4–5 minutes, seasoning with salt and pepper and breaking them up with your wooden spoon as you stir them. Add the splash of alcohol and let it bubble up for a few seconds.

Remove the offal and chop it up as finely as possible, so that you almost have a purée. Put this in a small Kilner jar and pour the butter over the top. If the pâté is not quite covered by the butter, melt a little more. Covering the offal with fat will prevent bacteria getting to it, thus preserving the pâté.

Store in a cool spot and eat for breakfast or lunch the next day, though be warned, you will not get much pâté from three birds – a tablespoon each perhaps.

'Devils on horseback' pheasant with bacon and apricots

Feeds 4

4 pheasant breasts
(from 2 pheasants)
12 plump, juicy dried apricots
(or fresh if you're lucky
enough to find a tree)
8–12 rashers streaky bacon
1 sprig of thyme (optional)
salt and pepper
butter or olive oil, for frying

This recipe is blissfully easy to make and uses the delicious flavours of sizzling bacon and caramelised apricot to complement the gamey flavour of pheasant. It uses only the breast of the pheasant, so try preserving the other parts of the bird in fat (see Duck confit, page 150) for a barren spell. The pheasant-shooting season starts at the beginning of October, a month when you can often be blessed with long, balmy evenings to enjoy your supper around the fire.

Enjoy this with chips, Potato and burdock root scones (see page 273), mash or Guy's bannock bread (see page 72) if there are no vegetables available.

Cut each pheasant breast in half across the middle lengthwise so that you have eight thin lengths of breast. Cut the apricots across in the same way.

Lay out a rasher of bacon and place on it a sprig of thyme (if you are using). Place a piece of pheasant breast across the bacon slice and lay three pieces of apricot on top of the breast. Season with salt and pepper and then wrap the bacon tightly around the pheasant to make a parcel. If you need more bacon, use another piece – it just needs to contain the apricots. Repeat with the remaining bacon, pheasant and apricot.

In a frying pan melt a little butter or oil over a high heat so that it is sizzling hot. Add the pheasant parcels and cook for 3–4 minutes a side until the bacon is crispy and golden, the apricot caramelised and the pheasant just cooked. The heat from the pan will seal the bacon around the meat.

Peking poached pheasant

Feeds 6

2 pheasant

1 cinnamon stick

5 cloves

10 peppercorns

5 star anise

1 small onion, peeled
and halved

1 teaspoon sea salt

a few dashes of soy sauce

damson sauce (see page 292),
to serve

a handful of hedge garlic and
hairy bittercress (or spring
onions if you can't find
any), to serve

a handful of pennywort
(tastes like cucumber –
see page 249), to serve

For the pancakes:

125g plain flour

a pinch of salt

1 large free-range egg

300ml semi-skimmed milk

a knob of butter

a little sesame oil, for frying

I love poaching freshly caught sea trout or salmon in the summer, but when it comes to meat most British people prefer to roast and fry more than anything else. This is a shame, as poaching gives an amazingly tender result, which is particularly useful when you are cooking game, as you can often end up with quarry that is old and tough. Poaching is also a thrifty way of cooking, as it enables you to scrape away every morsel of flesh from the bones.

Pheasant has a lovely gamey flavour that goes well with plums. The pancakes are quick and easy to make, so don't be daunted (but you could always buy some).

Put the birds in a large casserole and cover with cold water. Add the spices, onion and seasoning. Put the casserole over the heat, bring to the boil and simmer gently for 15 minutes, and then take off the heat. Leave the birds to cool in the liquid. When they are cool, strip the meat from the carcasses, shredding it as you go.

Meanwhile, to make the pancake mix, sift the flour and salt into a bowl. Make a well in the centre and break in the egg. Beat the egg with a spoon or whisk, gradually adding the milk and incorporating the flour from the sides of the bowl. Melt a knob of butter in a heavy frying pan and whisk it into the pancake mix. Heat a tiny bit more, or some sesame oil, in the pan and when it is hot and sizzling add approximately 30ml of pancake mix. Swirl around in the pan to make a small and very thin pancake. Cook on both sides until pale brown. If the pancake is very thick, thin the mixture with more milk. Make all the pancakes, keeping them warm in foil by the fire.

When you are ready to eat, toss the pheasant in the hot frying pan for 5 minutes and add a few tablespoons of damson sauce. Arrange the pancakes, pheasant, damson sauce and wild leaves on plates, and tuck in.

Duck prosciutto

Makes about 50 thin slices
  of prosciutto
4 duck breasts, with skin
thyme leaves from 2–3 sprigs
2 garlic cloves, peeled
  and whole
2 bay leaves
6–8 juniper berries
10 peppercorns
500g rock salt

This recipe and the following one are wonderful ways to preserve duck meat to enjoy later, but see my note on page 70 about bacteria. Use these only when it is really cold outside (or when you are in the luxury of your home with its fridge). You could also try making them with other game.

Try using this recipe as part of the Duck prosciutto salad on page 150.

Cut each duck breast in half along the natural division. Using a pestle and mortar, bash up the thyme, garlic, bay, juniper berries and peppercorns a bit to bruise the garlic and juniper and crush the herbs. Mix in the salt and scatter all over the breasts. Arrange the breasts in a single layer on a plate and put in a cool place (or fridge) for 2 days, turning them in the salt from time to time.

Wash the salt off the breasts and wrap each piece in muslin. Tie up the muslin with string and hang each breast in a cool, shady spot (our wall tent was perfect for this). Whatever spot you choose, make sure that rodents cannot reach it. Hang the breasts for a week and then hang them the other way up for another 8–10 days, re-tying as necessary. By this time the breasts should be very hard to the touch. You can keep them in a cool place for a further 2 weeks.

To eat, slice extremely thinly, so that the slices are almost transparent.

Duck prosciutto salad

Feeds 3–4
75g hazelnuts, shelled
2 English eating apples
    (preferably tart ones)
25 slices duck prosciutto,
    or cured ham, e.g. Parma
    or Serrano
200g watercress

For the dressing:
100ml extra virgin olive oil
2 tablespoons sherry vinegar
1 teaspoon honey
½ teaspoon Dijon mustard
Maldon salt and pepper

Hazelnuts go beautifully with game in salads, or indeed ground up in puddings or added to pâtés. I recommend huge experimenting with these sweet, indigenous nuts.

Warm the nuts in a dry frying pan over a medium heat for about 5 minutes, tossing gently to get an even colouring. You want them toasted a very light caramel colour.

Make the salad dressing by combining all the ingredients in an old jam jar or glass. Quarter, core and slice the apples and toss them in a tablespoon of the dressing to stop them discolouring.

Slice the duck breasts very thinly. Remove any thick stalks from the watercress. Toss the watercress and nuts in enough dressing to make them glisten and arrange piles on each plate. Top with slices of apple and duck breast, and *voilà*!

Duck confit

Yields 4 confit duck legs
4 duck legs, with skin
500g rock salt
2 garlic cloves, peeled
    and whole
thyme leaves from 2–3 sprigs
2 bay leaves
6–8 juniper berries
10 peppercorns
800g duck fat

This recipe uses the same ingredients as Duck prosciutto (page 149), with duck legs instead of the breasts, plus some duck fat, so if you have a glut of duck you could cook both recipes at the same time to preserve both the legs and breasts of the bird.

Trim the legs of any excess fat and set aside. Mix together the salt, garlic, herbs and peppercorns and rub all over the duck. Store in a dark, cool spot for 12–24 hours.

When you are ready to cook the duck, melt the fat in a large, heavy-bottomed casserole over a medium heat. Brush the salt off the duck legs and rinse the legs in water, reserving the herbs and juniper berries for cooking the duck. Pat the legs dry and slip them into the fat in a single layer with the reserved seasoning. They should be covered in the fat, but if you don't quite have enough, turn them from time to time during the cooking.

Bring up to simmering point and simmer for 1½ –2 hours until the meat is extremely soft. Carefully transfer the legs to a Kilner jar or earthenware pot and cover in the melted fat. The legs need to have at least 2½cm of fat covering them.

You can store them for 3–6 months, depending on how cool your camp is. To use, take the confit out of the fat and cook in a hot frying pan or oven until it is crisp. It is delicious with boozy prunes (see page 154), in salads or with mash.

Warm beetroot and pigeon salad

Feeds 4–6
450g beetroot
a large knob of butter
salt and pepper
8 pigeon breasts, seasoned
*   with salt and pepper*
100g hazelnuts or walnuts
*   (foraged or from the*
*   tuckbox), toasted in a*
*   dry pan*
2–3 teaspoons mix of
*   tarragon, chives, parsley,*
*   thyme (some or all)*
2 large handfuls of summer
*   leaves (e.g. hairy*
*   bittercress, watercress,*
*   chickweed, sorrel)*

For the dressing:
100ml extra virgin olive oil
1 tablespoon red wine vinegar
1 teaspoon Dijon mustard
a few generous pinches of soft
*   brown sugar*
salt and pepper

Woodpigeon are at their best in the late summer/early autumn, when they are plump from a season's feeding. If you take the breasts off (saving the carcasses for stock or potted pigeon – see page 154), they take minutes to pan-fry in a hot pan, making them perfect fast, camp food. Enjoy them for breakfast with coffee and eggs (if you have some) or use them in this salad.

Salad leaves like hairy bittercress, watercress, pennywort, chickweed and sorrel are plentiful in the late summer, and provide essential roughage and vitamins. At home, you can substitute rocket or other salad leaves. This recipe is also delicious made with duck breasts.

Halve the beetroot and slice each half into small wedges. Parboil in salted water for 15–20 minutes until just cooked.

Heat the butter in a heavy-bottomed saucepan on a fairly high heat and add the drained beetroot wedges. Season with salt and pepper and sauté until they start caramelising – this will take about 10 minutes.

Turn the heat right up, and add the pigeon breasts to the pan (and a little more butter if the pan looks dry) and cook them for 1–2 minutes a side. When you think they are cooked, prod them: they should still be a little pink and squidgy in the middle, as overcooking game makes it dry and tough to eat.

Remove the pigeon and beetroot from the heat and rest the meat for 5 minutes while you make the salad dressing. Mix all the dressing ingredients together in an old jam jar, together with any pan juices. Slice the pigeon and toss with the beetroot, nuts, herbs, leaves and dressing.

Potted pigeon with boozy prunes

Makes about 400g
2 pigeon
1 garlic clove
3–4 peppercorns
1 bay leaf and some thyme
3–4 rashers streaky bacon
3 wild garlic leaves, shredded
melted butter, to cover the
   potted pigeon

For the boozy prunes:
10 prunes
1 large glass red wine
   or brandy
50g soft brown sugar
a pinch of allspice

This is one of the most delicious game recipes and it is incredibly easy to make. You can also use it to cook partridge, pheasant, rabbit or any other meat you have. The poaching and shredding means that you use every last bit of meat on the animal and are left with a wonderful stock for a wild soup. When I cooked this with pigeon, there were masses of wild garlic in the woods, which I mixed with the shredded pigeon – a lovely addition.

Put the pigeon in a saucepan of simmering water with the garlic, pepper and herbs. Bring the water back up to the boil and simmer gently for 10 minutes. Allow the pigeon to cool in the water. Meanwhile sweat the bacon over a gentle heat for 5 minutes until it releases some fat. It should be cooked without being crisp. Cut into tiny pieces.

While the pigeon is cooking, put the prunes, wine, sugar and allspice in a small saucepan and simmer for about 15 minutes until the prunes are coated with a rich thick syrup.

When the pigeon has cooled, pull away all the meat from the carcass in shreds and mix with the wild garlic and the streaky bacon and its fat. Season to taste. Press the meat down into a small Kilner jar and cover with melted butter. Serve the potted pigeon with Guy's bannock bread (see page 72), toasted, and the boozy prunes. It should keep well in the sealed jar in a cool place, provided the meat is well covered by a layer of butter.

Pot-roast pigeon with cherries and hedge garlic

Feeds 6

3 tablespoons butter

4 pigeon

salt and pepper

1 large onion,
    roughly chopped

2 large handfuls of cherries,
    halved and stoned

1 handful of hedge garlic or
    2 garlic cloves, peeled
    and halved

3 bay leaves, preferably fresh

1 tablespoon very finely
    chopped tarragon leaves

zest and juice of 1 orange

1 large glass white wine,
    plus ½ glass water

4 slices bread, buttered

dandelion or watercress
    leaves, to serve

Game recipes are always associated with the winter, but pigeon is also a real treat in the summer. This recipe takes no time at all and uses the subtly scented hedge garlic. Wild cherries go brilliantly with the slightly gamey flavour of pigeon, if you can find them before the birds do – it is often the case that they are unripe one day and gone the next.

Prepare the fire for using the Dutch oven (or indoors, preheat an oven to 150°C/gas 2).

Melt the butter in a Dutch oven (or casserole). Season the inside of the pigeon with salt and pepper. When the butter is sizzling hot, brown the pigeon all over in the fat and set aside. Add the onion to the pot, cooking it until it is soft and translucent. Meanwhile stuff the pigeon with half the cherries and the garlic. Add the bay leaves, tarragon, orange zest and juice and the rest of the cherries to the onions, pour over the wine and season with salt and pepper. Bring the wine up to simmering point and then place the pigeons on the mixture and cover with the Dutch oven (or casserole) lid.

Put the oven in the coals of the fire, putting at least two-thirds of the coals on top of the oven and one-third underneath. Pot-roast for 20–25 minutes (or indoors, for about 25–30 minutes). Fry the bread and serve the pigeon on the fried bread with a salad of watercress or dandelion leaves.

Game soup

Feeds 4–6

a little olive oil, for sweating

1 medium onion, chopped

1 carrot, chopped

spice mix (see page 33)
   (optional)

2 garlic cloves, chopped

a bundle of herbs tied
   together (bay, rosemary or
   thyme and parsley would
   be good)

250g rice, potatoes or lentils

1 teaspoon redcurrant jelly

a squeeze of lemon juice or
   a dash of sherry vinegar

a dash of port, sherry
   or brandy, if you are
   carrying them

For the base:

1kg raw trimmings from
   game (e.g. pheasant,
   partridge, venison – one
   or a mixture) – giblets,
   bones, meat

2 tablespoons olive oil

1 large onion

1 carrot

½ bottle wine (save the
   other half for supper)

5 juniper berries

5 coriander seeds

1 fat garlic clove

another bundle of herbs tied
   together (as above)

This recipe uses a base of the bones and leftover bits of meat from any game that you have shot, transforming them into a warming and restorative broth. It is a great way to feed a hungry horde.

First make the base. Heat the oil in a casserole over a high heat and add the game trimmings, onion and carrot and brown for 10 minutes. Add the wine and let it bubble for a few minutes to reduce, before covering the lot with cold water. Bring to a simmer and add the rest of the ingredients. Simmer gently for a few hours while you go and do something else. Do not let the stock simmer too hard or it will boil dry.

Drain the base and throw away the bones (far from camp, so that you don't attract rodents). Heat more oil in the casserole over a high heat, add the onion and carrot and sweat for 10 minutes. At this stage you can add some spice mix if you feel like it. Add the garlic and herbs and cook for a few minutes before adding the carbohydrate. Stir for a few more minutes before adding the game stock.

Simmer for 20–25 minutes until the carbohydrate is cooked. Add the redcurrant jelly, lemon or sherry vinegar and a dash of booze if you have some.

Rabbit, apple and cider stew

Feeds 4–6

3 tablespoons olive oil

2 rabbits, jointed

salt and pepper

*6 eating apples, peeled, cored
    and cut into eighths*

2 large onions, finely chopped

*1 head of garlic, cloves
    separated and peeled*

3 bay leaves

5 sprigs of thyme

1 tablespoon brown sugar

*500ml cider or a mix of cider
    and water*

salt and pepper

Rabbit is one of my favourite things to eat. It is now possible to buy farmed rabbit but, as with most animals, this will never have as much flavour as its wild cousin, which has had the advantage of roaming freely, eating wild shoots and grass on its travels. If you are lucky enough to net a young rabbit, you will find that the meat is tender and succulent, with a lovely soft taste to it. Old rabbits tend to be tough, but slow cooking softens the meat.

In Somerset we did some work for Sifty and Ann on their cider farm and in return they let us set up camp in the orchard, and while we were there we shot some rabbit. Sifty's incredible home-made cider was perfect for this delicious, seasonal stew. Serve with mashed potatoes and a green salad.

Make sure your fire has lots of hot embers for a Dutch oven (or preheat an oven to 190°C/gas 5).

Season the rabbit joints with salt and pepper. Heat half the olive oil in a casserole pan or Dutch oven, brown the rabbit pieces all over and set aside. Add the rest of the olive oil and cook the onion, garlic cloves and apple on a medium–high heat for about 10 minutes until they turn golden and caramelised, seasoning them as they cook. Place the rabbit on the caramelised onion and add the bay leaves and thyme sprigs, so that they nestle alongside. Sprinkle over the sugar and then carefully pour over the cider or cider and water mix.

Bring the liquid up to a gentle simmer and taste for seasoning. It is much better to season earlier on in the cooking, so that the flavour has a chance to develop. Put the Dutch oven in the embers of the fire (or put the casserole pan in the preheated oven) for about an hour, making sure that over half the coals are on the top and checking after 40 minutes to see if the rabbit is tender. Cooking times will vary, depending on the age of the animal.

Slow-braised rabbit with olive oil, sage and lemon

Feeds 6
200g flour
salt and pepper
thyme leaves from 1 sprig,
* finely chopped (optional)*
2 rabbits, each cut into
* six pieces*
4 tablespoons extra virgin
* olive oil*
1 lemon, sliced
20 sage leaves, chopped
6 garlic cloves, sliced
1 chilli, deseeded and
* chopped*
½ bottle white wine
600ml game stock or stock
* made from bouillon cubes*
chopped parsley, to garnish

The gentleness of its flavour means that rabbit, like chicken, can sit happily with many different ingredients. My love affair with rabbit began when I first ate it in Italy, in a canteen just away from the main square in Sienna. The Italians like to cook it very slowly, often stewing it in olive oil for an hour to tenderise it. On our gastronomic tour, thanks to my precious herb garden I was able to cook the rabbits we caught ferreting in the Italian style. Serve this with sautéed ruby chard and some boiled potatoes.

Season the flour with salt, pepper and thyme (if using). Put the flour on a plate and dust each rabbit piece in the flour. Heat half the oil in a casserole over a high heat and brown the rabbit pieces all over.

Add the remaining oil to the casserole and add the lemon slices. Cook over a medium heat for about 5 minutes until they start to caramelise, and then add the sage, garlic and chilli and cook for another 3–4 minutes. Add the white wine and stock, and season. Simmer gently for 35–40 minutes or until the rabbit is tender.

Remove the rabbit from the casserole and increase the heat. Simmer the sauce until it has reduced to a syrupy liquid and put the rabbit back. Sprinkle over chopped parsley.

Rabbit Milanese

Feeds 4–6

2 rabbits

⅓ packet of cornflakes,
    bashed into fine crumbs
    (see right)

some flour, for coating

4 free-range eggs, beaten

1 tablespoon olive oil

a knob of butter

For the sauce:

olive oil

1 large onion, finely chopped

1 fat garlic clove, finely
    chopped

2 carrots, diced into
    ½cm cubes

2–3 courgettes, diced into
    ½cm cubes

wild thyme, fennel, chervil
    or rosemary

1–2 bay leaves

1 x 400g tin of plum
    tomatoes or 4–6 fresh
    tomatoes, chopped

salt and pepper

a pinch of sugar

This is a wizard recipe for when you have netted or shot a young, tender rabbit. It also works beautifully with turkey, veal or chicken. Making breadcrumbs in camp is a tricky business, so carry a packet of cornflakes with you wherever you go. Empty a third of them into a bag, put the bag on a chopping board and bash the cornflakes into fine crumbs with a bottle or rolling pin. Easy-peasy.

You can add whichever vegetable is in season to this simple tomato sauce. (It is particularly good with artichoke hearts, celeriac or parsnips, or with broad beans, peas and lettuce instead of the tomatoes). The rabbit crumbing and frying takes about 10 minutes. Delicious, fast camp cooking.

Cut the meat from the rabbit into 3–4cm pieces and lay the pieces between sheets of greaseproof paper. Bash them with a rolling pin or bottle until they are very, very thin.

To make the sauce, heat the oil in a heavy-bottomed frying pan over a medium heat and add the onion. Sweat for 5 minutes before adding the garlic, carrot and courgettes. Cook for a further 5–10 minutes before adding the herbs and tomatoes. Season with salt and pepper and add the pinch of sugar. Simmer for 20 minutes until the sauce is reduced and full of flavour.

Take three deepish bowls and fill one with the cornflake crumbs, one with the flour and one with the eggs. Season the rabbit pieces with salt and pepper and dip each piece into first the flour, then the eggs and finally the crumbs, ensuring that each piece is totally covered in crumbs.

Heat a tablespoon of oil and a knob of butter in a large frying pan over a high heat and when they are sizzling hot add the rabbit and cook for 2–3 minutes a side until crispy and golden. Serve with the tomato sauce.

Hare ragout

Feeds 4

olive oil, for browning

500g hare meat, chopped
   very, very finely

salt and pepper

1 large onion, chopped

2 carrots, cut into small cubes

3 garlic cloves, finely chopped

1 x 400g tin of plum
   tomatoes

a couple of sprigs of thyme

a few bay leaves

a pinch of allspice

a pinch of sugar

300ml red wine

a square or two of dark
   chocolate or 1 tablespoon
   redcurrant jelly

The hare is such a magnificent animal that I still hesitate to pull the trigger when I have one in my sights. Seeing one run through a field, with its lean, powerful body and long, graceful ears, is uplifting. In some areas a hare is a rare sight and I would really prefer to see one slip away to live another day, even if I am really hungry. However, if you are lucky enough to be in countryside where hare are plentiful, you might think of taking one home for the pot – they are utterly, utterly delicious. Though hare is not nearly so plentiful as rabbit, it is prepared in much the same way (see Guy's instructions for rabbit on page 134 for details.)

This ragout is wonderfully easy to make and tastes equally good made with pheasant meat, wild boar or even a mixture of minced pork and beef. Serve it on top of piles of steaming mashed potato or celeriac; it is especially tasty if you serve it with velvety pasta and a grating of Parmesan cheese on top.

Heat a little oil in a heavy-bottomed pan over a medium heat and when it is smoking hot add a third of the meat. Brown the meat on all sides and season with salt and pepper before removing and reserve. Repeat with more batches until all the meat is browned.

Heat some more oil and add the onion and carrots. Cook for 5–10 minutes, stirring from time to time so that the vegetables don't colour. When the onion is translucent, add the garlic, and after a couple of minutes the tomatoes, herbs, allspice, sugar and wine. Simmer for 10 minutes before adding the hare and chocolate or redcurrant jelly. Cook over a low heat until the liquid has reduced to a rich, thick sauce. Taste for seasoning.

Venison liver with dandelion leaves

Feeds 2
2 tablespoons butter
1 medium onion,
  finely chopped
1 venison liver, cut into
  1cm-thick slices
1 teaspoon flour
½ glass red wine
a splash of sherry vinegar
a dollop of cream
  (if you have it to hand)
salt and pepper
toast, to serve
a handful of dandelion leaves,
  to serve

Liver takes very little cooking. Flash fried in a smoking hot pan is the best way, ensuring that the texture remains soft and yielding to the bite rather than tough and grey, as I gather it was served to our parents at school.

Liver is incredibly good for you and I always think women in particular should eat more of it as nationally we suffer from low iron levels and liver is packed full of this essential mineral. Cooked right, it is exceptionally tasty.

Melt the butter in a heavy-bottomed frying pan over a high heat and fry the onion until it becomes translucent and golden. Add the slices of liver and cook for about 2 minutes. Remove the liver and keep it warm. Sprinkle the flour into the pan and stir it with the butter for 3–4 minutes over the heat to cook the flour. Stir in the wine, incorporating it bit by bit into the flour. Bring to a boil and simmer for a few minutes before adding the sherry vinegar and cream (if using). Season to taste with salt and pepper. Serve the liver on toast with the wine sauce poured over it and the dandelion leaves.

Venison braised with chilli and chocolate

Feeds 10

*2kg shoulder or haunch
    of venison*

olive oil, for browning

2 medium onions, diced

2 carrots, diced

5 celery stalks, diced

2 parsnips, diced

5 garlic cloves, chopped

2 dried chillies, crumbled

*500ml game stock (or stock
    made from bouillon cubes)*

½ bottle full-bodied red wine

*100g dark chocolate, finely
    grated or chopped*

1 tablespoon redcurrant jelly

For the marinade:

1 bottle full-bodied red wine

4 garlic cloves

1 sprig of rosemary

4–5 sprigs of thyme

*2 fresh red chillies, deseeded
    and finely chopped*

*3 tablespoons extra virgin
    olive oil*

10 juniper berries, crushed

salt and pepper

Braised venison is a wonderfully warming dish in the winter, especially when steeped with the flavour of chilli and chocolate. Although there seem to be a lot of ingredients in this recipe, you can make the marinade one day, cook the stew a day or two later and eat it several days later. Each stage is fairly quick, so by the time you eat it you scarcely feel as if you've had to work. It is a really delicious stew – my favourite, I think. At home I like to make double the recipe and freeze some for a rainy day – sadly not possible in a wall tent! Serve it with hunks of bread or mashed sweet potato.

Make sure your fire has lots of hot embers (or preheat an oven to 190°C/gas 5).

Cut the venison into 2.5cm cubes, removing large bits of fat or gristle. Put these into a double-layered plastic bag, along with all the marinade ingredients. Set aside for a day in a cool spot in the river (or in the fridge if you have taken your quarry home), turning every so often so that all of the meat comes into contact with the marinade.

When you are ready to cook, remove the venison from the marinade, setting the marinade aside for later. Heat a large casserole over a high heat until it is smoking hot. Pour in a tablespoon of olive oil and when it is very hot add the venison cubes, 6 or 7 at a time, so that you are not overcrowding the pan and thus bringing down the temperature of the oil. Brown the meat on all sides for 1–2 minutes, letting the pan get hot again between each batch and adding more oil if necessary.

When the meat is all browned, set it aside while you brown the vegetables. Add a tablespoon of oil to the casserole and sweat the onions for 5 minutes before adding the carrots, celery and parsnips. Cook for a further 10 minutes, allowing the vegetables to start caramelising without letting them burn. Add the garlic and cook for another 5 minutes.

Return the venison to the casserole, along with the reserved marinade and the rest of the ingredients. Bring up to a gentle simmer, stirring to melt the chocolate into the sauce. Cook in the Dutch oven (or preheated oven) for about 90 minutes or until the meat is tender and falling apart.

Flash-fried Sicilian venison steaks with pine nuts and raisins

Feeds 4

4 venison steaks, taken
*   from the saddle*
2 teaspoons black
*   peppercorns, ground*
2 tablespoons olive oil
½ glass red wine
5 juniper berries, crushed

For the sauce:
a large knob of butter
60g raisins, soaked in hot
*   water for 30 minutes*
3 tablespoons pine nuts
1 teaspoon redcurrant jelly
1 teaspoon red wine vinegar
1 glass red wine

Guy and I spit roasted a whole roe deer over a fire and served slices of the venison with this Sicilian-inspired sauce, which uses nuts and dried fruit from the store. It is a lot simpler and quicker, however, to pan-fry steaks cut from the saddle (or fillet), the tenderest part of the animal. Try not to overcook the venison, as it really ruins the texture and flavour. Red wine is an essential part of the sauce, so don't go off to camp without a bottle.

The sauce would be delicious with a roast haunch (leg) of venison for a fun Sunday lunch. If you do this, cover the meat with bacon fat to stop the lean meat from drying out.

I love eating this with puréed sweet potato or butternut squash and steamed greens.

Marinate the steaks in the pepper, olive oil, wine and juniper berries for half an hour.

To make the sauce, melt half the butter in a frying pan over a medium–high heat and fry the drained raisins and the nuts for 3–4 minutes until the nuts are lightly toasted. Remove the steaks from the marinade and add the marinade and the rest of the sauce ingredients to the pan. Simmer for 15 minutes until you have a lovely rich sauce.

Meanwhile melt the rest of the butter in a smoking hot, large heavy frying pan and cook the steaks for 2–3 minutes a side; the amount of time they need will depend on their thickness. Venison is best eaten pink in the middle, so err on the side of undercooking – you can always put the meat back on the heat if it is too pink for your liking. Pour over the sauce, simmer for 1 minute and serve.

Venison with potato scones and hawthorn syrup The wonderful marriage of hawthorn berries or rosehips with game is a recent discovery of mine. The rounded, fruity flavour of rosehip seems to melt into gamey meat such as pheasant, while hawthorn berries and venison are an ideal match. Nutritionally this makes sense too, as nature provides protein in the meat and vitamin C in the wild berries. Marinate and cook the venison as above and serve with Potato and burdock root scones (see page 273) and Rosehip and ginger syrup (see page 290) or Hawthorn sauce (see page 291) and you'll be in for a treat.

Spiced squirrel popcorn

Feeds 4–6

2–3 squirrel (or 2 chicken breasts or 300–400g pork tenderloin)

1 tablespoon fish sauce or soy sauce

50g arrowroot

vegetable oil, for frying

For the spiced salt:

1 teaspoon fennel seeds

1 teaspoon allspice

1 blade of mace

75g salt

1 teaspoon finely chopped thyme or sage leaves (optional)

Grey squirrel is a fine-tasting meat, not unlike free-range chicken. This is a wonderfully fast way to eat meat, ideal if you are tired and hungry. It will provide your body with protein, starch and calories. It is delicious dipped in home-made aioli (see page 295), and it is absolutely delicious with beer, if you can find a local brewery on your travels.

To make the spiced salt, using a pestle and mortar grind all the spices into a fine powder and mix this into the salt with the herbs (if using). Take the meat off the squirrel and cut it into thin slivers. Toss the meat in the fish or soy sauce and then in the arrowroot. Heat the oil in a large deep pan over a high heat until it is shimmering. Test the heat by touching the oil with a piece of meat. If it sizzles, the oil is hot enough to fry the squirrel. Do this in small batches, so that the pieces do not crowd the pan and thus bring down the temperature of the oil.

When the squirrel has turned crispy and golden, remove it with a slotted spoon and drain on some kitchen paper. Sprinkle the spiced salt over it and serve.

Barbecued leg of lamb with laver salsa verde

Feeds 6–8

1 leg of lamb (about 3–4kg)

4 tablespoons olive oil

*2 garlic cloves, very finely
    chopped*

*rosemary leaves stripped
    from 2 sprigs, very finely
    chopped*

zest and juice of 1 lemon

salt and pepper

For the laver salsa verde:

half a plastic bagful of laver

1 fat garlic clove, peeled

salt

juice and zest of 1 orange

*5–6 tablespoons extra virgin
    olive oil*

*1½ teaspoons capers
    (optional)*

*3 anchovies (optional, but a
    fine addition), chopped*

*1 tablespoon tarragon,
    chopped*

2 tablespoons mint, chopped

a handful of parsley, chopped

*1 tablespoon rosemary leaves,
    chopped*

a pinch of brown sugar

By including this recipe for lamb I am by no means exhorting you to go out into a field and shoot your supper, but Guy and I did get desperate for food occasionally and had to work out alternative ways of finding it. We spent a very wet and cold day in a field in Wales shaving swede heads for Colin, a farmer who had a herd of wonderful saltmarsh lamb, which fed on the marshes of the Gower Peninsula; we were rewarded with a leg of this rare animal in return. We made a barbecue in an old oil drum, sawn in half, which we laid in an old supermarket trolley, creating the ultimate mobile barbecue.

This salsa verde will last for several days in a cool place (or fridge). Serve the meal with roasted vegetables.

Remove all the skin and fat from the leg of lamb and take out the bone. Open out the meat with a sharp knife, so that it is a similar thickness all over. You will find more fat in the meat, which you will need to cut out. (Your butcher could do this for you: ask him to bone the leg and butterfly it.) Leave the leg in one piece or divide it into three or four pieces, if you prefer.

Put the meat in a shallow bowl with the olive oil, garlic, rosemary, lemon zest and juice and seasoning, and rub the marinade in well. Cover and leave in a cool place (or fridge) for a minimum of 1 hour, but preferably overnight, to allow the flavours to sink into the flesh.

A couple of hours before you are ready to start cooking the meat, wash the laver well and then put 200ml of water in a saucepan. Add the laver and cook over a low heat for 1–2 hours. If the laver starts catching on the pan, put it in a bowl and suspend the bowl over the saucepan, to which you have added simmering water. Cook until the laver has cooked down and looks like very well-cooked spinach. Drain and squeeze dry.

Using a pestle and mortar crush the garlic clove with a pinch of salt, being careful not to overdo the salt, as the laver is salty. Add the capers and anchovies, and then the herbs, and work into a paste. Work in the laver slowly and stir in the orange juice and olive oil. Add the sugar and check the seasoning.

When the barbecue is hot and ready for cooking, put the lamb on a grill over the fire and cook it for 10–15 minutes a side, if you have left it in one piece, or half that time if you have cut it into chunks. I like lamb pink, so I cook it for less rather than more time. Alternatively skewer chunks of the lamb on hazel spears (or skewers) and give each guest their own spear to cook it as they like it. When the lamb is cooked, leave it to rest for 5 minutes before serving it with the salsa verde.

Lambs' kidney and rosemary skewers

Feeds 4

4 lambs' kidneys

2 large onions, each cut into 8

8 bay leaves

150g bacon, cut into chunks

2 tablespoons olive oil

a drizzle of balsamic vinegar,
  red wine or sherry vinegar

salt and pepper

8 long branches of rosemary,
  soaked in water to stop
  them catching light

When I was butchering the saltmarsh lamb described above, I saw the heart-shaped kidneys nestling in the lamb's fat. Kidneys are such vital organs that they are surrounded in layers of billowing, white fat to protect them from harm. They are a real treat to eat when cooked properly but, just like the liver, they should not be overcooked.

We barbecued them alongside the butterflied lamb for 3–4 minutes on a really hot part of the grill and they were utterly delicious. If you can't find any rosemary, long, thin strips of hazel also make very good skewers.

Cut the kidneys in half horizontally so that you keep the shape. With a small, sharp knife, cut out the white membranes and slide the kidneys out of their protective layer of skin. This will stop them from being tough. Gently toss the kidneys, onions, bay and bacon in the olive oil and balsamic vinegar, wine or sherry vinegar. Season with salt and pepper.

Skewer the kidneys on to the rosemary branches, starting with a chunk of onion, then a kidney, then a bay leaf and finally a piece of bacon. You should be able to fit two lots on to each skewer. When you are ready to eat, put the skewers on the barbecue (or under a hot grill), allowing a couple of minutes a side.

> *'If you wish to be happy for ever, learn to fish'*
> Chinese proverb

THE AQUATIC GOURMET

It was early, just after dawn, when Tommi and I arrived at a river that darkly snaked and swirled its way between banks gripped by the roots of ancient pollarded willows. The valley still held its morning mist, and in a distant field I saw five Suffolk Punch draught horses standing very still, waiting for the sun to burn off the early-morning chill. Suffolk Punches are the smallest working horses in Britain, and these days they are a rare sight; to see five in one go was a privilege. As we watched, a heron lifted from his post and flew along the line of the river and a group of plump mallards glided shyly away, keeping their eyes firmly upon us. We crept stealthily towards the bank, staying low as we deftly flicked little brass spinners into the stream, aiming for the swirling depths beneath the tree roots.

We were after pike, a voracious predator that looks like a freshwater equivalent of the barracuda. Accompanying us was a man who had spent much of his life engaged in the pursuit of these aquatic assassins and was prepared to share some of his hard-earned experience. He was also the great-great-grandson of John Constable, who captured this landscape so perfectly almost 200 years earlier.

A spinner ready for the hunt; it looks like a wounded fish when it is being reeled through the water – utterly enticing for a hunting fish.

After just a few minutes Tommi let out a whoop with delight. The end of her fishing rod was pointing down sharply, and in the water I saw something glow in the darkness. It was the golden side of a fighting pike, flashing in the shadowy waters, and Tommi had it hooked hard. A perfect day of fishing had just begun.

By the end of the morning we had caught three beautiful pike. Tommi pulled in the largest, weighing in at 4 pounds. There were undoubtedly larger pike lurking in those mysterious depths, but we were using small lures in the hope of catching younger and therefore tastier fish. Back at camp, after Tommi had carefully seasoned them and wrapped them in foil, we baked the fish in the charcoals of the fire. We ate them with a wild mushroom sauce (see page 232) and they tasted delicious. Pike are not often eaten in Britain, which is a pity, as they are plentiful and if skilfully cooked make very good eating. They just have to be approached in an unbiased way.

Britain is a wet place, full of rivers, lakes and streams, as well as having an immense coastline. Scotland alone has over 15,000 lochs, never mind the endless miles of coastline and inland waterways. This wateriness is nirvana for the aquatic gourmet (or AG, as I shall henceforth call him or her), as it means that there is an abundance of perfectly delicious food waiting to be caught, netted, gathered or picked all around us. You just need to know how.

This section will describe how to catch and prepare a number of superb fish and shellfish that can be caught or gathered in British waters. However, I want to declare at the outset that, though I have fished all my life for pleasure, I am a complete beginner compared to those people who fish with an almost supernatural ability. Whether you are cooking, hunting, gathering or making camp, the only true way of learning is through your own experience. Nevertheless, I hope this chapter will give you enough information to set you off on your own adventures leading to many fabulous fishy meals.

The first step for the hungry AG must be to assess the surroundings. As Britain is an island, the first question is: are you near the sea? If so, what sort of coastline is it? Are you near a river estuary and sandy beaches, or is the coastline rocky and indented with areas of deep water bordered by patches of seaweed and sand? Are there harbours near by where an enterprising AG might be able to get on a fishing trip, or even hire a boat in order to hunt the offshore depths? If you are in the middle of the country, there are likely to be lakes and rivers near by which will provide good food. If you are in the midst of a sprawling metropolis, even canals and urban stretches of river can afford surprising opportunities.

Once you have fixed upon the most realistic spot to begin, you can start the fascinating exercise of identifying a particular fishy inhabitant of that stretch of water to be your target. At this point it pays to do your research, losing yourself in the task: read everything you can and subject local fishermen to barrages of questions regarding how, where and when they catch their prey.

What is certain is that, to become experienced, AGs must fish close to home and not restrict their aquatic hunting to far-off exotic places or the occasional holiday. The reason for this is simply that the most important factor in becoming a good fisherman is time – time not only to get to know your watery hunting ground but to also master the techniques of fishing that water.

Now this is where, in these rushed and stupidly busy times, fishing becomes a beautiful thing. Of all the areas of wild grubbing, fishing demands the most patience and time – in fact, when embarking on a fishing trip you should simply leave your watch behind. Don't plan to fish for an hour, as you certainly won't get lucky. Plan instead to spend the whole morning or evening, or even the whole day. Fishing teaches us a rare and rapidly disappearing skill: the ability to wait. In the process, you may be treated to great shows of natural action and come home with some incredible stories – it is amazing what you will see if you simply sit still.

Once, as a teenager, I was fishing at dusk on a quiet loch on my island home. Bats were flitting overhead, and I noticed one in particular beginning to fly in mysterious and swift circles. Suddenly from behind me I heard a whooshing sound and watched as the bat was caught in the open talons of a large buzzard. Some time later I caught a large trout and walked back through the woods feeling proud to bring a good fish back for my mother. I told her about the buzzard and the bat . . . she did not believe me.

An AG must be ready to swim for his supper. In northern waters use a neoprene hood. Without one your brain becomes cold and slow.

A minute's silence for the sea

The sea has always been our chief provider of fish, but before you read any further I ask you to close this book and sit in silence for one minute to meditate upon man's utter abuse of the ocean and her magnificent bounty. Many species of fish stand on the brink of extinction, all because we are too greedy and stupid to remember our duty, which should be to husband the great resources of this beautiful planet rather than destroy them.

Of course there are some very fine fishermen working off the coast of Britain: people who are careful and aware of their responsibilities. I have met some of them, and I admire the difficult and skilful job that they do. I have also met people who work in fish and shellfish farming, and it seems that much more attention is now being paid to the issue of ensuring that threatened stocks have a chance to re-establish themselves.

I take heart from the fact that we have achieved great things with our inland waterways, and that many rivers that once held nothing now contain growing fish stocks. In certain parts of the world's oceans I have marvelled as I have dived and snorkelled at the diversity of sea life, but in others – such as the Mediterranean – I have been sickened by the utter lack of life that has resulted from man's rapacious nature. Let us hope that we can get a grip of the issues that now threaten the great diversity of our oceans and act appropriately before it is too late.

There are over 50 different species of edible fish in Britain's rich sea waters, some of which are under great pressure. Covering the subject thoroughly is beyond the scope of this book; instead I will simply introduce a few choice species that are not under threat, which the AG can seek out without causing a decline in fish stocks. (On the Marine Conservation Society's website – see page 309 – you will find the names of suppliers who deal with responsibly sourced fish, so that you can enjoy a fish meal without feeling that each mouthful is contributing towards some kind of aquatic Armageddon.)

We'll start our salty foray on the foreshore, which offers an abundance of sublime grub in two main forms: seaweed and shellfish. The first aim with both is to find a good site that is open and unpolluted, so avoid foraging in sight of a refinery, sewage outfall or busy urban or industrial area.

Preparing to push nets for brown shrimp on Morecambe Bay.

Edible seaweeds

There are ten edible seaweeds that can be gathered off the coast of these islands: sea lettuce, kelp, intestinalis, sugar kelp, bladder wrack, carragheen, batter frond, pepper dulse, dulse and laver. The joy of gathering seaweed is that almost all these species can be harvested throughout the year, and they can be found in most rocky coastal areas. They are also extremely rich in minerals, namely iodine, bromine, iron, zinc and magnesium. Generally the bigger the weed, the more likely it is to be good for the pot. Here are some favourites.

Kelp *Laminaria spp* This luscious, leathery olive-brown seaweed has long fascinated me. When swimming in the sea off the Hebrides I often allow myself to stray into thick forests of this sensuous and slippery kelp. Forgive the Freudian diversion, but once you have experienced the subtle joy of kelp slipping seductively across your chest on a bright sunny day you will understand its unexpected allure.

Kelp grows all year round, and can be found wherever there is a rocky shoreline to a depth of 5 to 7 metres. It anchors itself on to rocks and forms mysterious underwater forests through which seals glide and sunlight creates brindled patterns as the plants sway with the ebb and flow of the tide. Although it grows all year, it is best to collect this weed in the spring, when its finely chopped blade-like branches can be added to salads as well as being used to thicken soups and stews. For extramural activity, kelp makes a very effective whip and can thus warm one nicely after a swim before being brought home to eat. I have suggested this use to my wife on occasion, but sadly she has firmly declined . . .

Sugar kelp *Laminaria saccharina* Unlike its cousin, this sandy-yellow kelp has no middle rib and is made distinctive by the crinkling that runs its entire length, reminding me of the front of one of those frilly 1970s-style dress shirts worn by people of dubious taste. It too anchors itself to a rocky shoreline, and has a lustrous, shiny quality that makes you want to bite into it raw. Best harvested in spring, sugar kelp is good in salads and soups, but its best use is as an exotic addition to a stir-fry. Young plants are always best – sometimes I nibble on the raw stems, which have a subtle, fresh taste.

Dulse *Palmaria palmate* This brownish-red or sometimes purple weed is a bit of a shape-shifter, appearing either as a single blade or as a number of strap-like fingers. It clings to the rock with a disc-shaped pad, unlike the rooty-looking anchors of kelp. As with all weeds, it can be eaten raw, and it is also very good stir-fried. Like laver, dulce has a Celtic following; in Ireland it is chopped up and mixed into mashed potato to make a dish known as champ. Bangers and champ: a good idea I think, and you heard it here first!

Laver *Porphyra umbilicalis*

Tommi and I enjoyed a memorable swim amidst breaking waves off a sandy beach on the Gower Peninsula in Wales. It was a cold grey day in October, and we were not even halfway through our gastronomic journey through Britain. Later on, having just managed to stave off hypothermia, we returned to the beach to collect laver, which is a famous Welsh standby.

Laver resembles a dark purplish handkerchief which becomes greenish with age (rather like my hankies, actually), and it can commonly be found on sandy shores throughout Britain. You can collect it all year round, although it is in its best condition during spring, and it can be eaten raw, although it is an acquired taste. It makes a good accompaniment to meat and is a delicacy in south-west Wales, where, mixed with oatmeal, it forms the basis of their famous laverbread. It is prepared by first thoroughly washing the laver to remove any sand and then simmering until it is soft and resembles a jelly.

Laver is treated as a great delicacy in Japan, and is sold in the UK as dried sheets called nori. It can also be used to wrap fish for baking – I like this idea, as it would keep the flesh moist while imparting a delicate flavour of the sea. Tommi and I bartered with a local Welsh farmer, trading labour – topping swedes – in return for a superb joint of saltmarsh lamb, which made the ideal accompaniment for this lithe little weed (see page 171).

Marsh samphire *Salicornia spp*

Another green hero of the foreshore (mudflats and estuaries in the south and east, mainly) is marsh samphire, also known as glasswort, which is at its best from July to early September. Resembling a mini cactus, samphire has a satisfying fleshiness that makes it look quite delectable.

Once washed, the young plants make a crisp addition to salads; or they can be boiled in unsalted water for no more than six minutes, as otherwise they will lose their lovely green colour. The gentle flesh can then be stripped from the plants and served with butter. There can be no greater complement to fish than this beguiling little plant, which straddles the shifting zone between the watery and dry worlds, and there is nothing more satisfying after catching fish than gathering its accompaniment right there on the shore.

Bladder wrack *Fucus versiculosus*

(Following pages) Broken-up kelp in a rockpool. A day's foraging on the foreshore feeds the AG's soul as he stumbles upon patterns and shapes artfully arranged by mother nature.

'Wrack' is an old-fashioned word for weed, and this weed keeps itself afloat with ingenious little bubbles or bladders of air that stipple the tips of dainty olive-brown, strap-like branches. Just like kelp, the bladder loves a rocky shoreline, but it is even healthier, being a rich source of iodine. Iodine is essential for the body to properly process proteins, and hence to heal itself. Bladder wrack can be used just like kelp, and if chopped and dried it makes a particularly nice addition to light-flavoured soups, as well as being a superb condiment.

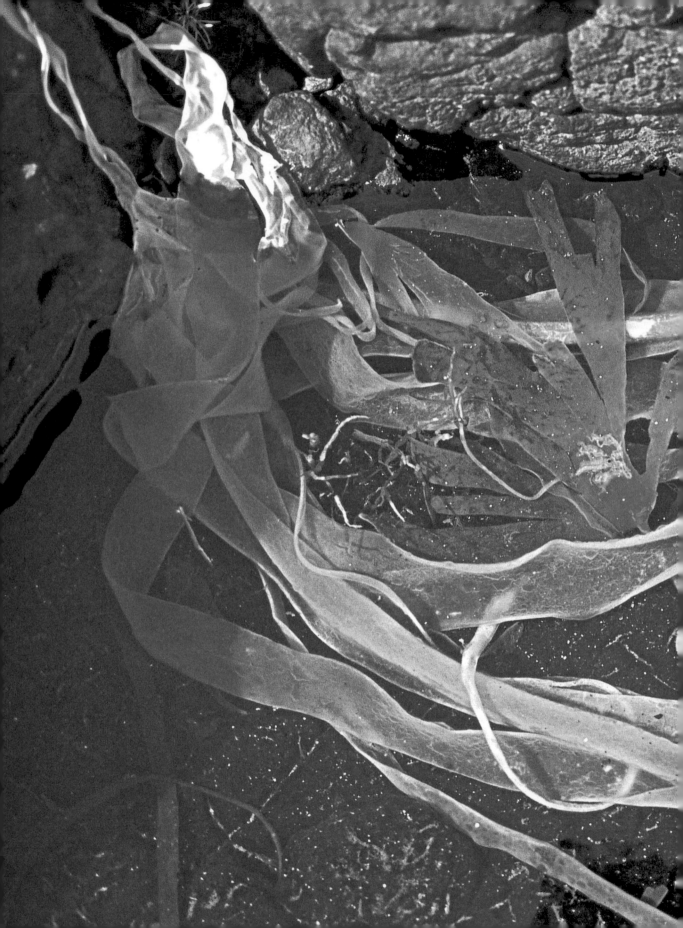

Sustainable shellfish

As with seaweed, if you can find a good patch of shoreline, free from sewage and other pollutants, there will invariably be rich pickings in the form of shellfish. I am a little picky (excuse the pun) when it comes to shellfish, and frankly believe that the soles of my shoes would make better eating than some species. The experience of chewing on a limpet, for instance, simply left me wondering why anyone would put themselves through it. The answer, of course, is that many wild foods were appropriated during times of great hardship and famine, when people had no other option.

In these more fortunate times I feel I need not even touch on some of the grimmer snacks that can be harvested on the shoreline – we'll leave them for the survivalists. Instead, I am going to present an entirely subjective list of goodies which Tommi and I both enjoyed. Our ethos throughout our journey was to put taste before anything else, and rather than asking 'Can we eat it?', we put the question 'Do we want to eat it?' If something tasted appalling, or made us feel like Jim Gunn or Robinson Crusoe, we simply spat it out and reached for the nearest shot of whisky.

A fisherman gives us a lift – without local knowledge and help the AG is nothing.

Blue mussels *Mytilus edulis* I free-dived for some of these beautiful mussels off a beach in Cornwall. I was specifically after mussels that are never exposed by low tides, and thus have grown large because they have a permanent feeding opportunity. These mussels are a sublime deep blue tinged with purple, and can be found from the high-tide mark right down to ten metres in depth.

Orange meat is found in the shell of a mature female mussel, while the pale cream meat comes from males or immature females. It generally takes about three years for them to reach maturity. The best time to scavenge for mussels is between September and April, when they are full of roe and milt (fish or shellfish eggs and sperm respectively); they should be left alone in summer, when they become gritty.

Tommi cooked the mussels in a surprising way (see page 212), placing them on a chopping block under an armful of straw, which I lit with a spark. Once the deep orange flame had burnt through, we blew away the ashes and found that the blackened shells had opened, revealing perfect mouthfuls of golden flesh.

The great joy for the AG is that mussels respond well to farming, and thus can be eaten with a clear conscience. Farmed mussels taste exactly the same as wild ones, as they enjoy exactly the same living and feeding conditions as in the wild – the farmer's only input is the provision of a place to cling to and access to good water.

If gathering your own mussels, be careful where you collect them – mussels are filter feeders and thus can build up concentrated amounts of toxins from the water. Find a spot a long way from man and his pollutants, and make sure that the mussels are below the high-tide line. Ask around locally about algal bloom, which occurs during a red tide and can affect the quality of mussels. If ingested, these mussels can lead to continual vomiting and even paralysis – hardly the ideal end to a dinner party.

Sensible precautions should be taken before eating mussels. Throw away any damaged ones or any that remain open after cleaning, as they could be toxic. Clean mussels thoroughly before cooking and remove any that float to the top of a bowl of water. During cooking the mussels should open; throw away any that don't.

A note about algal bloom All shellfish that feed by filtering nutrients from water are vulnerable to poisonous algal blooms. There are two types of algal toxin to look out for; both have the potential to make the AG's life hell and in the worst case could even lead directly to the grave. Diuretic Shellfish Poison (DSP) can float about in blooms in late summer and early autumn, and if ingested leads to vomiting and diarrhoea. Paralytic Shellfish Poison (PSP) is even worse, and could send dinner guests on a hellish journey that might end in paralysis or death. PSP occurs in algal blooms from spring to early summer and even into winter, and occurs only in mussels.

So the sad news is that filter-feeding shellfish are vulnerable to algal bloom all year round. Nevertheless, if you use common sense and forage only in open, well-drained areas where the water is clean and full of movement you should be fine. Ask knowledgeable local people whether there have been any algal blooms or red tides in the area. The internet offers good up-to-date information as well.

The native oyster *Ostrea edulis* The native oyster can be identified by its classic flat-topped shell with a rounded bottom, in contrast to pacific oysters, whose shells are crinkly all over. Pacific oysters are more often found for sale, but they are mere upstarts when compared to the classy native oyster.

Natives are the ideal size for eating after three to four years' growth; they are available from September to April, though best from late October to late February, when the sea is colder. Pacific oysters are available all year round.

It is against the law to collect more than twelve wild oysters per person. My feeling is that it is best to get hold of farmed oysters when you return to civilisation, as these taste exactly the same (and are just as arousing) as wild ones. The reason for this is that they are harvested when they are at the optimum age, which is about three to four years old, with the added bonus that they will be guaranteed free from the effects of algal bloom. Farmed oysters are fed in the same way as wild ones, and nothing artificial will have been added. In fact farmed oysters have started out wild in the first place, as they are captured when in their floating or 'spat' phase. The oyster farmer just allows them to settle and grow on the specially designed structures of his farm such as lantern bags.

King scallops *Pecten maximus* There are many different types of scallop, but the king is . . . well, the king. Scallops are found all around the British Isles and can grow to as much as 18 centimetres in diameter. They have a wonderful, reddish-brown shell that is typified by strongly defined ribs set out in equidistant lines running its length. The edible parts are the round abductor muscle and the orange and white roe (called coral), which make superb eating. The frilly gills and mantle tissue along the margin should be used only for soup or stocks.

The king scallop is typically found in areas of coarse sandy seabed between 13 and 30 metres in depth, where it lies partially submerged in sediment. It has also been found much deeper – well below 90 metres – and even in the intertidal zone (also called the 'littoral zone', where land and sea meet between high- and low-tide zones).

Harvesting scallops is best left to the most determined of AGs, as it involves diving, and moreover, in northern waters, the use of a dry suit. For these hardy souls, once you have entered the murky deep, spotting scallops presents quite a challenge, as they are masters of camouflage. They lie submerged on the bottoms, their large curved 'right-hand' shells planted in the seabed while their flat 'left-hand' shells are covered by a layer of sediment. It takes a while for your eye to become attuned: the trick is to get used to the seabed's normal appearance and then keep an eye out for disturbed patches which may give away the presence of a king. Sometimes you will be lucky enough to disturb one, and you will see it swimming away like a giant castanet, pumping its shell to fly away.

If you do not feel like sinking into the depths in pursuit of this delicacy, ask a fishmonger for 'diver-harvested' scallops, so you'll know that they have been hand-picked for size and quality, with no unnecessary damage to the surrounding seabed.

Oysters have been eaten in Britain for thousands of years, and were once a staple for many people, not a luxury. Like all shellfish, oysters must be alive before consumption. If the shell is open, the oyster is dead.

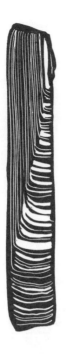

The razor shell *Ensis spp* Also sometimes known as the razor clam, this enigmatic shellfish resembles an old-fashioned cut-throat razor, and can grow to a length of 15 centimetres. It buries itself in coarse sand or gravel from the lower shore down to about 35 metres in depth, and is easily collected on beaches around the country. Razor clams hide in their vertical burrows with only two short tubes sticking up above the surface. They use these to suck in seawater as it rushes up the beach, allowing them to filter out bits of food in the water.

To gather this fine-tasting fish the AG needs to prepare a noxious saline solution: keep adding salt to a litre of water until it no longer dissolves, and then put it into a squeezy water bottle with a nozzle. Go out on to a beach at a low spring tide, and look for the small round holes in the sand that are the razor shell's giveaway. Squirt some of the liquid into the hole and all the others within a square metre or so, and then stand back and wait. If you are lucky, the razor shell will push its way out of one of the holes in disgust. Carefully take hold of the shell and prise the poor thing out of its hole, being quick, as they are great diggers, yet gentle, to ensure that you don't leave half the flesh behind. Pop the razor shell into a bucket of salt water while you gather more.

Razor shells are wonderful steamed, and also make great bait for various varieties of sea fish.

Cockles *Cerastoderma edule* The heart-shaped shells of the wondrous and bountiful cockle are found washed up in vast quantities along our beaches. This shellfish is so prolific that in the southern North Sea, for example, it is common to find up to 1,000 large cockles in a square metre of seabed; thus a wading bird consuming a normal amount of around 300 cockles a day would take more than three days to clear a square metre. Cockles can grow as large as 5 centimetres in diameter and have whitish brown shells that show 22 to 27 prominent radial ridges. They live on open sandy areas of the intertidal zone, feeding in shallow water when submerged and burying themselves just beneath the surface while the tide is out.

Cockles are best harvested in September or October, and are easily gathered with a rake and bucket or, to use a more traditional method, with your bare feet. Squidge the mud between your toes with a delicate treading motion to an approximate depth of 15 centimetres, and when you feel lumps, grab them fast. Be aware that the cockle is the Ferrari of the shellfish world and if you don't act quickly he'll be gone!

Clean the cockles well before cooking, discarding any that are open. Some people advise placing them overnight in a bucket of salted water with a handful of oats – the theory is that the cockles will eat the oats and in the process pass out any sand and rubbish in their bodies. They are most often pickled in vinegar, but can also be boiled or barbecued – best done outside, as they can be very smelly.

Crabs

These hardened gladiators of the deep have to live with two great weaknesses that make them vulnerable, despite their ferocious weaponry: their great taste when cooked and the relative ease with which they can be caught. I have memories of hunting for crabs as a child on the Chesapeake Bay in North America, using chicken necks lowered to the seabed on lengths of string. The crabs simply couldn't resist this treat, and after a while I'd carefully test the weight of each string to see if I'd drawn a crowd. Invariably they would be so lost in the feast that they wouldn't notice as I slowly raised them out of the depths and quickly scooped them up with a long-handled net just below the surface.

Spider crab

In Britain, I was once diving off Brownsea Island in Dorset in an aquatic pea-souper about 2 metres above the seabed. I couldn't see anything and was relying on the glowing compass that was guiding me back to the anchor chain. Then, through the clouds of murk, I saw beneath me scores of large spider crabs, reaching up towards me with their claws. It was an eerie sight and reminded me that anything that falls to the sea floor, be it animal or vegetable, will be scavenged by crabs.

On the west coast of Scotland, Tommi and I traded some scallops for a selection of edible, shore or green and velvet swimming crabs from a crab fisherman. These are the best eating crabs to be found in Britain, with the exception of king crabs, which are found only in the far north.

Edible crab

The edible crab (*Cancer pagurus*) is common throughout British waters, and easily identified by its brick-coloured carapace. Underneath the carapace it is custard yellow. The front edge of the shell has a kind of crimped effect, making it look like dough on the top of a pie ready for baking. The custard yellow gives way to black-tipped claws that are infamous for delivering a crushing pinch that gets tighter and tighter. Like all crabs, the edible crab can be found on all areas of seabed, and is an omnivorous scavenger par excellence. Eighty per cent of Britain's edible crab catch is caught off the east coast of the country between March and September, with peak catches in May and June. In winter the crabs head off for deeper water, coming back inshore later to moult. The white meat, brown liver and eggs are used for food.

Common shore crab

The common shore crab (*Carcinus maenas*) can also be found all over the country. It has a greenish carapace that gives it its other name, the green crab. It is most common in shallow to brackish water under stones, within the intertidal zone and on any kind of seabed, but can also be found right down to 200 metres.

The velvet swimming crab (*Necora puber*) – so called because the last segments of its rear legs are modified into flattened paddles for swimming with – is also very common. The carapace is covered in velvet-like hairs, which give it quite a grubby appearance. It has blue banded legs, but its defining feature is its blood-red eyes, which make it look somewhat threatening. The colour of its eyes and the general aggressive nature of this species may explain its alternative names of 'devil crab' and 'witch crab'.

Velvet swimming crab

The easiest way to catch some crabs, if the AG is so inclined, is to put on a mask and snorkel and swim out looking for them. Search about under overhanging rocks,

*Lay your crabs on wet seaweed:
it keeps them cool and fresh.*

around old piers and amongst seaweed. Often you can scoop up common shore crabs when swimming over sandy bays – the aggressive little scamps will stand up and raise their pincers towards you, ready, in true gladiatorial style, to fight to the death. In this position it is easy to catch them with one open hand: hold each side of the shell and push the crab down until you have a grip, and then put him in your net bag, keeping your fingers well out of harm's way.

Another way is to bait a creel (a fish trap commonly made from wire or string) and throw it in at a suitable depth. Note, though, that there are various laws that have to be adhered to, and handling a boat and creels if you are inexperienced is dangerous. This is a job best left to fishermen, who are trained in handling the boat, the sea and the catch. Also it is worth mentioning that, if you do throw a creel, beware the politics of the sea. Be subtle and don't go about in a manner that will irritate the fishermen; for example, it's not a good idea to throw your creel about close to a fisherman's creel. In short, if you don't want to go swimming for them, I would suggest buying crabs from a fishmonger or, if you are near a harbour, direct from a fisherman.

Sea fishing

Sea fishing Of course we could wax lyrical about every one of the many edible fish that swim in the sea around this island. If only we were writing this book in Elizabethan times – what a joy it would have been to discuss salmon, Atlantic cod, herring, plaice, Dover sole, halibut and even the once 'common' skate. Sadly, however, in these times of depleted fish stocks, all these species are endangered, and I don't want to contribute to endangering them further. So below is a list of some good sea fish for eating that you can catch without guilt, some of which you may not have come across before.

There are plenty of other fish in the sea, but every AG should take a responsible stance: ensure that if you kill a fish it is from a sustainable species. Many fish take many, many years to reach maturity, and taking even just one has a big impact for the breeding chain. Stop to ask yourself: is it worth taking a cod which has lived for 20 years, or a skate that may have lived as long as 50, just for one good meal? My answer is: of course not, let it go.

You must familiarise yourself with the appearance of every fish that you are likely to catch – get a good fish identification book, or fish with someone who is experienced. Also, you should make sure you are familiar with minimum landing sizes (see page 309) and put back any fish that don't come up to scratch: the European Union has set minimum landing sizes for all sea fish and shellfish, which must be strictly adhered to. In some cases there are additional restrictions set in the UK by DEFRA.

Rather than go into the detail of tactics here, I will refer you to those who know better: the aspiring AG's approach must be strategic, and before your first sea-fishing foray you must immerse yourself in a good book. Similarly, consult this for explanation of techniques and technical terms, which I do not have space to describe here. Thankfully, Britain is full of people who fish and each area will have its own band of specialists. Do whatever you can to join this gang. I recommend out-and-out bribery in exchange for being shown a good spot. Remember, the pursuit of knowledge in the real world must frequently involve a deal.

To get going you'll need some tackle, and a good fishing shop is the place to start, preferably in the area where you are planning to fish. That way you will pick up invaluable local advice as well as the appropriate tackle. Keep things simple. Tell the shop assistant that you want your gear to be soldier-proof – nothing complicated or new-fangled that will simply lead to problems. Do not become lured, like a fish, by bright flashy objects. Fishing has been going for a long time, and the tried-and-tested methods work best. All of the fish described on the following pages can be caught offshore as well as from the nearest beach, headland or estuary.

Atlantic mackerel *Scomber scombrus* This sleek, powerful silver fish enthrals me. It is one of the most beautiful of all fish, with a muscular body, small scales and a back that is beautifully coloured with deep blue set against a green background. Its belly is white or silver, and two dorsal fins, one anal fin and a row of freestanding fins on both sides of the tail complete this speedster's racing outfit. Mackerel are found in constantly moving schools, usually in the upper layers of the ocean. In the winter they sink to depths well below 200 metres, where they feed very lightly. In the spring and summer they rise to warmer waters with thoughts of love, ready for spawning around May and June. Related to the tuna and bonito, mackerel are superb to eat, and very healthy, their flesh being rich in omega-3 fatty acids. They are also very plentiful, and so can be hunted by the AG with a clear conscience.

A number of methods can be used to catch mackerel, which are relatively easily caught, either from a boat or from rocky shorelines. Spinners or hand-held long lines work well, sometimes using nothing more than feathers. Before heading out you should set a figure in your mind of how many you need, as once you find yourself in a school of these voracious predators you can heave in huge amounts. Set yourself apart from those idiots who keep going until they have plastic bags sagging with fish that they will land up feeding to the dog: catch what you need and then place the fish in an ice box ready to take back to camp, or better still cook them right there on the beach. As mackerel are oily fish they barbecue very well, and nothing tastes better than fish, eaten outside, that have been caught less than an hour before.

European sea bass *Dicentrarchus labrax* A freshly caught, lovingly cooked sea bass is my idea of gastronomic nirvana, and if you are in the south of this magnificent island you will have a good chance of catching one of these delicious fish. Bass can reach a weight of up to 10 pounds, and like many fish live to a ripe old age, up to 30 years. The minimum landing size for bass is 36 centimetres; however, many knowledgeable people have put pressure on the government to increase this to 45 centimetres, which would ensure that the fish could get big enough to have at least one spawning opportunity within its lifespan. Unfortunately, despite the common sense behind this proposal, which would help commercial fishing by encouraging stocks to increase before they reach the same sorry state as some other species, the government has so far refused to budge.

When fishing for bass, the AG must keep an eye on the almanac and the barometer, as success is all about working out where the fish will be feeding. If you wish to fish for bass off a beach there should ideally be an onshore wind of force three to five on the Beaufort scale; you will be casting your rod into an exciting environment for the bass, who will be patrolling about snapping up little crabs and flatfish that might be dislodged from time to time. The aftermath of stormy weather is a good time, and tides will also have a significant effect on where the fish can be found. A beach with big, ill-fitting boulders will often hold good bass hot-spots, as when the tide recedes it pulls food down and into nooks between the boulders.

At low tide take a walk to determine a good spot. Then, during the first couple of hours of the flood, drop a crab and hook out at about 35 metres. Peeler crabs – crabs that are just about to shed their shells before growing a new one – make excellent bait. They can be bought or collected on the shore, then frozen or kept in the fridge (some reading is required on this subject, as there is an art to keeping them in good condition).

Fish the middle tides just before the big springs, as things will be stirred up nicely then. Estuaries are also good, as the bass move up the main channels and swim into the little creeks in search of flatfish and sand eels. They can also be seen just yards from the shore, feeding on crabs in the weedy areas – toss a crab, hook in again and let it move about with the tide.

Bass can also be found in harbours and along breakwaters – in short, wherever water conditions are disturbed and food is stirred up. They love gullies that run parallel to beaches, and here an impatient AG can try spinning for bass with an ABU Toby Spoon or a slim little plug that makes a vibrating noise as it is reeled in. Spinning requires constant casting and movement, which is the perfect antidote to boredom.

When fishing for bass, always keep the rod in your hand so that you can strike hard when you feel the fish bite. Normally you will feel two little knocks on the rod; when this happens, pull the rod tip hard to set the hook in the fish's mouth. Good luck!

Pollack *Pollachius virens*

This handsome fish is a rather solitary member of the cod family who chooses the company of a school of fish only when spawning. Like all fish, the pollack is a smart dresser: he can be identified by the very precise tailoring of his lateral line, which bends downwards below the midpoint of the first dorsal fin. Sadly, however, his looks are somewhat let down by his pronounced under-bite. The pollack can reach a large size – over 10 kilos – and can be found from the water's surface right down to over 200 metres.

Catching pollack is all about understanding where and how they feed. The pollack has a preference for the dramatic when it comes to scenery, and thus can be found off the southern and western coasts of Britain, where cliffs tower and the air is full of the complex scent of a tumultuous ocean. Rocky indented shorelines and ancient and jagged scree that has tumbled into deep water are perfect hunting territories for him.

Pollack ambush their prey: they spend their time lying low and looking up, waiting for a suitable opportunity, and when that comes they rocket up, Jaws-like, towards their victim. In order to reach these hitmen of the depths, the AG must dress in rugged but light clothing and be prepared to clamber across rough, trackless terrain. If you are planning to fish off rocks, beware of leaving yourself too exposed and make sure that you will be safe should there be a particularly large wave.

Like most fish, pollack are very much affected by weather. A slightly overcast day with a light offshore breeze is ideal, as there will be enough light to highlight your lure, but not enough to dazzle the marauder below. Aim to be fishing at either dusk or dawn, around two hours either side of slack water. (Slack water occurs at high and low tide, when the water has least movement.)

When fishing from a rocky stand, cast off to one side and gradually work round until you have fished a complete arc. A spinner is most likely to be successful: cast out and let the rig sink, and then steadily retrieve, stopping every now and then to let the spinner drop down a few feet before continuing. You will lose a lot of lures fishing like this, but it will be worth it, as you will be much more likely to get lucky.

If a fish bites, you will feel a gentle, steady pull. Don't stop the retrieve, or else this surprisingly polite first bite will end up as a rude rejection as the fish spits out the spinner and swims off. If you play it cool and keep pulling, the hook will sink in and then the pollack will dive down hard. The battle for a fine plate of fish will have begun. I suggest that the AG buys a stash of ABU Toby (28g) spinners and then flattens out the barbs. This will not only help the hook to sink deeper but also allow you to return the fish to the sea undamaged if it is too small.

Gurnard The fascinating gurnard does not look at all tempting for the table; in fact, with its large head and headlamp-like eyes the gurnard looks more like some kind of futuristic vehicle than a fish. It does, however, make great eating, and has long been appreciated by the French. The gurnard is not fished commercially, yet it deserves to be as its flesh is white and firm, not dissimilar to that of red mullet.

It comes in two varieties, grey (*Eutrigla gurnadus*) and tub (*Chelidonichthys lucernus*), which can be distinguished by size and colour. The tub gurnard is larger than the grey, and has impressive pectoral fins and reddish colouring. The grey is greyish brown-coloured on its upper side and has a dark patch over its dorsal fin. Both species creep about sandy bottoms, using what appear to be six long fingers; these are actually called fin rays. They are usually found from the shore down to over 100 metres, although they are so odd-looking that you would expect to find them in the murky depths with all the other weirdos.

These fish patrol areas of clean sand or mud as well as junctions between sand and gravel; large specimens also lurk where steep cliffs fall into the sea. The rock ledges of Devon, Cornwall and Wales and the deep sea lochs of Scotland all offer big gurnard-hunting opportunities, but gurnard do not like a strong tidal flow, so seek them during neaps and middle tides.

The joy of fishing for gurnard is that you will not have to head out in bad weather, as they are best fished when the weather is sunny and the sea is calm. Gurnard are visual hunters, and they don't like the water too stirred up, so you can happily head out in a boat without any danger of suffering *mal de mer*. Being hunters, they like moving bait, and so whether fishing from a boat or the shore you must let the water flow move your bait.

To do this, cast up into the current and let the line spill out from your reel until you feel the weight hit the bottom. Engage the reel gear and hold the rod tip low, pointing at the sea; then watch as the current slowly brings the bait round in an arc. In a light current a 1-ounce lead will do; in deeper water (below 9 metres) use a 4-ounce; in very strong tidal zones you might even need to use a 10 ounce.

Gradually the line will draw tight. Gurnard do not bite hard, but you will know you've hooked one when, due to the weight of the fish, your line stops moving with the flow. The rod tip will also take a heavier set, giving you a feeling that something has happened within that subtle world of movement and mystery. Thank the gods of luck and chance: the sea is about to provide you with a gift.

You can also catch gurnard with a spinner: cast downstream, letting the line spill out but maintaining tension so that you can quickly pull in when the fish takes the spinner. This time you will feel the bite, as fish always take spinners at speed. A spinning rod with an 8-pound line would be perfect – use small flashing spoons, such as silver mackerel spinners, and bait the treble hooks with 2- to 7-centimetre slivers of white mackerel underbelly. When you take the gurnard out of the water you'll feel as though you are lifting a wind-up bath toy, as it will emit a buzzing sound caused by vibrations in its swim bladder.

Flounder *Platichthys flessus* It is a mystery to me why this robust flatfish is maligned by culinary snobs. They should be tarred and feathered in their own kitchens for such a slight on his fine character. The flounder is distinguishable from other flatties by a line of sharp bony spines along his lateral line, gill covers and base of his dorsal and anal fins. He makes great eating.

When Tommi and I were netting brown shrimp in Morecambe Bay during our gastronomic odyssey I caught a flounder quite by chance. I couldn't believe my luck

A lucky day: I was pushing that net for shrimp and the sea decided to give me a flounder.

as I lifted the net from the tea-coloured estuary water and saw the brilliant white underside of this fine fish, flashing from time to time as it thrashed in my net. The fish also alerted me that it was time to move on, as he had been brought in on the rising tide. Later Tommi cooked the fish in a pan over the fire with some brown shrimp thrown in (see page 226), and my love affair with the flounder reached new heights.

Flounder are found on both soft and hard sea bottoms, from the shore right down to around 100 metres in depth. Like most flatfish, they are tolerant of freshwater and can thus be found quite far up streams and estuaries. The time to catch flounders is during the rising tide, when they swim into estuaries to feed on bottom-dwelling creatures such as shrimp, small fish and brittle worms.

Arrive at your chosen estuary at low tide and spend some time looking the area over, keeping an eye out for channels carved by freshwater. Also look out for pools that have been left by the fallen tide, as these will contain shrimp and other creatures that are marooned and waiting for the liberating flood. When the water rises, the flounder will home in on these hot-spots, hoping to catch the hapless creatures as they make a run for it. Sometimes it is even possible to find actual flounder tracks, which appear as frilly patterns in the mud. Never recce an area of mud alone, however, as it can be dangerous. Sometimes you can do much from the shore with a powerful pair of binoculars. Try to line up your hot-spots with a recognisable feature on land, so that you can find them when all is submerged.

Into one of these marked spots, drop your bait. Use a size one Aberdeen hook and a half peeler crab that you have tied to the hook using elastic thread. A 10-pound line and paternoster rig will do. Some people use coloured beads and bits of shiny spoon, which can help, but a delicious crab bait is irresistible to most fish. Ask around locally, as some rivers seem to fish better with particular baits such as crab or ragworm.

The AG should then find a comfortable spot and wait. As I said earlier, such periods of waiting are one of the great joys of the AG's art, and they can be filled happily by reading, drinking, smoking or even making love if the weather is clement, the spot suitably isolated and your partner willing. Do not take your eye off the state of the tide, however: when it starts to rise you must be ready.

If you catch a fish below 2 pounds in weight, carefully remove the hook and let him go. If you must hold the fish, use a soaking wet towel and keep clear of gill covers. Try to do the whole thing holding the fish in the water, and use some long-handled, narrow pliers to pull the hook out. Push down to release the hook and then pull it out – do not rip and tear, as you may do irreversible damage.

Flounder can be caught all year round, and will keep you going when other species are going through a lull.

Freshwater fishing

There are many highly experienced people who fish Britain's rivers, lakes and reservoirs very successfully, and there is much superb food to be had in such places. Many of the fish that are caught in freshwater will also have a salty tale to tell, having migrated into the freshwater world from the sea. As with sea fish, the AG must exercise great care and restraint when hunting for freshwater grub. If a fish you catch is too small, don't throw it back: instead, gently remove the hook without tearing and place the fish carefully back into the water, thus ensuring that it lives to tell the tale. Always ensure that you have permission to fish, and be informed about the size limits that pertain to your area. Housekeeping is also important: never leave cut-off bits of line or hooks behind, as people or animals may get tangled up in them, causing great pain and suffering. Step lightly; be sensitive. And with luck you will come home with something perfect for the pot.

A word needs to be said here about permissions: all freshwater areas are owned by somebody and you need the permission of this person or body in order to fish there. On lakes you are likely to get better results by taking out a boat, and at many lakes where fishing is permitted you can hire one. You can find out details from notices posted around the area or from local fishing shops.

Pike *Esox lucius* Pike are everywhere (everywhere, that is, except Cornwall, for some reason). The pike is a killing machine, and lurks in dark places, using its camouflage to stay hidden until it can spring out and catch a small fish unawares. It has a classic predator's streamlined shape, with a long snout, many sharp teeth and its fins placed quite far back on its body, enabling it to mount an attack with maximum forward momentum. After reaching a size of about 10 centimetres, the pike becomes exclusively carnivorous, even catching frogs and birds if prey is limited.

Pike spawn in March and April, when females gather in deep channels to wait for the ideal temperature. They then move to the reedy edges of lakes and overgrown backwaters of rivers, followed by the smaller males. They spawn in about 15 centimetres of water or even less, thus protecting the eggs from invertebrate predation and exposing them to more warmth from the sun. In the cold months pike slow down, but in the summer they grow fast, hunting with great energy at night, in the early morning and at dusk, when the light levels are low and best suited to attack. In the first few years of life pike double in size, reaching maturity at around ten years. Pike can grow enormous if there is plenty of food around, and the females can reach over 30 pounds in weight. The males rarely grow over 6 pounds.

When Tommi and I were with John Constable, as described at the beginning of this chapter, he showed us how to hunt pike for the pot. Fixing dainty little spinners to a steel trace that he attached to a strong line, John fished with the grace of a true master. It was a joy to watch him, and no doubt due to his sage pointers we caught some very fine fish for the table.

Pike can be fished using a spinner or plug, which is always fun, or cunningly hooked dead bait (dead fish attached to hooks), in both cases casting towards a pikey-looking spot. It is truly a case of beating the fish at its own game. Look for where he would choose to lie in wait. Would it be in the middle of the stream? A more likely spot would be a reedy, dark bend or beneath an overhanging tree. Plop your spinner or bait in there, and then sit back and wait. Pack some gloves and some long-handled pliers for hook removal, as pike have teeth and will not hesitate to use them.

Perch *Perca fluviatilis*

This is a fish that dresses to kill and is as voracious as it is beautiful. It was introduced to Scotland and Wales, and it thrives there, as it does all over Britain. The perch's wardrobe is dramatic: he sports bright red fins, which contrast with the dark bold stripes that cross his bottle-green body. His fins all have firm leading rays that culminate in sharp points and his dorsal fin is large and tipped by very large and sharp rays. His gill covers, too, are razor sharp, and will cut quickly if you're not careful.

Like all hunters the perch has fine wide eyes and a mouth that is big enough to envelop other fish. Once big enough, perch switch to a fishy diet that helps them to grow faster, although a fish rarely gets bigger than around 5 pounds. (The British record for a perch is 5lb 9oz.) Perch spawn from April to May in sheltered stretches of water such as lake margins and lee bays, as well as the backwaters of rivers.

It is fun to spin for perch – visit a local fishing shop for ideas on a spinner – or you could consider using a worm and float on a 4-pound line. The trick is to plop your worm somewhere slow moving or slack, near snags and vegetation, as the perch is another one of those nasty ambush merchants. I used to spend more time spinning for fish when I was an impatient teenager with no concept of the pleasure of simply being still. Now I take a good book, a flask of coffee and a mind full of thoughts, and then happily cast out my float, lean back against a tree and daydream.

Trout

In Britain there are two species of trout that can be fished for: brown and rainbow trout. Trout belong to the sophisticated salmon family (*Salmonidae*) of freshwater fish and, like salmon, are great travellers, gliding easily from freshwater to salt and vice versa. I enjoy eating trout more than any other freshwater fish; just imagining that delicate pink meat placed lovingly on a plate beside some new potatoes smothered in butter and mint is enough to send me out fishing in any weather.

Brown trout *Salmo trutta* To call this trout brown is like describing a peacock as green: the first thing you'll notice, if you're lucky enough to catch one of these exquisite fish, is that it is anything but brown. Instead, it is dappled with many different shades of silver, blue and rusty red.

Apart from carp, which is not one of my favourites, the brownie is the most widespread freshwater fish in Britain. Rather like bored Ivy League graduates, some brown trout with itchy fins decide that a life of travel might be more exciting than hanging around in the same humdrum loch or river. These trout head downstream and off to sea, sometimes remaining out in the briny depths for up to 25 years, only returning to freshwater in order to spawn. At this point they are called sea trout, and sometimes can be mistaken for salmon, as they will have grown large and changed into silvery clothing instead of the more understated colouring of their freshwater brothers.

Brown trout spawn between September and October, when the temperature is cooling, and select a place where the river or stream flows fast enough to ensure that there are banks of clean gravel. The female digs a shallow trench, or 'redd', and lays her eggs there. Trout eggs take 150 days to hatch – the longest incubation period of any freshwater fish in Britain. The young will then spend at least one year in the stream before heading off for bigger rivers, lakes or even the sea. The size of a brownie is determined by the size of its home waters and the food that is available. The largest brown trout are found in lakes and have got to this size by becoming pisciverous: in the great former ice lochs of Scotland they chase schools of Arctic char in the gloomy depths, growing yet bigger with each silvery mouthful.

Rainbow trout *Oncorhynchus mykiss* Compared with the brownie, which has a long heritage, the rainbow trout is a brash outsider. Picture a discreet gentleman's club, a place of quiet conversation and sedate behaviour, patronised by some thoroughly good brownies (who, incidentally, beneath all their understatement, are capable of being very brutal – rather like their human counterparts). The door bursts open and in comes a large, well-fed American, badly dressed, talking loudly and polluting the air with noxious cigar smoke. 'How did he get in here?' a brownie might exclaim, and the rainbow reply: 'By not being so damn picky about the quality of my surroundings. Oh and, by the way, I've been here since 1884.' At which point an old brownie might tweak his subtle club tie and say, 'Well, dear trout, we have been here for over 8,000 years.'

The rainbow trout is a very successful species that was introduced to Britain and Europe from North America and is now the main breed of commercially farmed trout. Being not very selective about its living conditions, it can happily exist in water that would send a brownie floating belly up to the surface.

Spawning populations of rainbow trout have been found in Cumbria and Scotland, and they spawn later in the year than the brownie, between October and December. Although similar in shape to the brownie, the rainbow can be identified by the highly visible pink or violet blush that runs along its sides, and the black spots on its anal fins and tail. In rivers rainbow trout feed on the larvae of caddis and mayfly, and in lakes they become opportunists, often feeding on other fish when they reach a larger size. Rainbow trout can grow very large, yet, although faster-growing than the brownie, they are often held back by being in home waters that hold less food than the wild lakes and rivers of the brown trout's habitat. Some monster specimens are sadly infertile, expending energy on growth, not gonads. But just like the brown trout, they taste very good on the plate.

Fly fishing for trout There are many ways of catching a trout, and I must admit that my preference is for the schoolboy classic, worm and float, which has never let me down (although fishing with a worm is not permitted in many places – check the regulations on your permit). By far the most skilled method is fishing with a fly, however, and I am a great admirer of the art. The beauty of fly fishing lies in its simplicity, which seems uniquely suited to the aquatic environment, and in the skill of selecting the right fly and then making it behave realistically.

To become a skilful fly fisherman takes some commitment; to be successful, the AG must embark upon a lifelong journey of learning and discovery. You must first learn in detail about each fish's prey, and then imitate it accurately by placing a hooked 'fly' on the surface of a river or lake as lightly as if it had just wafted down from a leaf, not even breaking the surface of the water.

Fly fishers can seek out trout both beneath water and on the surface. The first method is called wet fly fishing, in which one attempts to catch trout feeding just below the water surface, or deep amidst the hidden pathways and eddies of a lake or river. The fly, also known as a lure, impersonates recently drowned flies, nymphs, pupae, larvae, small fish and other aquatic creatures. Great skill and patience are needed to fish a wet fly, but you can be rewarded with big fish. The aim is to methodically cover the lake or river, casting into areas that show signs of trout as well as places where they should be, gradually moving upstream or along the banks of the lake after fishing through each area. The dry fly method is all about skilfully presenting an artificial fly on the surface of the water, imitating a naturally fallen insect. This fly is light enough not to break the skin of the water, and is used to target trout that are feeding on the surface.

Both dry and wet fly fishing have many different nuances, depending on the time of day and types of water being fished. I am not even going to attempt to take you through the various aspects of casting, weight of line and fly types, as many books have been written on the subject (see page 310). This is a journey that the

There is a subtlety and beauty to fly fishing that can become a consuming passion – an artificial fly, if handled correctly, will land on the water as gently as a wild mayfly.

CASTING A FLY

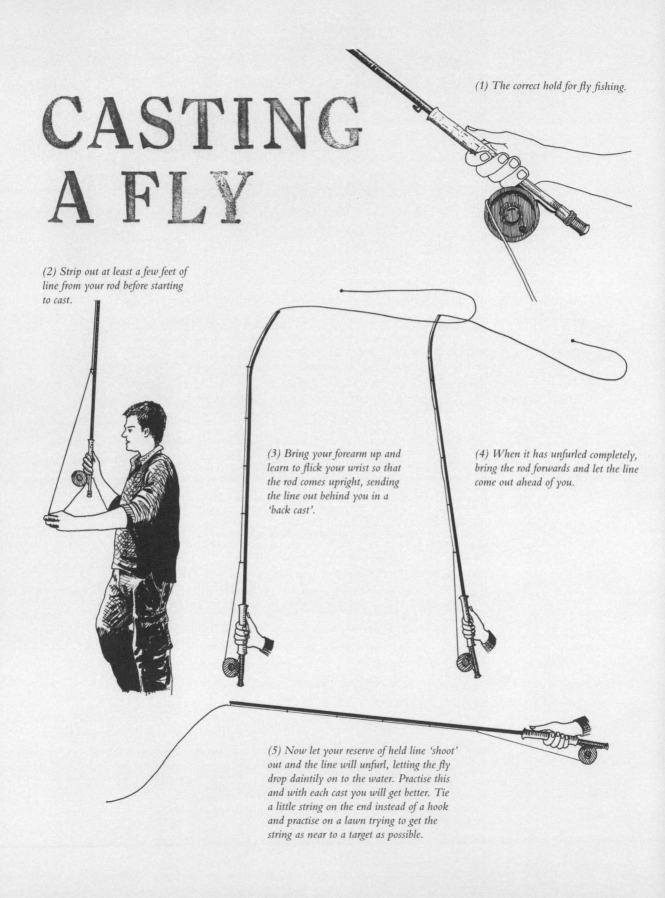

(1) The correct hold for fly fishing.

(2) Strip out at least a few feet of line from your rod before starting to cast.

(3) Bring your forearm up and learn to flick your wrist so that the rod comes upright, sending the line out behind you in a 'back cast'.

(4) When it has unfurled completely, bring the rod forwards and let the line come out ahead of you.

(5) Now let your reserve of held line 'shoot' out and the line will unfurl, letting the fly drop daintily on to the water. Practise this and with each cast you will get better. Tie a little string on the end instead of a hook and practise on a lawn trying to get the string as near to a target as possible.

AG must go on alone, but be warned: it may become a compulsive pursuit. It will teach you great things, as well as leading to some great fish meals, and who knows: you may even land up learning to tie your own flies. You might want to put in some family time before you begin, as pretty soon you will be sneaking out at every opportunity. Some of the greatest fly fishermen are women, who bring an uncannily light touch to the water and a sort of hesitancy that transfers neatly to the fly, making it look very real. Men – and I suffer from this – can sometimes be too confident in their movements, with the result that the fly slaps on to the water in an altogether unconvincing way.

Salmon *Salmo salar*

The Atlantic salmon operates on the opposite principle to that of the eel (see page 206), migrating from the sea to freshwater to spawn, and demonstrates incredible navigational abilities by returning almost invariably to the river of its birth and early youth. (Having said that, there are some examples of salmon that don't migrate: in Sweden, for example, there are lake-locked salmon called blanklax that have opted to remain in one place.)

Many believe that the salmon 'tastes' its way home, following minute chemical markers in the water. There is just one species of Atlantic salmon, which is native to this country and can grow very large: the biggest have been caught in the Russian Federation, Norway and Scotland. (The biggest rod-caught salmon to date in Britain, weighing in at 64lb, was caught by Georgina Ballantine on the Glendelvine beat on the River Tay in Scotland in 1922.)

The salmon spawns between November and December, and 90–95 per cent die after spawning, although some – usually females – manage to survive and spawn again, sometimes up to three times. The whole process is a hard business, and it's no wonder the fish frequently conk out: the males swim for miles up fast-flowing rivers and streams, leaping waterfalls on the way, and the females lay between 400 and 500 eggs.

When the eggs – known as alevins – hatch, the young salmon are still attached to a yolk sac. They emerge from the gravel in April, about 2 centimetres in length, and start to develop prominent markings on their sides; at this stage they are called parr. There is 95 per cent mortality in the first three months of life. After approximately two years in the stream the fish assume a bright silvery livery, the parr marks are obscured and the salmon smolts drop down the river to head for the open sea. These brave, silvery youngsters will live out at sea for several years; at this stage they are called grilse. Usually after two years at sea they return to the river to spawn, after which they are known as kelts. Kelts are very weak, and if caught should be returned to the water immediately. Thereafter they return to spawn around every 18 months, though some are so exhausted by the process that they spawn only once (see above). The normal lifespan of a salmon is five to six years.

Salmon meat is a delicacy prized by all. Throughout its life a salmon is attacked from all quarters by everything from goosanders to seals, otters and pike. There are many other dangers, from the effects of farming to overfishing and water pollution, and only 10 per cent survive to maturity. For this reason, sadly, I cannot recommend fishing for wild salmon. Instead I suggest that you find a pay-phone and enquire about organic farmed salmon, which minimises the impact to wild stocks and the environment. Wild salmon can also be bought from other countries where stocks are plentiful, such as Alaska; however, doubtless it won't be long before these stocks are also in trouble. So in conclusion, I would advise that you never buy wild salmon, and certainly not if it was caught in this country – if you do, you deserve to come back in your next life as a sand eel.

Signal crayfish *Pacifastus leniusculus* The 1970s were a truly hideous era, and along with tasteless clothes, offensive building design and wallpaper from hell came another garish innovation: the American signal crayfish. A series of farms were set up to supply restaurants in Britain, which sadly failed. This was all to the benefit of the crayfish, however, which flooded out into our waterways like a bunch of football hooligans, stuffing themselves with invertebrates and fish eggs, and spreading disease into our native white-clawed crayfish population, which has gone down by 49 per cent over the last 25 years.

The signal crayfish is an adept walker and climber, and is thus spreading into all sorts of waterways, where it will devastate salmon or trout spawning grounds, for instance. It is also a vandal, and burrows up to 1 metre into river banks, causing major bank collapse, which further impacts on native stocks. It is easily distinguishable from our native species by its size: whereas the white-clawed native grows to a maximum of around 12 centimetres from nose to tail, the signal can reach up to 30 centimetres. It also has bright red claws, in contrast with pinkish white undersides of the native crayfish's claws.

There are four other alien species of crayfish that are not helping much either: the red swamp, noble, spiny-cheeked and Turkish. In short, the AG will be doing our native stocks a favour by getting rid of as many of these invaders as possible. They are all very tasty and easy to catch: all you need is some bait and a simple crayfish trap. No skill is required, just a place to submerge your trap (crayfish traps are very cheap to buy) and the strength to pull it up. Of course nothing is ever that simple, as catching the large ones may lead to a proliferation of smaller ones, as you will have removed their main predator. Nevertheless, this is a shellfish that can be caught and eaten without guilt.

The common eel *Anguilla anguilla* I abhor eel meat, and find the creature utterly unappetising and unappealing. Tommi is a believer and a skilful eel cook, however, and thus I owe it to her to mention this slithering creature of the deep.

The common eel has a snake-like body and changes its colour throughout the various stages of its life. Newborn eels or larvae drift in the Gulf Stream for a while before making their way to our coasts over a period of about three years. As they grow, they change into miniature adults called elvers or glass eels, so called because

Wherever there is water there are eels, and if you can learn a few culinary tricks with their meat you'll never go hungry.

they are completely transparent. Arriving in Britain, they head for brackish and fresh water, and their backs turn brownish black while their bellies turn yellowish brown. At this point the eel is referred to as yellow eel, and it becomes part of the hidden lives of our rivers, wriggling through the darkness of our freshwater channels for up to 25 years.

Then, fully grown and strong, the eel heads for the sea, neatly changing its outfit for the job and becoming nearly black with a silver-white belly. It is now called a silver eel. Its growing days done, it is time for it to travel. In readiness for the sea the eel's snout becomes longer and the eyes get larger. It heads off on a grand journey that ends at the Sargasso Sea in the mid-Atlantic. A great spawning takes place, and then the larvae head for the coast, catching the Gulf Stream to begin the cycle all over again. The life cycle of this shape-shifting creature, moving from colour to colour and zone to zone, is still shrouded in mystery. We still do not know how the silver eel finds its way to the Sargasso Sea.

But those without eel prejudices do know how to catch them. The best way to catch eel is in an eel basket, usually made from willow. Unless you happen to be skilled in basket making, it's probably best not to try to make your own: ask a basket maker to make you one. Once you have your basket, drive round looking for a dead rabbit or other roadkill, and then stuff this grisly relic into the basket. The aim is to lure eels into the basket with the promise of some grub – and because of the cunning design of the basket they won't be able to find their way out again.

Throw the trap into a good deep section of river, lake, reservoir or waterway, not forgetting to tie the basket to a tree or something permanent. Be aware that there are restrictions on the sizes of eel baskets that can be used and the locations where they can be placed, so that other species are not unwittingly trapped: consult your local authority for further details.

Eels inhabit about 99 per cent of our freshwater system, and thus almost any spot will contain some of these creatures. When choosing a spot, however, try to target an established area of water, as eels take time to grow; thus the older the river, the larger the eels. Eels are territorial, so if you are lucky enough to catch one, leave that particular spot for some time before returning, as the odds are that you caught the eel that once held sway over that section of water. If using a rod and line, get a good strong line with a 14-pound breaking strain, as eels can swim backwards and thus exert a big pull. Also carry a long-handled net that is wide enough to bag the eel.

Preparing and gutting fish

Fish are the easiest creatures to gut for the pot: everything is packaged perfectly and can be removed with minimal effort.

Should you decide that your fish is good enough for the pot and its size is legal, then do not waste any time: kill it immediately. Simply put, to kill any fish you need to hit it hard on the head. If done deftly, two or three sharp whacks are all that is needed. Some people carry a small truncheon called a 'priest' for the job. I usually just find a good stout piece of wood.

Ever since I gutted my first fish as a child (a yellow perch caught in the Potomac River in America) I have marvelled at how well packaged fish are. They are very simple to prepare for cooking and the intestines come out quickly and cleanly, leaving a useful cavity that can be stuffed with all manner of gastronomic delights.

To gut a fish, first wash it in fresh or salt water to get rid of any slime, dirt or blood. Hold the fish with its back resting in your hand or against a surface, so that the underside is exposed, and then locate the vent. This is the anal hole, which is found down towards the tail. Place the end of your knife in this hole with the blade pointing up, and ease it along the fish's body until you reach a point just below the gills. Take care to not cut too deeply, or else you may pierce the digestive system and taint the flesh. Having opened the body cavity, you will have exposed the neatly packed innards.

Pull the guts out and then reach for the oesophagus to which they are all attached. Cut this as close to the head of the fish as possible, and discard the innards. Now you will have an empty body cavity. You will see a long dark line running along the spine: this is called the kidney line, and can be removed with a knife or spoon.

Flatfish have a very small rounded internal cavity that is easily found on the fish's underside. To gut them, follow the same procedure.

Once you have removed the innards, wash the fish inside and out. Some people cut off the fins and head, others don't – it all depends on the recipe. I love to cook fish in the simplest way possible, so I tend to leave it intact.

Scales Not all fish need to be scaled. To find out if your fish needs scaling, run your knife up its body from the tail towards the head at an almost 90-degree angle. If your knife catches on large scales, it needs to be scaled; if it moves smoothly over the fish's body, there's no need. Scaling a fish is easy. Hold it by the tail and use your knife to rub along its body towards the head, aiming not to cut but to lift the scales. The scales will scatter off. Keep going until they are all gone and you are left with just slippery skin. This job is messy but utterly satisfying.

Bleeding fish Some people cut the fish at the tail or below the head while it is still alive and then drop it into clean water so that it bleeds. They do this to get better-looking fillets, which appear less dark and bruised. I totally disapprove of doing this, no matter what anyone says. If you are going to kill an animal, you have a duty to do so as quickly as possible and without causing unnecessary pain and suffering. If you bleed live fish, you will sully your soul and generate bad luck for the future.

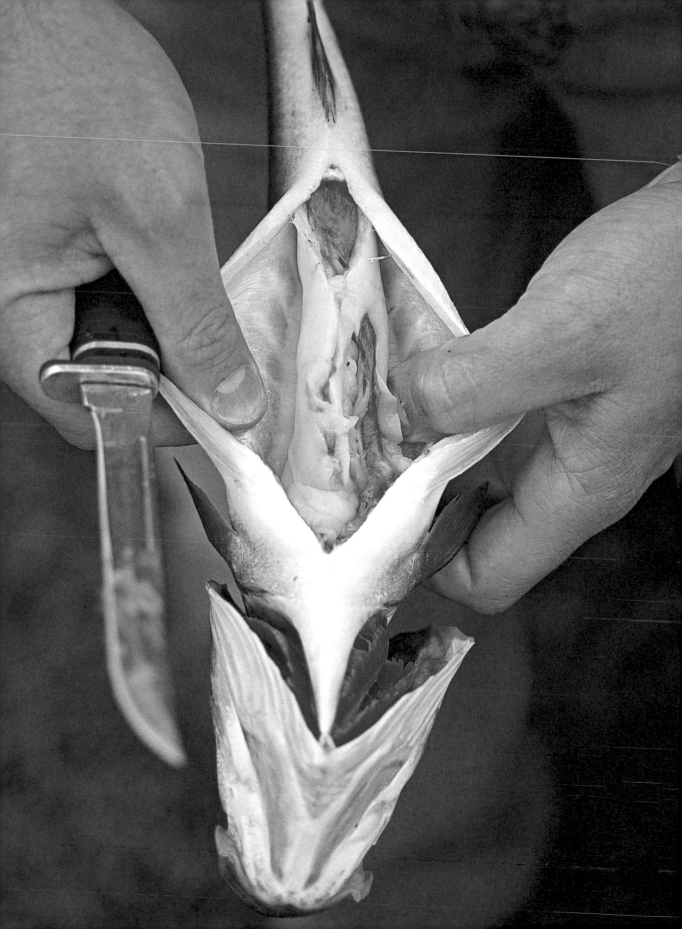

Recipes

For me, fishing is one of the most relaxing pastimes. It is true that the short, charged burst of adrenalin caused by the fish taking the bait is hardly peaceful: a fight for life versus supper ensues and it can be a physically exhausting tussle for both fish and man. However, despite one's supper being at stake, from the moment you get a rod in your hand and a quiet spot along the river or on a fishing boat, a tranquillity descends over the setting. In Wales the perpetual rain threatened to dampen our morale as well as our tents. Squatting in a downpour in waterproofs by the side of a river for hours did not immediately appeal to me as an enjoyable pursuit, but to my surprise I loved it. If a fish is caught the reward is not just food, but a sense of fulfilment, often tinged with regret that such a beautiful creature has been sacrificed.

Of course not all fishing is the same. Deep-sea fishing for scallops demands complete attention: the scuba gear has to be rigorously monitored and levels of oxygen checked. But what lies waiting is a bewitching sight: the dance of the scallops across the seabed under the silent blanket of water. Shrimping is also an icy-cold business in winter, but one is taken out of the usual helter-skelter pace of life. The roar of the tractor engine dragging nets across the beach is deafening and often monotonous but it is a perfect foil to the stillness of the dawn sunrise over the sea.

If, as I hope, you are tempted by these recipes, but you do not have the means to go out and fish yourself, do enquire about where your purchase has come from when you shop. The more we ask about how and where fish are caught, the more our shops and fishmongers will be forced to think about these questions too. The simple goal is to ensure that these healthy, protein-rich creatures survive for our grandchildren in decades to come. The Marine Conservation Society has an excellent guide to the right fish to eat. Please do get into the habit of checking it when buying fish for supper.

Mussels on the beach

Feeds 2
1 garlic clove, peeled
salt and pepper
1 teaspoon thyme leaves,
*   chopped*
1 teaspoon parsley, finely
*   chopped*
1kg mussels, debearded
75g butter

The first meal that Guy and I ate together on our journey was a bowl of mussels, which we cooked on Guy's chopping block using a French method called l'éclade. We rested the chopping block on the sand, so that it lay flat, and hammered in four nails in a 3cm square in the middle. Around the nails we arranged the mussels in ever-increasing circles, with their hinge side down and curve facing outwards, starting with the biggest mussels. We then covered them with about 30cm of straw and lit it. (If you have no straw to hand, you could use a large amount of dry pine needles.)

By the time the straw had burnt down, the mussels were cooked. They had a delightfully smoky flavour and needed nothing more than a little thyme butter and some fresh crusty bread. (A bottle of chilled white wine wouldn't go amiss with them either.) Fast, fresh food, from sea to plate in less than 10 minutes.

For sensible precautions to take when cooking mussels, see page 187.

Using a pestle and mortar, crush the garlic with a teaspoon of salt. Season with pepper and add the herbs and then the butter. Beat it into the herbs and garlic until they are thoroughly combined.

Arrange the mussels on a chopping block and cover with straw, as described above, and light the straw. Have the thyme butter covered and waiting as close to the fire as possible to warm it. When the straw has burnt completely, blow away the ashes and discard any mussels that haven't opened.

Unless you don't mind the odd bit of ash, at this point wash the mussels in a bucket of sea water. Toss them in the thyme butter and eat them immediately.

Pan-fried scallops with samphire and dandelion

Feeds 4
75ml extra virgin olive oil,
*   plus some for frying*
½ teaspoon honey
3 tablespoons sherry vinegar
½ teaspoon Dijon mustard
salt and pepper
a large handful of
*   marsh samphire*
12–20 scallops
a large handful of dandelion
*   leaves (pick only the*
*   youngest), washed*
at least 12 sage leaves

Scallops are at their best when cooked really fast on a high heat. Pan-frying does this to perfection, caramelising and blackening the slightly sweet flesh on the outside and allowing the inside to stay as soft as butter. Marsh samphire has a delicious tangy flavour, a little like capers; it is often known as the asparagus of the sea. (If you cannot find any for this recipe, substitute a couple of tablespoons of capers. It is also delicious in the Fennel and samphire mayonnaise on page 294.)

The bitter flavour of dandelions beautifully complements the sweetness of the scallops and the tanginess of the samphire. This recipe would also be delicious with the addition of some shredded hedge garlic. For a feast, serve five scallops per person, but be warned: they are very rich.

Mix the olive oil, honey, 2 tablespoons of the vinegar and Dijon mustard together and season with salt and pepper. Pick through the samphire, taking out any woody stems. This takes a while – be warned! Bring a saucepan of salted water to boil and blanch the samphire for 2–3 minutes. Refresh under cold, running water (a stream is perfect for this).

Season the scallops with salt and pepper. Heat 1 or 2 tablespoons of oil in a heavy-bottomed frying pan over a high heat until smoking hot. Add the scallops in batches – if you have too many in the pan at a time you will lower the heat and boil the scallops instead of frying them. Fry for 1–2 minutes on each side until the skin is golden and almost burnt.

When you have cooked each batch, transfer the scallops to a warm place by the fire and add more oil to the pan. When the last lot have just gone into the pan, add the sage leaves, a splash more olive oil and the samphire. Fry for a couple of minutes.

Put all the scallops back in the pan and add the remaining vinegar, swirling it around to assimilate all the pan juices (and flavour). Arrange the scallops over the dandelion leaves and pour over the juices from the pan, samphire and sage. Top with the samphire and sage and drizzle over the dressing. Check the seasoning before eating.

Grilled scallop salad with wild garlic and anchovy sauce

Feeds 4
2 good handfuls of
hawthorn leaves and
dandelion leaves
16 plump scallops
olive oil, for brushing
salt and pepper
crusty bread, to serve

For the sauce:
10 anchovy fillets
juice of 1 lemon
1–2 tablespoons wild garlic,
finely chopped (or a
chopped garlic clove)
1–2 tablespoons rosemary
leaves, very finely chopped
5 tablespoons extra virgin
olive oil

The sweetness of scallops goes beautifully with the saltiness of anchovies. Add some wild leaves and you have a really good, simple salad. Hawthorn leaves have a rather good, slightly nutty flavour. They are in season only in April and May, just when wild garlic is coming up. Dandelion are also at their best at this time of year, before the leaves get too tough and bitter. If you find a patch of dandelion, blanch the leaves by covering them with a bowl for a day or so – this will reduce any bitterness.

These scallops are also delicious sandwiched in some fresh, crusty bread.

First make the sauce. Using a pestle and mortar, mash the anchovies with the lemon juice. Add the garlic and rosemary and mix. Transfer to a cup and stir in the olive oil. Wash the hawthorn leaves well. Brush the scallops with olive oil and season them well with salt and pepper. Grill them over a hot fire, griddle pan or barbecue for 1–2 minutes a side until they are lightly charred. Toss the leaves in a little lemon juice and scatter the scallops on top. Drizzle with the sauce.

Stone-grilled razor shells with lemon and olive oil

Feeds 4
at least 20 razor shells,
washed
extra virgin olive oil
juice of 1 lemon
a little hedge garlic, finely
chopped (optional)

Razor shells are one of the more delicious types of clam and look great on a plate in their long shells. They are often ruined by overcooking: typically they need only a couple of minutes of cooking. In Spain and Mexico fish and shellfish like this are often cooked on a plancha, a flat griddle that is heated over the fire.

You can re-create the effect in a dry, heavy frying pan, but better still you can cook your shellfish right by the water's edge, using stones instead of a griddle. Make a big fire and when it is getting good and hot, place large, flat stones directly on it. In 10–15 minutes the stones will be ready to cook on, but do be careful, as they can sometimes crack. If indoors, heat a heavy-bottomed frying pan or griddle instead.

Place the clams on top of the stones (or the hot frying pan/griddle) hinge side down. As they open, pick them up and turn them so that the meat is in direct contact with the stones. Grill them, flesh side down, for 1 minute before turning them again.

Drizzle the clams with a little oil and then transfer them to a plate. Drizzle over a little more oil and lemon juice to taste and sprinkle over the hedge garlic (if you have found any).

Fried oysters po'boy sandwich

Feeds 2

12 oysters (you could manage happily with 8 or 10)

flour

salt and pepper

½ teaspoon cayenne pepper

1 free-range egg, beaten

200g cornflake crumbs (see page 161)

bread, crusty if possible, like baguettes

olive or vegetable oil, for frying

mayonnaise (see page 294), to serve

Tabasco

juice of ½ lemon or a dash of sherry vinegar

wild leaves or lettuce, the crisper the better (pennywort would be good, or dandelion)

When we were on the west coast of Britain we did some raiding of oysters, and in exchange for a bit of work, we were given a royal amount of them. I have always wanted to make an oyster po'boy sandwich – the idea of fried oysters sandwiched in crusty bread with lashings of mayonnaise is too tempting. I spent some time in County Cork, Ireland, in my twenties, much of it oyster shucking, so while Guy made the fire, I set to work on the oysters. A little cooking later and we were feasting on what is probably the best sandwich in the world.

To shuck an oyster, scrub the shells well using an oyster knife or some equivalent, with a short, sharp, sturdy blade that can be used for prising open the shells. Discard any oysters that don't smell good.

Wrap your non-shucking hand well in a tea towel so that if the knife slips, it doesn't cut you. Take the oyster with your towel-wrapped hand. Place it on a board with the flat side facing up and the thinner, sharp end pointing away from you. Wiggle the knife blade into the small crevice that forms at the pointed end of the oyster, between the two halves of the shell. Once you have managed to insert the blade into the crevice, wiggle it more, prising the two sides apart from each other. You will now have a very narrow gap between the two halves.

Slide the knife along the very top of the flat half, in order to cut the muscle of the oyster that holds the two shell halves together. Once the muscle is cut the halves will fall apart from each other. Cut the oyster away from the shell, making sure you don't leave any behind and the oyster is shucked. Keep the oysters in a bowl as you shuck them.

To make the sandwich, season the flour generously with salt, pepper and the cayenne pepper. Drain the oysters (drink their water, if you wish) and toss them in the seasoned flour. Then coat them in the egg and roll them around in the cornflake crumbs. If it is windy or raining, you can do this very easily by tossing the oysters in the flour, eggs and crumbs in three separate plastic bags.

Meanwhile wrap whatever bread you have in aluminium foil and put it in the fire (or an oven at 180°C/gas 4) for 5 minutes to heat through. Heat about 3 tablespoons of oil in a heavy frying pan over a high heat until smoking hot. Add the oysters and fry for 1 minute a side or until crisp and golden. Cut open your baguettes and lather them with mayonnaise. To make each sandwich, stuff in oysters and some green leaves, dress with lemon or sherry vinegar and a shake of the Tabasco bottle, and tuck in. Delicious.

Sicilian shellfish stew

Feeds 6

5 tablespoons extra virgin
   olive oil

3 medium onions, sliced

250g potatoes (if using
   instead of crostini), cut
   into 1.5cm chunks

1 x 400g tin of plum
   tomatoes, chopped

3 garlic cloves, finely chopped

a few sprigs of thyme

a few bay leaves

a clutch of parsley

1 tablespoon coriander seeds,
   ground

1 dried chilli, crumbled

1kg filleted fish (e.g. a
   mixture of gurnard, sea
   bass and red mullet)

2 glasses dry white wine

salt and pepper

1 teaspoon brown sugar

400g mussels, clams or
   cockles, cleaned

1 tablespoon fresh mint,
   to serve

For the crostini:

Guy's bannock bread (see
   page 72) or baguette slices

1 garlic clove, halved

olive oil

For the fish stock:

bones and shells of the fish

a handful each of thyme and
   wild fennel

3 bay leaves

2 garlic cloves

2 dried chillies, crumbled

This recipe is a foolproof way of combining various fish that you may have caught out at sea and near the shore. At home I like to use various types of fish too. Gurnard is vastly underrated: with a lovely, intense flavour, it seems destined for soups and stews – you just need to have a pair of tweezers to get rid of the bones. Coley, bass and mullet are also delicious simmered together, and in addition I've also used firm-fleshed fish such as pollack and hake. Pacific-caught halibut and salmon are OK to use, but do avoid these fish if Atlantic-caught, as they will be from threatened stocks (so if in doubt, avoid these species altogether). Cockles, clams or mussels added to the pot complete the stew.

If you don't have any bread to make the crostini, add potatoes to the stew instead and serve with dollops of Aioli (see page 295).

Put all the stock ingredients in a saucepan and cover with 1½ litres of water. Place over a high heat, bring to the boil and simmer gently for 10 minutes. Strain and set aside.

In a large casserole, heat 1 tablespoon of olive oil over a high heat. Add the onions, potatoes, tomatoes, garlic, herbs and spices and sweat for 5–10 minutes. Pour over the stock, the rest of the olive oil and the wine, season with salt and pepper, and add the sugar. Bring to the boil and simmer for 10 minutes before adding the firm-fleshed fish. Simmer for another 5 minutes before adding the soft-fleshed fish and shellfish. Cover the pan and simmer for another 5–10 minutes. Check the seasoning and discard any shellfish that haven't opened.

To make crostini, roast some bannock bread on the fire or toast slices of the baguette, rub the cut side of a garlic clove over the bread and drizzle olive oil over each piece. Put the crostini into bowls and ladle the stew on to the bread, making sure everyone gets some fish, vegetables and shellfish. Scatter some mint over each bowl.

Sally's potted crab

Feeds 6
130g butter
a pinch of salt
1 teaspoon freshly ground
   black pepper
a good pinch of cayenne
   pepper
½ teaspoon ground mace
1 tablespoon double cream
   (optional)
450g crabmeat

Sally, my aunt, makes the best potted crab in the world. If you mean to store this, leave out the cream, but if you are going to eat it relatively soon, add the cream and spoil yourself. Serve with plenty of toast.

Melt two-thirds of the butter in a saucepan over a high heat and add the salt and spices. Add the cream (if using) and the crabmeat, and heat through for a few minutes. Spoon into little pots. Melt the remaining butter until it foams. Spoon off any white solids on the surface and pour the clarified butter over the crab. Leave to set and then keep the pots in a cool place (or fridge). Eat within 3 or 4 days.

Poached crab with lightly spiced mayonnaise

Feeds 3–4
100g salt
½ medium onion
1 teaspoon black peppercorns
a few sprigs of parsley
a few bay leaves
4–5 green or edible crab
Spiced mayonnaise
   (see page 294), to serve
wedges of lemon, to serve
brown bread and butter,
   to serve

On a beach north of Oban we came across a fisherman who had netted such a large haul of crab that he was only too delighted to exchange some for the scallops that Guy had caught earlier in the day. So we had a slap-up dinner of poached crab, mayonnaise and pan-fried scallops. Simple and delicious.

When you are ready to eat, fill a large saucepan with water, place it over a high heat and bring it to a rolling boil. Add the salt, onion, herbs and peppercorns and simmer for 5 minutes to flavour the water. Put the crabs in the pan, fasten a lid on top and simmer according to which crab you are using (see cooking times on page 220). Serve on a board, with a hammer to crack the shell and something long and skinny to poke out the flesh (such as chopsticks, small knives or clean sticks). Be careful to remove the dead man's fingers, which are the gills covering the meat when you lift the crab lid off.

Then all you need is a bowl of mayonnaise, wedges of lemon and some brown bread and butter.

Cooking times for crabs

All cooking times for crab are for boiling in water, a method which ensures that the crabs are killed immediately.

Edible crab Fifteen minutes for the first kilo and 5 minutes per kilo thereafter.

Common shore or green crab About 5 minutes, but watch their claws – they're aggressive creatures.

Spider crab (a favourite of the Spanish because of the sweet, delicious meat) The same as the edible crab.

Velvet swimming crab (the prettiest of all crabs) These turn a lovely coral colour when boiled for about 5 minutes.

Mackerel with wild rose ras al hanout

Feeds 4
4 mackerel, filleted
salt and pepper
2 tablespoons Wild rose ras
*   al hanout (see page 291)*
olive oil, for toasting and
*   frying*
3 tablespoons raisins
3 tablespoons pine nuts
200g rice
1 medium onion,
*   finely chopped*
1 garlic clove, finely chopped
salt and pepper
1–2 tablespoons coriander
*   leaves*

Mackerel is one of my favourite fish, but only if I can get it fresh. After a day out of the water, it starts to lose its wonderful flavour and declines in quality faster than any other fish. A mackerel should glisten and shine with freshness, both in its eyes and on its body.

Mackerel are at their best in the summer, at about the same time that wild roses are in bloom. Go and gather some wild rose petals and make the very quick and easy Wild rose ras al hanout spice mix on page 291.

This dish is delicious with a salad of leaves and diced apple. If you have no time, instead of rice use couscous, which cooks in 5 minutes but will not absorb so much of the seasonings. I have also tried this recipe with langoustine and it is exceedingly good.

Rub both sides of the mackerel fillets with salt, pepper and 1 tablespoon of the spice mix. Set aside to allow the flavours to sink in.

Meanwhile heat a drizzle of olive oil in a saucepan over a medium heat. Add the raisins and, after a few minutes, the pine nuts. Toast these until the nuts are golden brown and the raisins puffed up. (Be careful not to take your eyes off them or the nuts will invariably burn.) Set aside.

Add a tablespoon of olive oil to the pan and when it is hot, add the onion and the remaining tablespoon of ras al hanout. When the onion has turned translucent, add the garlic, fry for a few minutes and then pour in the rice. Stir-fry for a few minutes before covering with boiling water. Season with salt and pepper, and simmer until the rice is tender, adding more hot water if the rice becomes dry.

When the rice is almost done, heat a little more oil in a frying pan over a high heat and when it is really hot, add half the mackerel fillets. Fry the fillets for a couple of minutes a side, until the flesh has just turned from translucent to opaque. Keep the fillets warm while you cook the rest.

Toss the toasted pine nuts and raisins and the coriander in the rice, and check the seasoning. Serve a pile of rice on each plate, topped with a couple of fillets placed across it.

Mackerel ceviche

Feeds 2

2 mackerel fillets, skinned

juice of ½ lime (or lemon, failing the lime)

½ red onion, finely diced (or spring onions)

a scattering of diced chilli, with seeds if you like it hot

1 heaped teaspoon fresh chopped herbs (coriander works best, but parsley is also delicious, then mint and then basil)

salt and pepper

a drizzle of extra virgin olive oil (optional)

This recipe can only be made with really, really fresh fish. Consider doing it only if you can get off the boat after fishing, prepare the fish within an hour or two and have it on the plate an hour after that. If all these things are possible, you will be rewarded with a melt-in-the-mouth experience that you may well find yourself recounting to your grandchildren some time in the future.

This ceviche is equally delicious made with scallops (cut in halves or thirds across the middle), bass, coley, Arctic char, cod or any other firm-fleshed fish. It is very good with barbecued sweetcorn, if you can find any: the sweetness offsets the heat of the dish.

Cut the mackerel fillets into thin strips. Arrange in a shallow bowl and squeeze over the lime or lemon juice. Scatter the onion, chilli and herbs over the mackerel and season generously with salt and pepper.

This ceviche can be eaten at once, as the Peruvians like it, or left to marinate for a few hours, but only if you have a cool place (or fridge) to store it in – try putting it in Tupperware and leaving it secured in a cool stream. A drizzle of extra virgin olive oil over the top just before serving is an excellent seasoning.

Sea bass baked in salt

Feeds 4–6
a few lemons
1 line-caught sea bass
  (about 2–3kg)
salt and pepper
at least 3–4kg coarse,
  rock salt
a handful of wild fennel

Baking fish in salt has been a revelation to me. The salt bakes into a hard crust around the fish, allowing the fish to steam bake in its protective shell. The fish's scales and skin protect the flesh from the salty layer.

When the fish is cooked, break open the crust to reveal the perfectly cooked, white flesh and eat with mounds of home-made mayonnaise, aioli (see page 295) or salsa verde (see page 171) and some of Guy's bannock bread (see page 72), freshly cooked. The only proviso is that you must cook the fish when it is fresh. You will need lots of rock salt too.

Light a large enough fire to produce charcoals for 20–25 minutes of cooking in a Dutch oven (or preheat an oven to 200°C/gas 6).

Cut one of the lemons into slices and stuff them, together with the wild fennel, inside the fish. Season the inside with salt and pepper.

If your Dutch oven is large enough to fit the fish lying flat, pour about half the salt into the pot. Otherwise instead of the Dutch oven use a wider frying pan or a baking pan, with an accompanying lid, and put the salt on that. Place the bass on top of the salt and then pour the remainder of the salt over the top of the fish. It does not matter if the head and tail are poking out a bit, but the body must be thickly covered.

Splash a little water over the surface of the salt crust and put the lid on the pan. Bury the Dutch oven or baking pan in the coals (or put the pan in the oven) for 20–25 minutes. After 20 minutes, take off the lid and stick a knife into the fish through the salt (a skewer is good for this). If the knife or skewer comes out warm, the fish is cooked. Let it rest for 5 minutes and then crack open the salt crust. Serve with lemon wedges.

Flounder with brown shrimp sauce

Feeds 2–3
salt and pepper
200g brown shrimp
100g butter
1 blade of mace
a good pinch of allspice
a pinch of cayenne
Maldon salt
½ glass white wine
a good dash of sherry vinegar
1 flounder (about 400–500g)
a small clutch of flat-leaf
*   parsley, roughly chopped*
bread, to serve

The flounder's reputation doesn't match that of the sole, which, because of a chemical it releases after it is caught, has a delicate flavour that is prized amongst fishermen. Nevertheless, we were ecstatic to catch one off the coast of Cumbria on a perishingly cold morning in late November.

We had been going to net the regional speciality, brown shrimp. Although we had managed to cadge a lift on a tractor to where the shrimp swim, Guy was unable to get hold of any waders. Unfazed, he set off in his wetsuit into the freezing sea. Ever the successful hunter, he came back an hour later not only with teams of shrimp but also with the best-looking flounder I have ever seen.

I will never forget cooking it on a fire in the pouring rain. Dripping in the buttery shrimp sauce, it was delicious. It made one of the best breakfasts I've ever eaten, perhaps because it was such unexpected bounty.

Bring a large pan of salted water to the boil. When it is simmering add the shrimp and cook for a few minutes until they have turned from translucent to pinky brown. Drain and shell them. Be warned: this is quite a fiddly job, so get some helpers.

Melt all but a small knob of the butter in a saucepan over a high heat and add the spices, along with a healthy few pinches of Maldon salt. Bring to a simmer and cook for about 5 minutes until the butter begins to brown. Cook for a further minute or two and then add the white wine and vinegar. Let the sauce simmer a little and then add the shrimp. Take off the heat and check the seasoning (you may want to spice it up a little more).

In a large frying pan, heat the remaining butter over a high heat until it is sizzling hot and add the flounder. Cook for 2–3 minutes before turning and cooking for a further 2–3 minutes on the other side. Pour over the shrimp sauce and scatter over the parsley. Eat at once, mopping up the sauce with hunks of bread.

Brown shrimp toast with watercress For a handsome lunch minus the flounder, make the sauce as above and serve it on toast with some watercress, livened up with a little vinaigrette of olive oil, sherry vinegar, honey and mustard.

Potted shrimp Potting involves covering the shrimp in butter, which sets and keeps out air and moisture, thus preserving the shrimp. Substitute shrimp for crab in Sally's potted crab recipe on page 219 or use this recipe, leaving out the wine and cooking the butter for less time so that it doesn't brown.

Pan-fried lemon sole with sorrel sauce

Feeds 2
1 large handful of
* sorrel leaves*
1 lemon sole (about 400g)
salt and pepper
a large knob of butter
1 small onion, finely chopped
1–2 tablespoons white wine
* or water*
250ml double cream
lemon juice, to taste

At one point on our travels in Cornwall, we had a catastrophic time, thanks to torrential rain and gales. The fish weren't rising for love or money, and I spent a very wet day scouring the forest for mushrooms, chestnuts, berries and anything else I could get my hands on. I was rewarded by banks and banks of sorrel; sorrel is normally in season in the spring but this crop had come out in abundance in October.

Later on that day the weather changed and we finally caught a few lemon sole. We bartered one for some cream and feasted on the other with this simple but exquisite sorrel sauce. The lovely citrus flavour of sorrel is seriously good with fish.

Trim large stalks from the sorrel, roll up the leaves and slice through with a knife into ribbons. Season both sides of the sole with salt and pepper. In a frying pan heat half the butter over a high heat until it is hot and foaming, and add the sole, skin side down. Cook for 2–3 minutes and then turn to cook the other side for another few minutes. Take out the fish and keep it warm.

Add the remaining butter to the pan with the onion, and sauté the onion until it starts to soften. Add half the sorrel ribbons, stir around for a minute and then add the white wine or water, letting the alcohol (if you are using wine) sizzle off. Add the cream and simmer until reduced to a rich, creamy sauce. Season with salt and pepper and add lemon juice to taste. Stir the remaining sorrel into the sauce, pour the sauce over the fish and serve.

Quick sorrel hollandaise If you have no cream, you could make a quick hollandaise sauce with eggs and butter instead. Melt 250g pack of butter and let it come to the boil. Beat 4 free-range egg yolks in a bowl with a few tablespoons of water and suspend the bowl over a pan of hot water. Beat the egg yolks with a wooden spoon and pour in the butter, little by little, just as you would when making a mayonnaise. This hollandaise is dead easy to make and, as long as you don't let it get too hot, when folded into the sorrel and onion mixture in the recipe above it will be delicious over your fish.

Barbecued salmon

Feeds 10
1 salmon (or sea trout)
  (about 3–4kg)
1 lemon, sliced
any wild herbs you can find
  (e.g. fennel, chives, hedge
  garlic)
sea salt and pepper
olive oil

Salmon is a king among fish, though sadly nowadays very few of us get to taste the real thing. It has been so overfished that most of us only ever experience farmed salmon, which is vastly inferior in both flavour and texture. Sea trout is a good alternative, or try barbecuing rainbow trout.

When you have meat of this quality, simple cooking is always the best way to show off the fine flavour. Barbecued salmon is sensational. If wild garlic is in season, wilt some in a little olive oil and serve it under slices of the barbecued salmon. If not, all the fish needs is a salsa verde (see page 171), Fennel and samphire or Lemon mayonnaise (see pages 294 and 295), a green salad and perhaps some boiled potatoes to create a real feast.

Stuff the cavities of the salmon with the lemon and wild herbs. Season it well with sea salt and pepper and rub some olive oil into the skin.

When you can easily hold your hand over the fire at a hand's length for about 10 seconds the fire is ready for the salmon. Put the salmon down on a grill over the fire (or under the grill if you are indoors) for 20–22 minutes a side. The larger the fish, the longer the cooking time will need to be, but the flesh can still be pink in the middle, or rare like beef.

Note: If you prefer, fillet the fish into two long fillets. Season and oil as above and first cook the fillets skin side down for 5 minutes and then finish them off with a few minutes on the other side. This way you will be able to tell more easily how cooked the salmon is. Cut into slices and serve.

Fishcakes with wild garlic aioli

Feeds 4–5
600g potatoes, whole
  and unpeeled
salt and pepper
60g butter
500g fresh fish (e.g. trout
  or salmon)
2 tablespoons wild fennel
1 medium onion,
  finely chopped
2 teaspoons capers, chopped
zest of 1 lemon (optional)
1 free-range egg, beaten
flour
a quantity of Wild garlic
  aioli (see page 295)

Fishcakes are a cinch to make and remind me of when I was small: we used to have mini ones, made with any leftover fish, and we would always fight over the last ones. The solution is to make bigger cakes and make sure everyone gets one. Although I love Thai fishcakes, I can never resist the classic English ones. These are just the things to keep the wolf from the door.

Instead of Wild garlic aioli, try serving these with Fennel and samphire mayonnaise (see page 294) or the salsa verde on page 171.

Put the potatoes in a large saucepan in well-salted water and boil for 15–20 minutes until tender. Peel and keep next to the fire to steam dry for a while. Melt 1 tablespoon of the butter in a frying pan over a high heat and cook the fish for 4 minutes a side or until the flesh starts flaking off. Mash the potatoes and add the rest of the butter. Stir in the flaked fish, fennel, onion, capers, lemon zest, and salt and pepper to taste. Add half the egg to the fish mix, to bind the ingredients. If the mixture is soft and firm, do not add more egg; otherwise fold the rest of the egg into the potato mixture.

Turn out the mixture on to a floured surface and dust your hands with more flour. Shape the mixture into cakes (small or large is up to you) and dust each with flour to coat. Leave the fishcakes in a cool place (or fridge) to firm up for 20 minutes. When you are ready to eat, fry them on both sides (larger ones will take longer) until golden and heated through. Serve with the wild garlic aioli.

Baked pike with wild mushroom sauce

Feeds 8
butter, for buttering foil
1 pike (about 2–3kg)
salt and pepper
1 medium onion, sliced
1 small bunch of fennel
  or thyme leaves
2 fresh bay leaves

For the mushroom sauce:
50g butter
1 medium onion,
  finely chopped
250g mushrooms
liver from the pike
  (optional), chopped
salt and pepper
80ml double cream
thyme leaves from 1 sprig
juice of ½ lemon

While pike is considered a huge delicacy in France, in Britain it is rather underrated. This is a pity, since not only is it delicious but it is also great fun to pit one's wits against such a wily adversary. As Guy explains on page 200, fishing for pike is a game of patience and skill, for me made all the more exciting for having such a prize to cook.

We dug a shallow pit and made enough charcoal to go into the pit to cook our pike. If you are clever, you can cook a sauce on the fire while you are making the charcoal. Watch out, when filleting the fish, for Y-shaped fish bones.

This wild mushroom sauce is absolute heaven with pike. In the last century the French put anchovies with pike to add depth to its flavour. Here I have used the pike liver, which gives it a really gutsy, slightly piquant flavour. Even Guy, who hates pike, fell in love with this dish, and it couldn't be easier to make.

Prepare your pit (or preheat an oven to 200°C/gas 6).

To bake the pike, pour boiling water over it and scrub away the scales and then place it on a double layer of aluminium foil, which you have buttered generously. Season the inside and out of the fish with salt and pepper and lay the onion and herbs inside. Wrap the fish up tightly and place amongst the charcoals in the pit (or in the oven). Bake for 20–25 minutes until the flesh flakes away easily from the bone.

Meanwhile, make the sauce. Melt the butter in a saucepan over a medium heat and add the onion. Sweat for about 10 minutes until the onion has turned translucent. Turn up the heat and add the mushrooms and liver (if using). Cook for another 10 minutes, and season with salt and pepper. Add the cream, thyme and lemon juice, and simmer for 5 minutes.

Baked pike with hollandaise sauce

Feeds 8
pike and ingredients for
*   baking as on page 232*

For the hollandaise sauce:
50ml white wine vinegar
1 shallot or small onion,
*   sliced*
10 peppercorns
1 bay leaf
3 free-range egg yolks
250g butter, cut into 1cm
*   (approximately) cubes*
1 horseradish root, peeled
*   and grated (see page 296),*
*   to serve*
a small handful of parsley,
*   finely chopped, to serve*

This sauce is a classic English combination of hollandaise sauce and freshly grated horseradish. Making hollandaise sauce is nothing like as tricky as people make out; in fact, it is quick and easy. Just make sure you keep the heat constant – neither too hot nor too cold – over a pan of simmering water and use free-range eggs (apart from the ethical considerations, battery ones always seem to split in sauces).

Bake the pike as in the recipe on page 232.

Shortly before the pike is ready, make the hollandaise sauce. Put the vinegar in a small saucepan with an equal amount of water, the shallot or onion, peppercorns and bay leaf. Cook over a high heat until all but 1 tablespoon of the liquid has evaporated. Sieve this into a glass bowl and beat in the egg yolks.

Put the bowl over a pan of simmering water, preferably one that you are using to boil some spuds or some other vegetable that you can enjoy with the pike. Beat in the butter, one cube at a time, slowly incorporating it into the yolks to form a thick, creamy sauce. If you try to keep the temperature of the sauce even, you shouldn't have a problem with splitting. If the sauce is getting too hot take it off the heat for a few moments and if it is getting cold increase the heat under the water. Serve with plenty of freshly grated horseradish and some chopped parsley.

Crayfish with borlotti beans

Feeds 4–5
extra virgin olive oil
4 garlic cloves, sliced
1 tablespoon fennel seeds
1 small dried chilli, crumbled
450g crayfish
1 glass white wine
salt and pepper
1 tablespoon of sherry
vinegar or a squeeze
of lemon
Lemon mayonnaise
(page 295), or wedges
of lemon, to serve
wild leaves, to serve

For the beans:
200g dried borlotti beans
(or cannellini beans or
chickpeas)
1 teaspoon bicarbonate of soda
2 bay leaves
1 teaspoon coriander seeds
1 teaspoon peppercorns
2 garlic cloves, peeled
and halved
salt

Crayfish is a wonderful freshwater crustacean, delicious with home-made mayonnaise and especially good in curries. We have two types in Britain: the native, a small and endangered species, and the signal, a much more aggressive species brought over from America to farm for the restaurant industry. The signals' bigger size makes them excellent for eating but alas, soon after they were brought over they escaped into our rivers and have all but decimated our native stock.

There is nothing so thrilling as a night-time raid on crayfish, but do make sure you are carrying out your midnight mission in rivers inhabited by the invading signals, not our rare native species. An ingenious method involves an old bicycle wheel, wrapped in one of the net bags used for carrying onions. Place the wheel inside the bag and put a piece of meat (of bait) in the bottom. Leave the top of the bag open, and tie a rope under and around the netted wheel. Hang it from a nearby branch so that the wheel is suspended in the river and completely submerged in the water. The next day it should be awash with lunch. And what a feast it will be.

Fill a box with handfuls of nettles and empty the crayfish into the box. Weight the fish down with heavy objects and leave for 24 hours. This will empty the crayfishes' intestines, which can leave their flesh tasting bitter.

Soak the beans overnight in enough water to cover by at least 10cm, with a teaspoon of bicarbonate of soda. The next day, put the beans in a saucepan in the same water, with the bay leaves, coriander seeds, peppercorns and garlic, and put them on to boil on a high heat. Simmer for 45 minutes until cooked and tender. Drain them, reserving the cooking water.

Salt the bean cooking water and bring it up to a fast boil. Empty the crayfish into the boiling water and simmer for 10–12 minutes. Drain away the water.

Heat 2 tablespoons of oil in a saucepan over a high heat and add the garlic, fennel and chilli. When the garlic is soft but not coloured, add the wine and simmer for about 5 minutes, seasoning well with salt and pepper. Add the beans and heat through, stirring them into the sauce, and again check for seasoning. Add a tablespoon of sherry vinegar or a squeeze of lemon if the sauce needs sharpening up.

Serve the beans with dollops of the lemon mayonnaise or lemon wedges and a good drizzle of olive oil. Have the crayfish on the side, with a hammer to enable you to get at the flesh. Make sure everyone tucks in to get their share!

Warm salad of smoked eel, potato and bacon

Feeds 4
salt and pepper
½ medium onion,
    finely sliced
400g smoked eel
400g waxy potatoes, peeled
    and cut into bite-sized
    pieces
125g streaky bacon or
    pancetta, cut into pieces
1 large handful of watercress
horseradish cream or grated
    fresh horseradish (see page
    296), to serve (optional)

For the salad dressing:
150ml extra virgin olive oil
2 tablespoons sherry vinegar
2 teaspoons Dijon mustard
a few large pinches of
    brown sugar

To crudely smoke the eel, you can use the kippering technique described on pages 240–1, as long as you pierce the cleaned and gutted eel with sticks down the length of the body to keep the gut flaps open. For more precise instructions, consult a reference book, or alternatively buy it in a good fishmonger or deli.

Mix the salad dressing ingredients together and season with pepper (add salt only at the end when the salty bacon and eel have been added). Add the onion slices to the dressing and let them sit for 15 minutes. This will take away some of the astringency of the onion.

Cut the eel into 3–4cm pieces. Cut the potato into similar bite-sized pieces, put in a saucepan and cover with water, and boil for about 10–15 minutes until tender. Toss them in all but a tablespoon of the dressing and onion while they are still warm. Fry the bacon or pancetta over a high heat until it is hot and crispy.

In a bowl combine the eel pieces, bacon or pancetta and potatoes. Taste and adjust the seasoning. Serve with piles of the watercress, dressed with the remaining dressing, and dollops of horseradish cream or gratings of fresh horseradish.

Pan-fried eels with rosemary oil

Feeds 3–4
1 small eel, skinned
  (see right) and filleted
3–4 tablespoons flour
salt and pepper
60ml extra virgin olive oil
rosemary leaves stripped from
  1 long branch
a splash of sherry vinegar
Maldon salt and pepper
bread, to serve

We spent a fine day fishing for eel on the Severn estuary, underneath the Severn bridge. By the time we reached the bridge the Santana was close to running out of vegetable oil and we had no money to pay for the toll across the Severn. Luckily we managed to barter an eel breakfast that I cooked for some local fishermen for the toll, though to this day I can't quite understand why they took pity on us. Thanks to the piping-hot, rosemary-scented eels, we were able to cross the Severn in one piece.

Eels in Britain have a sweeter flavour than those on the Continent, where they have always been regarded as a great delicacy. Despite the decline of the old English dish eel pie, jellied eels are still available in parts of Britain, as are a few 'eel, pie and mash' shops.

Eels are difficult and horrible to kill. In order to skin them easily you need to nail its head to a post, make small cuts to the skin around the neck and pull the skin away from the body with pliers. This process rules out the very simple method of killing them by chopping off their heads. They come out of the water covered in a slime that coats your hands like a second skin and makes them impossible to grip. The first time I killed an eel I spent ages trying to get a grip on the poor creature and then bashed him over the head totally unsuccessfully. I felt like a yob and was close to tears as the animal moved around trying to escape from me. I managed to kill him quickly after that and have since found this much better method, which is easier for all concerned.

Put the eel in a big bucket and douse it in a generous sprinkling of salt. This kills it quickly and also gets rid of much of the slimy membrane. To clean it, put on a pair of rubber gloves, rub more salt all over the eel and rinse in cold water. It is now ready for cooking.

Cut the fillets of eel into 2cm pieces, season the flour with salt and pepper and toss the eel in the seasoned flour. Heat the oil in a large frying pan over a high heat until it is shimmering and then throw in the rosemary leaves, standing back to avoid spitting oil. Let the rosemary colour a little without burning and add the eel pieces. Stir-fry the eel for a few minutes, until the flesh turns from translucent to opaque, before adding a dash of sherry vinegar. Pour out on to a plate and eat with hunks of bread.

Pickled eels in vinegar

Makes about 1 litre
1 eel, without the head
(450–700g)
flat-leaf parsley leaves, stalks
removed, to serve
brown bread and butter,
to serve
lemon wedges, to serve

For the court bouillon:
3–4 fresh bay leaves
1 tablespoon coriander seeds
1 teaspoon peppercorns
1 medium onion, sliced
1 rosemary sprig (optional)
2 tablespoons sherry vinegar
3 tablespoons salt
1 teaspoon soft brown sugar
1 carrot (optional)
1 celery stalk (optional)

Natural jellied eels, East End style. These pickled fish are incredibly good for you and really delicious. I also think it is fun to make your own natural jelly, which comes from the collagen in the eel's bones.

Cut the eel into 3–4cm pieces. Make a court bouillon by putting the ingredients all into a saucepan over a high heat with 1 litre of water and bringing them to a simmer. If you have a carrot or a stalk of celery, throw them in too. Simmer for 15 minutes to flavour the cooking water.

Strain the court bouillon, pour it back into the pan and add the pieces of eel. Gently simmer for anything up to 20 minutes, depending on the size of the eel. You want to turn the heat off when the eel is not quite cooked, as it will finish cooking in the poaching liquid – this can take as little as a few minutes, if the eels are tiny.

Leave the eel to cool in the liquid and then pour into a Kilner jar. There should be enough gelatine in the eel bones to jelly the liquid, but it doesn't matter if the eels don't jelly up entirely – I like the home-made relaxed texture of naturally jellied eels.

Serve the eels with the parsley leaves, torn-up bread and butter, and lemon wedges.

Kippers

During our travels I became totally engrossed in the subject of preserving, my bible being *Preserved* by Nick Sandler and Johnny Acton. Guy and I were enthusiastic amateurs in this department and made a stab at kippering in an attempt to preserve some mackerel that we had caught. It turned out to be slightly more complicated than we had first thought.

Cold smoking is a method used to smoke bloaters, haddock, cod and salmon in temperatures not much higher than 32°C. The surface of the fish is protected from bacteria by the smoking, but the inside of the meat isn't touched. For this reason cold-smoked fish is often also cured in brine or a salt-sugar solution to preserve it, or cooked again when it is time to eat.

Kippering traditionally hot smokes the fish. The method relies on the fish being rubbed with salt, sugar and spices and then dried out in hot smoke. First the fish is heated at one temperature to condition it and then the heat is gradually increased to hot smoke and cook the meat through. The salt and sugar cure draws water out of the fish (which is where bacteria multiply), the heat from the hot smoking penetrates the meat and kills the bacteria, and the smoking forms a protective coat

over the fish. The smoking temperature needs to start at around 30°C for the first hour and then gradually rise to 80°C (see below).

The increase of temperature stops the skin becoming hard and dried out with the inside still wet. The fish should turn from translucent to opaque. Be careful, though, as oversmoking makes the fish tough and inedible and undersmoking leaves it raw. If you want to get serious about preserving, you might think about investing in a good smoking thermometer. We tried our best to control the heat in our stove pipe and had some successful, but other less successful, attempts.

Barbecuing fish is much easier, since you only have to cook the fish at one temperature until the flesh flakes away and is cooked, but it does not preserve the fish for a rainy day. The AG is thus greatly aided by acquiring the knack of kippering which will also produce the king of breakfasts.

Kippering works well with mackerel, herring and eel, all very oily fishes, and also with salmon and trout, so have a go with whichever fish you have spare. Meat can be kippered as well as fish, although I confess we didn't get as far as kippering pigeon breast on the journey. To kipper fish, find a cure that suits your palate and the fish you are kippering. An approximate cure might measure three parts of coarse sea salt to four parts of brown sugar, flavoured with bay leaves, pepper, allspice and juniper. Hunt around in old recipe books and find a cure that works for you. It is great fun to master and the resulting kippers make a delicious breakfast, grilled on the fire. You can use the same technique to smoke eel – see page 236.

First fillet your fish and cut it into smallish pieces. Score the skin with a razor blade or sharp knife without cutting into the flesh. Place the fish in a shallow bowl with the cure, layering the pieces and evenly sprinkling the cure between the layers. Leave to cure for 12 hours. Although the salt and sugar cure will draw moisture out of the flesh and stop any decomposition, do try to keep it in a cool, dry place (or in the fridge if you are indoors).

After 12 hours, rinse off the cure with cold water and place the dried pieces on a work surface. At this stage you can paint the fish with a sugar syrup for a few hours to get a sweet cure or proceed straight to the smoking.

Hang up the fillets (by threading one end of each with wire) down the stove pipe, with the thicker pieces closest to the heat, and smoke for 3–4 hours over oak, beech or alder wood. The last of these woods is my favourite of the three, as it gives both meat and fish a lovely sweetness.

The temperature in the stove pipe is hard to record but you should be aiming for smoking the salmon/mackerel/trout/eel for 1 hour at 35°C, 30 minutes at 49°C and finally for 1 hour at 77°C. Timings and temperatures will vary depending on the thickness of the fish.

*'Every dawn signs
a new contract with
existence'*
Chinese proverb

THE
PACIFIC
GOURMET

For the gourmet with a pacific inclination, there are endless opportunities to forage amongst the greenery that clings so seductively to this fascinating island. Much good food can be found through foraging, as thanks to the very diverse geography of Britain, there are numerous different kinds of edible plants, many of which are ancestors of the cultivated crops we can buy today; even plants that you might once have regarded as weeds can be enjoyed at the table. Thus the pacific gourmet (or PG for short) can lift mushrooms from the cool shade of a high country stand of conifers in the morning, and just a few hours later can be gathering hazelnuts and blackberries from a kindly thicket set deep within a sheltered river valley. The great joy of foraging is that there is often vast abundance. Yet with this bounty come duties of care and respect, and I will outline later some rules that the PG must observe.

There are many superb guides available to those wishing to forage for their grub, some of which are listed on page 310. I will not attempt to do what they do and list every individual plant that can be gathered and eaten in Britain. Many so-called 'edible' wild plants are, in my view, just too marginal and labour-intensive to justify the culinary pay-off. One can, for example, pull up vetch and eat the roots, but unless you have literally fields of vetch spread out before you, gathering sufficient is tedious and the resulting harvest depressing in the extreme. I think it is doubtful whether it is worth it, particularly when there are other so much tastier and more plentiful plants around.

Also, though survivalists may get a kick out of eating such bizarre titbits, bear in mind that in the past much wild grub was gathered only when people were starving. Stone Age man may very well have eaten vetch roots, but luckily we PGs don't have to (unless, of course, you find yourself on a camping trip that has gone very wrong – in which case you may find yourself digging with the best of them). So don't feel that you have to gather and eat every possible wild plant just because you can. Instead, make sensible, informed judgements about the relative ease or difficulty of gathering the plant, how plentiful it is and whether it will really be good to eat. Remember that you are a PG, seeking out only those foods that truly make top-class ingredients. We want to see you returning home with a basket of plenty: a selection of the best vegetation, nuts, berries and fungi that will reward your efforts without testing your stomach.

One man's weed is a PG's delight

As a child I used to enjoy studying those pictures that, when you shifted your vision slightly, suddenly revealed a new and unexpected image. Learning to recognise edible wild plants can transform the countryside around you in a similar fashion. Once you have stored up some knowledge, hedges, for example, become more than just barriers on either side of the road and are transformed into larders bursting with delicacies. (Just beware of harvesting at the side of busy roads, to avoid the noxious substances in vehicle exhaust fumes as well as dust and the danger of becoming road-kill.) The edges of fields, woodland and heath will similarly yield great possibilities, and you will become more connected to the countryside than ever before.

In this section, I will introduce our favourite wild plants, which can be easily gathered in the countryside around you.

Common nettle *Urtica dioica* This 'weed', which we are constantly trying to eradicate from our gardens, is actually the superhero of the plant world, and one of the most important native plants for wildlife in the UK. Its vicious character is what has ensured its survival, as few grazing animals will touch it, leaving it to be enjoyed by numerous species of insects and birds, including some of our most colourful butterflies. People have long eaten nettles, and until the latter half of the twentieth century they were also used to produce clothing, cordage and medicine. Tommi loves nettles and bravely picks them without gloves, as she has some odd theory about the gloves affecting the flavour – I think it came from her aunt (see page 268).

The nettle is best harvested before it flowers (between March and May) and the early spring shoots are always good. Later you can pick the tops and youngest leaves, but leave the leathery old leaves. Cook it as spinach or in soups, and rest easy – those stingers will disappear. Nutritionally the nettle is an excellent source of vitamin C, calcium, magnesium and iron, but it can taste somewhat bland when cooked, so use it with other ingredients.

Sorrel *Rumex spp*
This is a delicious salad green that can be found from February through to May on grassland and areas of open woodland. It likes an acid soil and thus is less common in the south of the country. Like the nettle, sorrel is a perennial plant, and has strong upstanding stems with leaves that look like Indian arrowheads. Young leaves are best, as usual, and also more nutritious, with greater quantities of vitamin C. Sorrel has a clean, fresh taste with a citrusy tang. It is wonderful as part of a salad, added to a fish dish or, as discovered by Tommi, in an omelette made with freshly laid eggs (see page 269).

Burdock *Arctium minus*
This is the burdock of 'dandelion and burdock' fame (see page 76), although in commercial brewing it has now been replaced by synthetic derivatives. We usually first become acquainted with its dried flower heads, which stick with passion to any clothing that allows its hooked bracts a hold, hoping to be given a free ride. (In fact, the Swiss inventor Georges de Mestral reputedly studied the tenacious clinging tendencies of burdock hooks when developing Velcro.)

Burdock is biennial, and its stems have many rising branches that hold large, hanky-like leaves that become rather dusty and leathery as the year progresses. The stems are hollow, with dramatic purple thistle-like flowers clustered at the top.

The young leaves can be cooked as (you guessed it) spinach, and the stems can be steamed as asparagus. Its roots can also be eaten, though you need some determination to dig them up (burdock often grows in very hard ground), and then boiled or sautéed in butter. The taste is mild and quite agreeable. The root is best harvested in autumn, but gather the stems and leaves as early as you can – between May and July.

Chickweed *Stellaria media*
Tommi and I were foraging in a hedgerow in Yorkshire when we came across bounteous quantities of this plant. The beauty of chickweed is that it's available all year, full of vitamin C and, most importantly, tastes great – rather like raw peas.

It's not very fussy where it grows: areas of wasteland, hedgerows and rich, deep-soiled parts of the country are all likely spots. It is annual or biennial, light green in colour with tiny white flowers, and grows in a kind of disordered mat. Chickweed can be cooked as spinach, or young, fresh plants can be added to salads. It is best in early spring, or in the autumn before the first frosts – in the summer it becomes rather chewy and burnt out.

Hedge garlic, garlic mustard or Jack by the hedge
Alliaria petiolata This fascinating and unexpected plant favours shady, damp areas such as hedgerows, woodland and river margins, and can be found throughout Britain. It is biennial, with an erect stem, heart-shaped leaves with toothy margins and small white flowers. The best time to harvest the leaves of this plant is March and April, before it flowers, but you can also find the odd cluster in autumn. It tastes great in salads – with a mild garlicky flavour that won't leave the PG with bad breath – and is also good with meat and fish. Some people suggest frying it with bacon, which sounds good to me. It is also used in herbal medicine to treat conditions such as gangrene and ulcers, but I'm not sure I'd recommend home treatments for such serious complaints – probably best to talk to your doctor first!

Watercress *Nasturtium officinale* Watercress makes a superb soup or
a tasty spinach substitute, and it is packed with vitamin C and iron. This perennial plant can be found between April and November. Many times I have passed by a watery ditch flowing from a field full of livestock and been tempted by the lush growth of watercress that crowds the surface of the water. Yet if I ate this cress (or at least if I ate it uncooked) I would run the risk of catching liver fluke, a nasty condition that is definitely best avoided.

Whether wild watercress is safe to eat or not is routinely debated by the sides of ditches around the country. For some reason, few people seem to know anything about liver fluke, and for many it is shrouded in confusion. In view of the importance of this subject, let us put down our foraging baskets for a moment and get to grips with the facts.

The dark mystery of liver fluke The liver fluke (otherwise known as *Fasciola hepatica*) is the Hannibal Lecter of the worm world, a nasty little flatworm that targets the liver. In Britain it is commonly found in the liver ducts of cattle and sheep, where it lives off hepatic bile and lays up to 500,000 eggs a day. These eggs are passed out of the animal's system and transferred by run-off water from the fields into ditches, where they cling to any vegetation in the stream, including watercress.

If you eat this watercress raw, you may ingest the eggs, which will cause a condition called fascioliasis. Early symptoms include vomiting, abdominal pain, fever and diarrhoea; later symptoms, in the worst scenario, may include death. I imagine the PG's epitaph: 'He died for his love of salad.' Obviously this is unlikely, but nevertheless it is a serious concern, and people do regularly contract liver fluke from eating watercress gathered from the wild. The answer is to avoid gathering greenery of any sort from ditches that may have had contact with animals (that is, almost all), or simply to cook it.

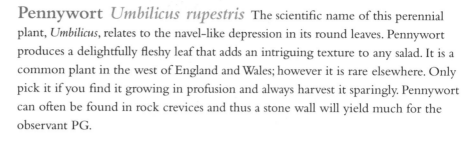

Pennywort *Umbilicus rupestris* The scientific name of this perennial

plant, *Umbilicus*, relates to the navel-like depression in its round leaves. Pennywort produces a delightfully fleshy leaf that adds an intriguing texture to any salad. It is a common plant in the west of England and Wales; however it is rare elsewhere. Only pick it if you find it growing in profusion and always harvest it sparingly. Pennywort can often be found in rock crevices and thus a stone wall will yield much for the observant PG.

Golden saxifrage *Chrysosplenium oppositifolium* This is an

exquisite plant, small and creeping with a tiny yellow flower. It grows in damp areas such as bogs, alongside ditches and damp woodland, and can be found throughout Britain, except in the far north. This perennial plant can be picked between April and September, and the leaves may be lightly boiled or steamed, providing a firm but delightfully substantial vegetable. Do not pick it unless there is quite a bit around.

Hairy bittercress *Cardamine hirsute* Also known as jumping cress or

popping cress, because its seeds pop out of little capsules and spread everywhere, hairy bittercress makes a great-tasting watercress substitute, without the worry of liver fluke. It is a tenacious plant that can be found throughout the year, growing on rocks, scree and walls and even creeping up between paving slabs in our cities. It is easily identified, having tiny white flowers and watercress-shaped leaves covered in tiny transparent hairs, and tastes much like watercress, although slightly less peppery. It is particularly good in salads.

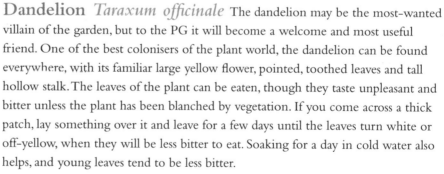

Dandelion *Taraxum officinale* The dandelion may be the most-wanted

villain of the garden, but to the PG it will become a welcome and most useful friend. One of the best colonisers of the plant world, the dandelion can be found everywhere, with its familiar large yellow flower, pointed, toothed leaves and tall hollow stalk. The leaves of the plant can be eaten, though they taste unpleasant and bitter unless the plant has been blanched by vegetation. If you come across a thick patch, lay something over it and leave for a few days until the leaves turn white or off-yellow, when they will be less bitter to eat. Soaking for a day in cold water also helps, and young leaves tend to be less bitter.

This perennial plant also has other uses: very young unopened flowers can be pickled in vinegar as a rustic caper substitute, and the root can be pulled up, dried and then crushed to form – in my opinion – the best coffee substitute of any (see Tommi's recipe on page 78).

Dandelion roots are best harvested in the autumn, as the roots have swelled while the plant has spent the spring and summer packing away nutrients in order to ensure its winter survival.

Reedmace *Typha latifolia* This is an attractive, tall reedy plant that is typically found on the margins of lakes and ponds or in shallow water up to 15 centimetres deep. It is common throughout England and Wales, but rare in Scotland. Typified by a large cluster of tiny flowers that form a pleasant extended group, it looks and feels like a dense velvet badminton racquet handle. The roots, which extend over large areas, can be baked by being placed in a hot stove in the fire. You can then suck off the starch from the fibres for a bearable, if rather desperate, snack. They can also be boiled and eaten like potatoes. In the spring young shoots rising from the base can be steamed or lightly boiled to make a superb vegetable. The immature flower shoots can also be eaten raw, cooked or made into soup; they taste not unlike sweetcorn. As with all root crops, the ideal time to harvest this perennial plant is in the autumn.

The PG's herb garden

Britain is full to the brim with useful herbs and flavour-enhancing plants. One only has to walk through a group of trees or to push through rough ground on a hot day to realise that our countryside almost shimmers with the scents and oils of plants, and many of these seemingly unremarkable-looking herbs can work wonders in our cooking. Here is an utterly subjective list of a few favourites.

Water mint *Mentha aquatica* Travelling south down the A1 late one night, I made a diversion into the Lammermuir Hills in Scotland. I decided to bivouac by the Whiteadder River and laid my bedroll down in a sheltered place beside the water. My weight crushed the plants beneath me, infusing the air with the beguiling, soft-edged perfume of water mint. This plant grows wherever it is wet, and it is best to search for it on the banks of rivers and streams. Small clusters of lilac-coloured flowers stand over green leaves tinged with purple. This mint can be slightly bitter, but it is good as a flavouring or as a gentle addition to a foraged tea.

There are over ten other types of wild mint in Britain, as native species have hybridised with garden varieties. It is a perennial, and is best gathered between April and October.

Wild thyme *Thymus serpyllum* This herb can be found growing in thick carpets that spread over dry grassland areas or wherever the ground is free draining – for instance, near dunes and on heaths. It is a highly recognisable perennial and can be found throughout Britain. The leaves are laid out opposite one another on either side of a dainty reddish stem, and at the end of each stem dense clusters of tightly packed purple flowers appear. Wild thyme is not as strong as the cultivated species, but very delicious, and easily dried. A hint of thyme sprinkled over a poached egg makes all the difference, and of course it does wonders for poultry.

Mint picked from beside a burn in the Hebrides. This gentle herb is a perfect digestive.

Bog myrtle *Myrica gale*

If you are ever wandering across a moorland area in Scotland on a sunny summer's day, you will notice a distinctive herbaceous scent wafting through the air. This is the rich aroma of bog myrtle, a deciduous shrub that seeps resin from glands on its twigs and leaves. The leaves are oval with a greenish-grey colouring; the female shrubs flower with red catkins and the male with orange catkins, followed by berries in late summer. The leaves are very good for stuffing poultry and game, and the berries can be dried with the leaves and used to flavour soups. Bog myrtle also works well as an insect repellent and is much disliked by the notorious Scottish midge. The best time to collect the leaves is from May to September, and the berries from July to October.

Wild garlic or ramsons *Allium ursinum, Allium spp*

Many a shady woodland walk can be quite taken over by the heavy pall of garlic when banks on either side of a path are covered in this dense, fresh green growth. Wild garlic has long, luscious pointed green leaves surrounding a light green stem, terminating in a cluster of white flowers, and can be found in spring and early summer wherever the soil is moist or neutral. The PG should not find this perennial plant hard to find and will probably be guided to it by scent alone. Catch it before it flowers, and take only the leaves, taking care not to denude an area of growth. The leaves are mild, and when chopped bring a gentle garlic taste to any dish. They can also be used to wrap meat and fish, and in many other ways. The bulbs can also be used as garlic.

Horseradish *Armoracia rusticana*

Tommi is nuts about this root, and who can blame her, as its pungent flavour is a great companion for meat and fish. It occurs as far north as southern Scotland, and favours rougher parts of the country such as waste ground and roadsides, and grows even among the ruins of collapsed houses or piles of rubble.

To dig it up (this can be done at any time of year) the PG will need stout shoulders and a good strong spade or fork. It is a perennial plant, and you can identify it by its leaves (dark green and oval-shaped with saw-tooth) or its flowers, which are white and often occur above the fruits, which are small oval pods. The root, however, is what this plant is all about. Once you have dug it out of the ground, peel away its brownish outer layer to reveal the white inside, which is used to make the famous horseradish sauce. Beware: horseradish is extremely powerful, and you only need a very small quantity. As Tommi grated the root, I felt as though we were taking part in a street protest and were being gassed by the authorities.

Marjoram *Origanum vulgare*

This is a herb that is much loved in the Mediterranean, and often used in Greek cuisine. From April through to September this perennial plant can be found in Britain, growing in wasteland, grassland, hedgerow and downs, chiefly in the south. It lends a sublime flavour to soups and

Magical, subtle fennel. This delicately flavoured herb is also as tough as they come and can grow anywhere.

salads, and all sorts of other dishes if used with imagination. The leaves, which are reminiscent of basil, grow in an opposite pattern on either side of a reddish hairy stem. Its flowers are white or pinkish in colour, and grow in clusters at the ends of stems.

Fennel *Foeniculum vulgare*
From March through to November this deliciously scented perennial plant can be found on wasteland, verges and wherever there is free-draining soil. It is common in coastal areas of southern Britain. Giving off its seductive liquorice scent, the plant has a distinctive spindly shape with bronze, feathery leaves and clusters of yellow flowers. The seeds can be eaten, and taste warm, sweet and agreeably aromatic. Traditionally, fennel leaves are used with fish dishes, especially oilier fish, as the astringent qualities of the herb offset the oiliness, as well as adding flavour. The stem can also be eaten, and is good in salad.

Ideal herbs for the PG's tea break
Sometimes the business of living outdoors can feel rather brutish, and members of your party may need the unique form of comfort and reassurance that can only come from a cup of tea. If you see that friends and family are on the wane, immediately settle them beside a fresh fire, hang a full kettle of water over the flames and set off in search of suitable greenery. Many plants can be used to make tea, but whether they make a nice tea is another matter. Here are a few, road-tested by me and Tommi, that offer a guaranteed pep-up.

Yarrow or milfoil *Achillea millefolium*
From May to October this dainty-looking plant is on hand to provide tired PGs with a gentle and revitalising herbal pick-me-up. It can be found in meadow and pastureland, along roadside verges and in hedgerows throughout Britain. It is a perennial with white or even reddish flowers (depending on the mineral content of the soil), which appear at the tops of long and graceful and erect stems. The leaves are delicate, upwardly pointing feather-like structures, and have a cooling scent when rubbed between the fingers.

Chamomile *Chamaemelum nobile*
Chamomile is perennial, and can be found mainly in the south of England on heaths, wasteland and wherever there is free-draining sandy soil – Tommi came across some perfect chamomile in Dorset. It is the small, daisy-like flower heads which appear in June and July that are used to make tea. Chamomile can be distinguished by its sweet scent, rather reminiscent of apples, and by a kind of hairy down that appears below its leaves, which also have a feathery look.

Lime *Tilia europea* This fine tree grows on all but the poorest of soils and is abundant throughout Britain. It is deciduous, and its oval leaves have sharp-toothed edges that often become sticky with honeydew. In the summer the PG must look out for the flowers, which are dainty and gently perfumed, and grow in hanging bunches of up to five. Pick as many flowers in full bloom as you can, and then lay them out on a flat surface in a warm but aerated place. After two to three weeks the flowers will be dry and ready for making into tea.

Berries

These are the holy grail of foraging: easily accessible, richly rewarding in terms of colour, texture, nutritional value and flavour, and easy to store and preserve. Here are some favourites, but beware: there are others who rely on nature's bounty more than you. If it is in short supply, take little or nothing, and let the wildlife take the prize. If there is a glut, gather and be grateful.

Blackberry or bramble *Rubus fruticosus* This storm trooper of a wild perennial grows just about everywhere, including woodland, hedgerows, scrubland and heath. The stems are extremely strong, and with the thorns removed make excellent quick-tying withies. The fruits start out as hard green little clusters and then gradually ripen from red until their peak, when they become sweet and black. Almost everyone in the countryside picks blackberries, either as a light snack while walking or as part of an organised foraging mission; the PG must be prepared to fight for his harvest. My advice is to rise early and attack a good thicket long before other foragers have stirred in their beds – this way you'll just have the birds to contend with. This prolific berry can be picked from late August through to October.

Blaeberry, whortleberry or bilberry *Vaccinium myrtillus*
The discovery of a thick patch of berries is always a moment of profound joy. I often pass a spot in the Highlands where, just by chance, I stumbled across an immense thicket of blaeberries beneath an open stand of Scots pine. I park my car where it can't be seen (being naturally very secretive about my sources) and sit amidst that perfect patch of berries, gorging myself like a black bear in autumn.

From July to September this dainty dark blue berry usually has a clouded surface that can be rubbed into a shine, almost as if it has been gently waxed to keep it fresh. (This clouding, which makes the berry appear almost frosted, is actually a white-coloured bloom of natural yeast.) You will generally see the vibrant fresh green bush first, and then spot the berries next, as they seem to hide beneath the undersides of the many bright green oval leaves that make up the foliage of this attractive evergreen shrub. Even the twigs are green. The berries are a rich source of vitamin C and can be used in many ways, though they taste best in my opinion simply eaten straight from the plant.

The universal blackberry: never underestimate its uses.

Wild strawberry *Fragaria vesca* When first you spot a wild strawberry, take a moment to admire its delicate and vivid beauty: wild strawberries are like tiny ruby-red jewels. They are often found in woodland or in the shelter of hedgerows, where the dark background makes them shine out even more intensely.

They can be found from the end of June through to August, and have an intense fragrance and flavour that shames some of the commercial varieties. The plant is perennial, so if you find a good spot you will be rewarded year after year, though you will have stiff competition, as the berries are highly prized by all foragers. They are small, but because they are very intense in flavour you don't need many. Eat them fresh, accompanied perhaps by large dollops of deliciously yellow clotted cream.

Raspberry *Rubus idacus* This exquisite perennial plant can be found on most acid and neutral soils throughout Britain, and in woodland, scrub and high ground in the southern part of the country. It looks just like its domesticated relative but the berries may be smaller, sometimes tinted with orange and – as with many wild varieties – more intense in flavour. Wild raspberries can be found from July through to September, and need little work to make a very classy addition to the PG's table.

Rosehips *Rose canina* The PG can seek out dog-rose bushes between September and December. Wait until the hips are pure red, not orangey in colour before picking. A hundred grams of rosehips reputedly provides the vitamin C equivalent of a kilo of lemons – during the Second World War people were encouraged to make jelly from rosehips in order to boost their immune systems. The hips should be opened up and the seeds removed and discarded before the flesh is dried. Alternatively, if you want to use them fresh, there is no need to remove the seeds; just push them through a sieve.

When Tommi and I made camp in Scotland, she cooked up a wonderful rosehip and blackberry sauce (see page 288), which made a surprisingly good accompaniment to meat. Rosehips also make a lovely syrup, which is delicious with ice cream or in drinks, and a superb tea. Allow the tea to stand for a while, so that as much vitamin C gets into the fluid as possible.

Rowan *Sorbus aucuparia* The rowan or mountain ash tree is famous in the Celtic fringes of our islands for its long association with protection from evil. Planting a rowan beside one's house is still said to bring good luck to the dwelling and its inhabitants. Each vibrant berry even has a pentagram (five-pointed star) opposite its stalk – what more proof is needed of the tree's magic? The berries can be harvested from July/August through to November, and make a great jelly that goes wonderfully with game.

Juniper *Juniperus communis* One of the first colonisers after the Ice Age, this ancient native shrub can now only be found in areas of grassland. The dark green leaves take the form of needles and have a bluish tinge. The berries take three years to ripen, and thus dark blue-black ripe berries mingle with bright green unripe ones during the autumn, and can be picked well into the winter. The ripe ones are similar in size to peas, and have an aromatic and resinous scent. Juniper berries are, of course, one of the main flavourings for gin, but their spicy flavour also works well with strongly flavoured meat, and even with fish, if you don't overdo it. They can also be used in sweet dishes.

The ones that got away Redcurrants, blackcurrants and gooseberries can also be spotted regularly in the wild, as they have managed to escape from the clutches of various gardens and set up home in woodlands and hedgerows. Just as the gardener has benefited from wild stock, so sometimes nature's pantry benefits from introduced species, although of course these escapees often wreak havoc.

Nuts

Our nation's truly great antiques are not paintings or furniture but the trees that surround us. As if they do not already give us enough, in the form of paper, furniture and the very air that we breathe, these magnificent plants offer yet another glorious gift: nuts.

Sweet or Spanish chestnut *Castanea sativa* From October through to November, in woodland areas PGs must keep their eyes peeled for chestnuts. They lie beneath one of the most beautiful trees that can be found in a deciduous forest, often scattered thickly on the ground, waiting to be collected. Common in the south of Britain, the sweet chestnut tree has distinctive spear-shaped leaves with sharply toothed margins. Its nut grows up within a very well-protected home with an outrageously spiky outer case. Often there will be as many as three nuts within this vicious case, which can be opened with a gloved hand or by standing on it gently till it pops.

Roast chestnuts are one of the most warming and tasty snacks around, perfect when roasted in the embers of a campfire (see page 74). Do not confuse them with the very shiny horse chestnut, which, though good for a game of conkers, cannot be eaten.

Walnut *Juglans regia* Walnut trees are utterly beautiful and invariably full of wildlife, as their nuts are highly prized. With this in mind you might want to approach a tree with a shotgun, in the hope of catching a grey squirrel as well as harvesting a good stash of walnuts. The trees, which are generally large and spreading, are fairly common in the south of Britain but rarer in the north. The

walnut itself is found within the fragrant green flesh of a spherical green fruit.
Gradually this fruit dries out and splits, revealing a hard-cased walnut within. You
can eat the nuts when they are 'wet' around July, but it is best to wait for them to
dry on the tree and pick in the autumn. The green fruit will stain your hands brown,
so wear gloves.

Hazelnut *Corylus avellana*

This little tree is very obliging, helping out
around camp with all sorts of problems (see page 41); and it is even generous
enough to provide the PG with a tasty snack. The hazel is common throughout
Britain, and it produces nuts in the autumn, beautifully packed for consumption
within leafy husks that look as though they were designed by Robin Hood's tailor.
When ripe, these little woody treats slip effortlessly from their frilly casing and lie
on the ground, ready to be scooped up. Hazelnuts, sometimes called cobnuts, offer
50 per cent more protein, weight for weight, than a hen's egg and are very tasty
eaten raw, as well as making a great addition to everything from bread to
chocolate sauce.

Beech & oak *Fagus sylvatica, Quercus robur*

Some people rave
about beechmast and acorns, but I have found both rather unhelpful when it comes
to providing good nut yields.

Beechmast need to be collected in large quantities to be of any use and often
they are dried up and empty; or the squirrels and woodpigeons have got there first.
With this in mind, I would probably concentrate on the wildlife that enjoys them,
and wait by a beech tree for a chance to bag some meat instead of bothering with
the mast.

Acorns, produced by oak trees, are good-sized nuts, but so bitter that they need
quite a bit of work to be made palatable. Some fanatics suggest burying acorns deep
in the soil until the following spring, believing that by this method the bitter tannins
will leech away. I have never tried this, but am willing to be persuaded, though it
seems a lot of work for very slight reward.

The enigmatic mushroom

In Wales we were lucky enough to meet a Belgian gentleman, recently returned from the Congo, who took Tommi off for a gastronomic stroll through the woods. I chopped wood and banked the stove before sinking into a gentle slumber as a kettle of water slowly came to the boil. I was woken by Tommi when she returned triumphantly, bearing a basket filled to the brim with the most exquisite mushrooms of every conceivable shape and colour. That night she made a delicate mushroom soup (see page 302) that we sipped in silence, staring into the stove as a storm rolled in.

Earlier that day, after an utterly unsuccessful fishing expedition, we had been wandering through the woods in the hope of finding something worth eating. We were lucky enough to stumble upon a few beefsteak mushrooms, growing as bracket fungi on the trunk of an oak tree. These astonishing mushrooms are well named, as they really do resemble meat, in both taste and texture, even 'bleeding' when they are cut or squeezed. We carefully removed a few and then cut them into thin strips, which Tommi gently pan-fried over the fire (see page 301). They tasted like ox tongue, and I believe we could have fooled someone into believing that they actually were meat, such was the likeness between the two.

Book after book has been written about the mysterious and complex world of mycology, and people with many letters attached to their names have brought great knowledge and experience to bear on the subject. When it comes to mushrooms I freely admit that I am a tenderfoot, and at the first stage of learning about these exceptional potential ingredients. Although I collect mushrooms for my own consumption on my island home off the west coast of Scotland, my knowledge is not deep enough to provide the PG with the best advice.

In order to successfully and, more importantly, safely forage for mushrooms, it is imperative that you have a very good identification book (for some recommendations, see page 310), as many mushrooms are poisonous. Rushing out and gathering armfuls of fungi is tempting, but may lead to mistakes that could literally be fatal. Imagine watching your guests collapse into a very deep, coma-like sleep after enjoying your mushroom soufflé, then springing up in a 'berserk' state of mind with no control of their limbs, every movement vastly exaggerated to the point that the act of crossing a leg becomes a full-blown kick. It would be even worse to cook up a stew of what you believed were nice young puffballs only to realise that they were in fact destroying angels. These mushrooms will kill fast, and by the time symptoms appear six hours or so after consumption, their gruesome work will be done and your (and your guests') liver and kidneys will be past repair . . .

As well as consulting an identification guide, the first few times you go out looking for mushrooms, go with someone who really knows their fungi, as it is difficult to be precise in identification and fungi are very variable in appearance, depending on age and environmental conditions. It is a well-known fact that some of the most poisonous species are the most innocuous in appearance, and most cannot be accurately identified simply by looking at pictures. As a general principle,

The delicious Penny bun (or cep); remember to watch out for worms in the stem, though.

I avoid all mushrooms with gills, as these are more likely to be poisonous. In addition, you should not collect endangered or rare species, and when picking any mushrooms always leave a few behind.

If you approach fungi correctly, you will discover a universe of flavours and textures, and the best places for mushroom hunting are coniferous and deciduous woodland. My advice is to start with a few easily identified species and then gradually get more adventurous as your knowledge increases. Wild mushrooms grow throughout the year, but autumn offers the most abundant and varied yields, particularly following a wet summer, when the crop is more plentiful. Below are my three favourites, which are relatively easy to find and make excellent eating.

Don't collect fungi in a plastic bag, as they will decompose – use a paper bag or, better still, a basket. When you return home with your hoard, have a good look through them and discard any that are soggy or maggot-infested or have a musty smell. Don't wash them, as mushrooms absorb water and will become soggy, but wipe to remove any debris and, using a sharp knife, cut away damaged or soiled bits and cut off tough stems. You'll only need to peel them if the skin is slimy. Once they're prepared, use them as soon as possible.

Chanterelle *Craterellus cibarius* Chanterelles grow particularly well
in Scotland and other northern countries, where they are highly prized. The bright apricot-orange colour makes the chanterelle relatively easy to spot, but there is an inedible (though not deadly) variety that looks very like it, the false chanterelle, so it is essential to know the difference. This beautiful mushroom can be gathered from July through to September and can be found in beech, birch and oak woodland, and also in coniferous woodland such as pine.

Chanterelles don't dry well, so use them fresh. Clean carefully with a soft brush and trim the bases. Sauté in butter with garlic and parsley and serve as a side dish, or add to omelettes or pasta dishes.

I recently came across a tennis-court-sized patch of these mushrooms when out walking with my family, and I have been put under considerable pressure to reveal the location. So far I have held out, but I might let Tommi in on the secret, as she has suffered enough from my smoky fires to deserve a few favours.

Horn of plenty *Craterellus cornucopioides* Brown-black in colour,
horn of plenty have a characteristic trumpet shape and a firm, almost leathery texture. They need very careful cleaning, as they can be gritty. They have no treacherous look-alikes but can be hard to spot, as they blend into the undergrowth like snipers. If you find one there will be more, so keep looking: work around the first one in ever-increasing circles. This mushroom tastes better than almost any other, in my opinion. It can be gathered from August to November, invariably near oak and beech. Slice it lengthways to remove insects and dirt.

Penny bun (or cep) & bay & birch bolete *Boletus edulis*

Penny buns (known as ceps in France, porcini in Italy) are highly prized, and both these and the bay and birch bolete are outrageously good to eat. Penny buns dry very well, and add a rich and rewarding flavour to any stock, soup, risotto or casserole. They can be collected from July to November, close to oak, beech and pine woods. Where there is one there will be more, so prepare yourself for a glut by learning how to dry these lovely fungi. When sorting through them, keep an eye out for worms, as sometimes they can become infested with a tiny transparent worm that can only be spotted by its black head. At first it looks like a poppy seed, but shortly afterwards you will mournfully realise that there is a body attached. The stems are more often infested than the caps.

Bay boletuses can be found in the same sort of country, although they are at their peak in September and October. Birch boletuses are found only in birch woodland, between August and September.

Tips for safe mushrooming

- Do not ever eat a mushroom unless you are absolutely certain of its identity. If in doubt, leave it out.
- If you are not sure about a particular mushroom, don't even touch it – you can pick up toxins from some species just by licking your fingers after handling them. Use a stick or knife to examine the mushroom.
- Keep a small portion of any mushroom you have collected – in the fridge if you are at home – so that if someone who eats has a bad reaction, you can identify the source.

Recipes

Guy and I had an amazing journey through Britain, and as we explored the West Country, Wales, Suffolk, Yorkshire, the Lakes and Scotland we found that we could eat incredibly well even if we had no meat or fish in our bag. We found hawthorn bushes, horseradish, wild garlic, hedge garlic, not to mention many other wild leaves, as well as walnuts, cobnuts, sweet chestnuts and fungi galore. I wish I had another year to explore Britain: I would discover more wild leaves, cook with more berries and find more types of mushrooms.

If I had the room, I would list every edible leaf, nut, berry and flower that Britain has to offer, but I'll have to leave you to explore further for yourself. Here I am giving you a little glimpse of the ingredients that we found and the food that we were able to eat while we were our little travelling band — Guy, Juno his faithful hound, the wall tent and me.

Nettle vichyssoise

Feeds 4
50g butter
4 leeks, white parts only,
  washed and sliced
half a plastic bagful of
  young nettles
900ml game stock (or stock
  made from bouillon cubes)
3 medium potatoes, peeled
  and chopped
salt and pepper
300ml double cream
wild chervil, hedge garlic or
  wild garlic, finely chopped,
  to serve

The last time I went nettle picking I felt rather foolish. I have often gone nettle picking, armed with a sturdy pair of Marigolds to protect my hands from the sharp nettle stings, but last year I was speaking to my aunt Sally about the subject and she assured me that plastic gloves ruin the taste of the nettles and that you should always pick nettles bare-handed. I was very excited by this information and relayed it to anyone who would listen.

The first opportunity I got to test the hot tip was in Cornwall. I spent a rather painful couple of hours gathering nettles for supper, determined not to use gloves. Though the soup was delicious, I'm not quite sure the sacrifice affected the flavour. I shall have to try it again with Marigolds and make a comparison.

Melt the butter in a large pan over a medium to low heat and add the leeks and nettles. Sweat for 10 minutes without allowing the vegetables to colour.

Add the stock and the potatoes, season with salt and pepper, and cook for a further 20–25 minutes.

Pass the soup through a sieve and add the cream. Either re-heat and serve, garnished with the wild herbs, or chill in a container in the river (or fridge) and eat cold, garnished with the herbs. Both ways are delicious, but if you eat it cold it should be very cold or else it's horrid.

Nettle and mushroom soup Nettles are also delicious with mushrooms. I made a nettle and mushroom soup very successfully by substituting 600g parasol mushrooms for the leeks and potatoes. Sweat the mushrooms and 2 finely sliced onions in the butter. Add the nettles and some wild thyme after 10 minutes. Sweat for a further 10 minutes before adding the stock. Simmer for 10–15 minutes.

Sorrel omelette

Feeds 2
6 free-range eggs
salt and pepper
40ml milk or cream
a knob of butter
a large handful of sorrel

This is a wonderful dish to eat in the wild because it takes minutes to cook on an open fire but tastes as if a Michelin-starred chef has spent years concocting the recipe. It has a light, sophisticated, delicious flavour and melts in the mouth. If ever there were a need to cheer up a partner-in-crime, some wild sorrel and a few eggs would sort things out. This omelette is unfathomably good with Pan-fried beefsteak mushrooms (see page 301). Also exquisite is Quick sorrel hollandaise (see page 228), poured over poached or boiled eggs.

Whisk the eggs together, season with salt and pepper and add the milk or cream. Heat a heavy, non-stick frying pan over a high heat until it is smoking hot and add half the butter. When the butter has melted and is sizzling, pour in half the egg mixture. Swirl it around so that it coats the whole pan and let it cook for about 20 seconds.

With a wooden or plastic spatula (a metal utensil will scrape the non-stick), tip the pan while scraping the eggs up away from the tilt and let the runny eggs pour down into the bare part of the pan. Add half the sorrel and cook for a further 20 seconds, and then repeat the tilting and scraping all around the pan.

When the top is still slightly runny (this bit is open to discussion, but my father swears that a wet omelette is the only answer), tip the pan towards a waiting plate and roll it up and out on to the plate. Remember that the eggs will keep cooking after they have left the pan. Repeat with remaining ingredients to make the second omelette.

Wild hop risotto

Feeds 4–6
2 generous handfuls of
wild hops
1 small handful of wild
garlic leaves and flowers
125g butter
1 large onion, finely chopped
400g risotto rice
150ml white wine
2.5 litres simmering water
or a light game stock
(or stock made from
bouillon cubes)
100g Manchego cheese,
Parmesan cheese or
goats' curd

Wild hops are the wild man's asparagus. Slender slithers of greenery, they are delicious gently fried in butter and eaten on toast. They are best picked in the spring when you can get the tender young shoots. They grow in dark, damp areas, often right next door to wild garlic. I found a bumper crop at Great Glemham, in the heart of the Alde Valley in Suffolk. With the neighbouring garlic they made the most wonderful risotto. I confess it was extremely tempting to use nettles in the risotto too – if you can't find the hops, use nettles or some slices of lovely, local asparagus.

Separate the tips of the wild hops from their stems – about 5cm – and cut into 1cm lengths. Put aside for the finished risotto.

Finely chop the remaining stems and shred the wild garlic leaves. Melt just under half the butter in a large pan over a medium heat and sweat the onion and hop stems for about 5 minutes until the onion turns translucent. Add the rice and half the wild garlic, and stir for a few minutes.

Pour in the wine and let it simmer for another minute or two before adding a cupful of stock. The secret of the risotto is in its stirring. Stir the risotto with a wooden spoon until all the liquid has been absorbed. Add another ladleful and repeat, always stirring and adding more stock only once the previous lot has been absorbed by the rice.

After about 15 minutes start tasting the risotto. It should be fluffy and puffed up on the outside, with a light bite on the inside. Add the wild hop tips and half of the remaining garlic. Keep adding stock, but in smaller quantities, for another few minutes until the grains are cooked to perfection and the risotto looks creamy and tempting.

Remove the risotto from heat and let it stand for a few minutes to cool. Beat in the remaining butter and the cheese. Scatter the remaining wild garlic leaves and flowers over it and eat at once.

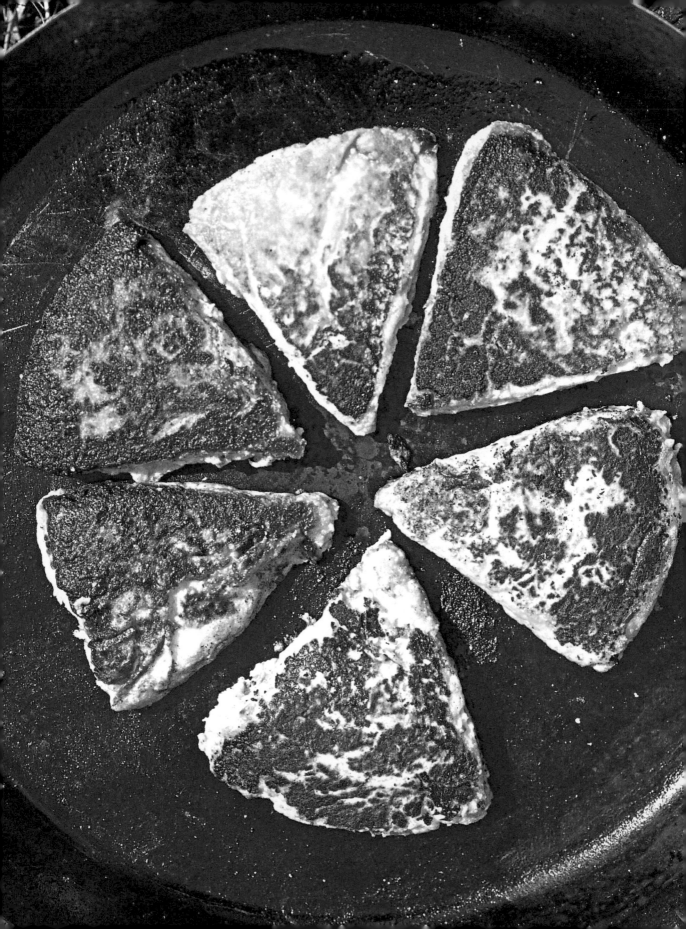

Potato and burdock root scones

Feeds 4
450g potatoes and
    burdock root
90g butter, melted, plus
    some for frying
1 teaspoon salt
130g flour

The burdock root is supposed to be incredibly good for you, clearing toxins from the bloodstream; it is also high in fibre and a natural diuretic. It is very popular in Japan, where it is stir-fried with carrots and dressed with soy sauce, mirin and sesame oil, or pickled in sushi.

It is best to soak the root in water for 10 minutes before cooking it, to get rid of a slightly 'muddy' flavour to the root. Once cooked, it tastes like artichokes and is great for bulking up vegetables. We combined it with potatoes to come up with these classic Scottish scones, which are glorious with the venison saddle recipe on page 168. See also page 76 for a classic British soft drink recipe.

Peel the burdock root, chop it up into chunks and soak in water for 10 minutes. Peel the potatoes, cut them into similar-sized chunks and boil them with the burdock in salted water until tender. Drain and leave to steam dry for 5 minutes. Mash the vegetables or rub them through a sieve, together with the melted butter and the salt.

Sift two-thirds of the flour into a large bowl and work into the burdock and potatoes, kneading with your hands until you have a smooth, pliable dough. Add more flour if necessary. Sift the remaining flour on to a wooden chopping board and turn out the dough on to the board. Roll out the dough so that it is about 1cm thick, patting it into a round circle with floured hands. Cut into six triangles.

Heat a little more butter in a large, heavy-bottomed frying pan over a high heat until sizzling and add the triangles. Cook over a medium heat for about 10 minutes a side until golden brown and hot all the way through.

Chestnut, thyme and potato soup

Feeds 4–6
250g chestnuts
50ml olive oil, plus extra
*   for the fried sage leaves*
*   (see below)*
1 large onion, finely chopped
450g potatoes, peeled
*   and sliced*
thyme leaves, stripped from
*   2–3 sprigs*
1.5 litres games stock
*   (or stock made from*
*   bouillon cubes) or water*
salt and pepper
fried sage leaves, to serve
*   (see right)*

I can remember the first time I discovered a crop of sweet chestnuts. At first they looked like conkers, spread in a thick carpet under the tree. On closer inspection I realised that they were conkers' edible cousin, sweet chestnuts.

These chestnuts are a real forager's find, packed with carbohydrates and natural sugars, and incredibly versatile as an ingredient. They are not only good in soup, as here, in purée, and in puddings (see page 289), but also delicious in salads – toss thin shavings of chestnuts with some wild leaves – and you can even make bread with them

Bacon, if you have any to hand, is a delicious addition to this soup recipe.

Put the chestnuts in a dry frying pan over a high heat and toast them for about 10–15 minutes, until they are browned on all sides and the skin has started to crack. Take them off the heat and when they have cooled down a little, roll them between your palms to get rid of the skin. Roughly chop them.

Heat the oil in a casserole and add the onion. Sweat for 5 minutes before adding the potatoes and thyme leaves. Sweat for a further 10 minutes, stirring to prevent the potato from catching on the bottom of the pan.

Add the chestnuts and cook for 5 minutes before adding the stock or water. Simmer, covered, for at least 20 minutes, until the potatoes are cooked through. Season with salt and pepper.

Next make the crispy sage leaves: heat about 2 tablespoons of olive oil in a small pan until hot and add a handful of sage leaves. Fry for about a minute, removing them before they burn. They should turn a lovely golden colour.

You can serve the soup chunky as it is with a few crispy fried sage leaves on top, or pass it through a sieve to get a smoother, more silky soup.

Wild leaf salad with caramelised onion and toasted walnuts

Feeds 2–3

a handful of walnuts, shelled

1–2 tablespoons olive oil

2 medium onions,
  finely sliced

salt and pepper

a pinch of sugar

2–3 handfuls of wild leaves
  (e.g. hairy bittercress,
  hedge garlic, dandelion,
  chickweed, woodland
  sorrel)

For the dressing:

75ml extra virgin olive oil

1 teaspoon Dijon mustard

½ teaspoon soft brown sugar

1–2 tablespoons
  sherry vinegar

This salad was invented at a low moment in Yorkshire, in a howling gale, when we had nothing else to eat. Guy managed to get a fire started in a small clearing in the wood. Somehow, in the wind and the rain, I managed to stop most of our carefully collected wild leaves from blowing away. It seemed mad then that the only food we could gather that day was enough to make a salad, and we dreamt of putting pieces of pink pigeon breast amongst the leaves, but in the end the salad was surprisingly good, and very restorative with some hot yarrow tea (see page 74) and a nip of whisky from Guy's hip flask.

Heat a dry frying pan over a medium heat and add the walnuts. Cook, tossing occasionally, until toasted and smelling delicious. Set aside. Add the oil to the pan and when it is hot add the sliced onions. Season with salt and pepper, add a pinch of sugar and cook over a medium heat for 15–20 minutes until golden brown and caramelising.

Combine the salad dressing ingredients and season with salt and pepper. Toss the leaves in the dressing and then strew the caramelised onions and toasted walnuts over them.

Celeriac chips

Feeds 2

2 celeriac (or potatoes,
*   beetroot, parsnips, etc.),*
*   peeled and cut into*
*   similar-sized chips*
salt
vegetable oil, for frying
*   (see methods)*

My feelings towards home-made chips are akin to those I have for home-made mayonnaise: they are such a treat if you have the time or inclination. Happily in the outdoors, without the distractions of television and other electricity-dependent pastimes, there always seems to be more time to make such things.

In Yorkshire we were put to work digging some allotments in exchange for any vegetables on offer. We were rewarded with armfuls of young celeriac. Chipped, they were the most delicious accompaniment to the grouse we shot. The real, deep-fried chips take hours and need a lot of oil. Although traditionally you would blanch them in the oil, we parboiled them in water first, which saved time and precious firewood. They are well worth it if you have the oil (and enough wood for a long fire). Otherwise try the second method, which uses less oil and takes less time – cooked this way the chips are still damned good.

These are delicious with the spice mix on page 33.

The deep-fry Bring a large pan of well-salted water to the boil and parboil the chips for 10 minutes. Drain the chips, dry them and salt them well.

In the meantime bring a large saucepan of oil to simmering point. The temperature needs to be hot enough to brown the chips, giving them a delicious, crunchy outside and a light, fluffy middle, and the chips will cook more quickly if they are not crowded. If the pan is small enough for the chips to be crowded, cook them in two batches. Deep-fry the chips until they brown – this may take as long as 30 minutes. When they look cooked to perfection, scoop them out with a slotted spoon and wrap them in foil. Put the bundle by the fire to keep warm. Cook the remaining chips at the same time as you cook whatever else you are going to eat, and then tuck in. The chips do not normally last very long.

Note: If you have plenty of oil, you may wish to cook two batches at once in two separate pans, so halving the cooking time (and use of wood). You can filter the oil at the end of cooking (and pour it back into your car, if it is a type that runs on vegetable oil).

The shallow-fry If you are cooking outside this method is much easier, though the chips won't have quite the same crunch as they do when deep-fried. Pour about 200ml of oil into a very wide, heavy frying pan. Put over a high heat and heat the oil until it shimmers. Empty in the chips and salt and pepper them well. Put a lid on the frying pan and cook, stirring occasionally, until the celeriac is tender. Remove the lid, stoke the fire and cook the chips for a further 15–20 minutes until the chips have browned nicely on most sides. Serve at once.

Red-wine-poached pears

Feeds 4
300ml red wine
1 cinnamon stick
3 bay leaves
zest of 1 lemon
50g soft brown sugar
6 pears, halved, cored
*   and peeled*
double cream, to serve

This is the easiest pudding to make and one of the most delicious. All you need is some red wine and sugar, a few spices and a crop of pears recently fallen from a tree. The pudding is made even better by a really good custard, but since this is a bit of a bore to cook outdoors you could opt for some thick double cream instead. I would as happily serve this pudding at a dinner party in London as eat it in the woods, having just poached the pears on the fire.

Put all the ingredients except the pears into a large, shallow saucepan with 300ml of water. Bring to a simmer and then put in the pears. Cover and simmer gently for half an hour or until the pears are tender (the amount of time will depend on how ripe they are). When they are cooked, take them out and keep them warm. Simmer the syrup briskly until it has reduced by half. Serve the pears with the warm syrup and the cool cream.

Bread and blackberry pudding

Feeds 6

8–9 slices of white bread,
  crusts removed

450ml milk

2 tablespoons butter, plus
  extra for dotting

½ teaspoon salt

½ teaspoon cinnamon

½ teaspoon nutmeg

zest of 1 lemon (optional)

2 free-range eggs

125g soft brown sugar, plus
  extra for sprinkling

4 tablespoons sherry
  or brandy

100g blackberries
  (or wild strawberries,
  redcurrants, etc.)

a quantity of Rosehip and
  ginger syrup (see page
  290), to serve (optional)

double cream, to serve

Some of my favourite bread-and-butter puddings have been brought to the table puffed up and quivering, more soufflé than bread pudding. This pudding is not one of those. Cooked on a fire, it will never be the soufflé-like creation that you can make in an oven at home, but it will be a rich, decadent pudding, full of the flavours of the wild. In fact, it will probably be the best one you have ever tasted, cooked and eaten in the elements. Laden with blackberries and other foraged fruits, it is a thoroughly British pudding.

Cut each slice of bread into four triangles. Heat the milk in a saucepan over a high heat until it is quivering – do not let it boil. Stir the butter into the hot milk and whisk in the spices, zest, eggs, sugar and sherry or brandy. Take off the heat and allow the bread to soak in this mixture for 10 minutes. Butter a frying pan liberally and scatter a little more sugar over it. Layer the bread slices in the pan in a pretty pattern. Scatter over the blackberries.

Cook, covered, over a medium heat for about 25–30 minutes, checking every so often that the bottom is not burning. Sprinkle extra sugar over the top and dot with some extra butter. Then turn the pudding out on to a plate and slip it back into the pan on the sugar side, and cook for another 30 minutes. Serve warm, drizzled with rosehip and ginger syrup if you have any and thick double cream.

Wild strawberry and petal fool

Feeds 4–6
450g strawberries, hulled
  and halved
40–60g soft brown sugar
finely grated zest and juice
  of 1 orange (optional)
a handful of flower petals
  (e.g. violets, rose,
  marigolds, lavender)
a little mint, freshly chopped
300ml double cream
toasted nuts or fried
  breadcrumbs caramelised
  in sugar, to serve

Fools are wonderful, seasonal puddings, designed to use up gluts of fruit. While winter fools have slightly negative connotations for me, with an endless supply of pears and apples always to be used up, summer fools seem to appear in short bursts of colour through the fleeting summer months. This nursery way of cooking fruit has never lost its charm for me, and how easy it is to do on a camp fire!

Put the strawberries into a saucepan with the sugar, orange zest and juice and half the petals. Put on a low heat for 15 minutes, until the strawberries are quite soft. Add the rest of the petals. Taste for sweetness and rub the strawberries through a sieve, or if you prefer a rougher fool, mash them up a bit with a rolling pin or old bottle. The purée should be a lovely sloppy consistency. If it is too juicy, put it back on the heat for five minutes to simmer off some of the liquid.

Beat the cream with a whisk until very softly whipped and fold all but a few tablespoons gently into the strawberry purée. Top with toasted nuts or some fried breadcrumbs that have been caramelised in sugar, and the reserved cream.

Other fruit fools Try this recipe with raspberries, gooseberries (my favourite) or plums. Try it with anything, in fact, but each fruit will need slightly different amounts of sugar. Add cautiously – you can always put in more sugar, but you can never take it out. Rhubarb fool is delicious with chopped whole strawberries – just as strawberry fool is delicious with poached rhubarb – though it is rare to find them both at the same time.

Apple purée

a large knob of butter
4 large cooking apples, peeled,
cored and sliced
sugar to taste
lemon juice to taste (optional)

Apple purée is a movable feast. Because no two apples are the same, no two apple purées taste the same either. You can use apple purée in puddings or serve it as a relish to go with pork, cheese or game.

Consider this a master recipe from which you can start improvising. You can spice it to make a sauce that is delicious with pork or cook it with spices, chillies, onions and raisins to get a chutney effect – see below. Keep it tart as a counterbalance to sweeter things (tart apple purée with sweet caramelised walnuts works very well – see page 285) or make it sweet to have on its own with cream. Play around with both cooking and eating apples – go and explore your local orchards and discover the huge range of apple varieties and tastes in Britain.

Melt the butter in a pan and add the apples. Cook on a low heat until they are soft and start breaking down. Add sugar and lemon juice (if using) to taste.

Apple compote To make a cold compote, follow the master recipe but leave out the butter. Add a cinnamon stick at the beginning of cooking for a little flavour.

Spiced apple sauce Add spices (cinnamon, allspice, cloves) and one small, chopped onion to the butter at the first stage and cook for 5 minutes or until the onion has turned translucent. Then proceed as for the master recipe, adding a splash of vinegar instead of lemon juice.

Apple chutney Apple chutney uses the same ingredients as Spiced apple sauce above, but far more sugar, and the sweetness is balanced with the addition of more vinegar. You might also like to add raisins, chilli and more onion to the mix. Experiment away with fruit and vegetables you have to hand.

Apple fool Fold apple purée into softly whipped double cream to make a rich apple fool.

Apple and caramel walnut tart

Feeds 8

a quantity of Apple purée
(see page 284)

double cream, to serve

For the pastry:

250g plain flour

25g icing or caster sugar

125g butter, cold from
the fridge

2 free-range eggs, separated
(reserving the whites for
glazing the pastry)

For the caramel walnuts:

250g walnuts

250g sugar

120ml water

60ml double cream

1 tablespoon apple brandy
(optional)

This is definitely not a pudding to make when out camping, but I couldn't resist including it, as it was such a high point on our travels. When we were staying with Sifty and Ann on their cider farm in Somerset, every morning we woke up to the smell of freshly crushed apples. Not only did we help pick apples but we also collected walnuts from their enormous tree. To thank them for the stay, we made a slap-up feast of all our foraged and hunted food and this tart was for pudding. Do try it at home. It is exceedingly good.

By all means buy the pastry, as long as it is made with butter and not margarine. Personally I enjoy making it, and really it takes no time at all. The secret is to make the pastry first, very quickly, handling it as little as possible. The butter should be cold and the pastry should sit for at least half an hour in the fridge (while you get on with everything else).

Preheat the oven to 180°C/gas 4.

Whiz all the pastry ingredients apart from the egg whites in a food processor (or rub the butter and sugar into the flour by hand and then mix in the egg yolks) and add water in splashes so that the dough just comes together in a ball. Turn out on to a clean surface and bring together, and wrap in cling-film. Pat into a flat circular shape and put in the fridge to rest for 30 minutes or more.

Meanwhile make the caramel walnuts. Put the walnuts on a baking tray and into the preheated oven for about 5 minutes until they look lightly toasted. Put the sugar and water in a saucepan over a medium–high heat. Swirl around so that the sugar dissolves, but do not stir or else you'll create fiddly sugar crystals everywhere.

Let the syrup start bubbling and slowly it will go a golden caramel colour in patches. Swish around more, so that the caramelising syrup is evenly dispersed. It will soon start turning dark brown. Wait until the caramel is right on the edge of turning black, so that the bitter caramel flavour offsets the sweetness of the sugar to give a wonderful, complex flavour. You will be able to tell when it is about to start burning, as the syrup will begin to smoke and turn really dark. At this point quickly pour in the cream and brandy (if using) and take the pan off the heat. Be careful, as the caramel will bubble up. Chill the pan in some iced water and stir in the walnuts.

Meanwhile roll out the pastry and line a 24cm tart case, pricking all over with a fork. Freeze for 10 minutes to stop shrinkage when you cook it. Line the pastry with greaseproof paper. Cover the paper with a single layer of uncooked beans and put in the oven for 12–15 minutes.

Remove the greaseproof paper and the baking beans, and brush the shell with beaten egg whites to seal the pastry. Return to the oven for another 5 minutes to take on a pale golden colour. Remove and allow to cool.

Spread the apple purée over the base of the tart and then spoon the walnut caramel on top of the purée. Serve with lashings of double cream.

Rosehip and blackberry sauce

2 large handfuls of rosehips
1 large handful of
   blackberries
about 200g of brown sugar
   (depending on the
   sweetness of the
   blackberries)

Discovering how beautifully the flavours of rosehip and blackberry combine was a complete accident. By the time we got to Wales in mid-November we were getting worried that we were going to run out of food. We had game, but I wanted to add nutritional value to our meals, as we had no vegetables.

I found what seemed to be the last clutch of blackberries in the country. No longer sweet (they made the mouth pucker), they still had a hint of their former taste. I combined them with rosehips to make this sauce, which I urge you to try. It is the perfect partner with pheasant. Try poaching the pheasant as on page 148, shredding it and placing a little on top of a potato rösti. A little swirl of this syrup completes the happy mouthful.

This sauce works very well if you substitute rowan berries for the rosehips or the blackberries. Rowans seem to go very well with venison.

Simmer the rosehips, blackberries and half the sugar in a saucepan, together with water to cover, for 15–20 minutes. Pass through a sieve into a bowl and then put the sieved contents back into the cleaned saucepan. Add another 200ml of water and bring to simmering point again, tasting and adding more sugar if the sauce needs it. Reduce the sauce until it looks thick and syrupy.

Chestnut and blackberry cream pot

Feeds 4–5
250g sweet chestnuts
milk (optional)
250g blackberries
4–5 tablespoons sugar
1–2 tablespoons brandy
  (or whisky) (optional)
double cream, to serve

I love this pudding. It is so quick to make, once you've shelled the nuts, and needs little added to it to be really delicious – the perfect forager's pudding. The chestnuts and blackberries are both in season in the autumn and sometimes grow right next to each other. They are high in natural sugars, making this a surprisingly healthy pudding, provided you don't mind a little cream. I like this with lots.

Shell and peel the chestnuts (see page 274), and then put them in a saucepan, adding enough water (or milk if you have it) to cover. Cover the pan and simmer the chestnuts for about 20 minutes until very soft. In a separate pan add the blackberries, a tablespoon of sugar and a splash of water. Put on the heat and shake around until the sugar has dissolved. Cook for another minute or two and taste, adding more sugar if you think the blackberries need it.

Drain the chestnuts and rub them through a sieve into a bowl. Beat the rest of the sugar into the purée, together with the brandy (or whisky) if you have any. Brandy and chestnut purée is a very good thing indeed.

Spoon a small mound of chestnut purée into whisky glasses. Spoon the blackberries and some of their juice over the purée. Finally pour over cream. Whoever said camp living had to be grotty?

Rosehip and ginger syrup

4 large handfuls of rosehips (about 600g)
5–7cm piece of ginger, peeled and sliced very thinly
500g soft brown sugar

I first tried this syrup when I was staying with my friend Jason Gathorne-Hardy at his wonderful home in Suffolk. His mother, Caroline Cranbrook, has spent decades building up plant and flower species in their walled garden at Great Glemham. The syrup came from the rosehips of a particularly fragrant wild Gallica rose that she cultivates there. This syrup, as well as being full of vitamin C, is delicious on my camp bread-and-butter pudding (see page 280). Try it also with yoghurt or, for a middle-Eastern flavour, with pheasant or pigeon.

Roughly chop the rosehips and put them with the ginger slices in a pan with 1 litre of water. Bring to the boil and simmer gently for 5 minutes and then let them stand, off the heat, to infuse for 15 minutes.

Put the liquid through muslin or a sieve, return the rosehips and ginger to the pan and cover them with another litre of water. Bring to the boil and simmer for 5 minutes. Let them stand for another 15 minutes and sieve into the first liquid.

Discard the rosehips and put the liquid on to simmer with the sugar, until the sugar has dissolved, and then reduce the liquid by at least half until it starts to look thick and syrupy. Store in sterilised bottles or Kilner jars. It will keep for about a month.

Rose petal syrup

300g freshly picked rose petals, whites removed
300g caster sugar
juice of 1 lemon

Wild roses flower in June and July and Jason makes wonderful rose petal jellies and jams that you can use to sweeten your tea in the morning or enjoy drizzled over lightly spiced barbecued pigeon or duck. I managed to get some pointers from him about the best way to make it. According to Middle Eastern food writers, the half-moon white part of the rose petal that resembles the whites on fingernails has very little scent and they cut these off before making jam, to get a fuller flavour.

Fill a large pan of water with half a litre of water and put on to boil. When the water is boiling, put half the rose petals into it and leave to infuse for an hour or two.

Strain the liquid and pour back into the pan with the sugar and remaining rose petals. Put the liquid back over the heat and stir until the sugar has dissolved. Add the lemon juice and bring the syrup to a slow simmer, and keep it simmering until it has reached setting point. To test for setting point, pour a little of the jam on to a cold plate and after a minute push it with your finger. If the jam wrinkles, it is ready to pot.

Pour the jam into jars that have been sterilised in boiling water. Half a kilo of rose petals makes approximately one jar.

Wild rose ras al hanout

Makes ½ jar
a handful of wild rose petals
2 cinnamon sticks, broken
  into several pieces
1 teaspoon cloves
1 tablespoon coriander seeds
1 tablespoon cumin seeds
1 tablespoon fennel seeds
1 tablespoon mustard seeds
1½ teaspoons cardamom
  seeds (or seeds from
  12 green pods)
3 star anise
1 teaspoon ground allspice
  (or 3–4 allspice seeds)
1 teaspoon black peppercorns

Wild rose petals are dried and used in aromatic spice mixes such as the Middle Eastern ras al hanout. Add this blend to slow-cooked lamb and wild plums. One or two teaspoons are enough for a big stew. Rub it into pheasant, partridge or pigeon before spit roasting (see page 66) or spatchcocking over a barbecue. It is delicious stuffed into pitta bread with spring onion, coriander leaf, yoghurt and a drizzle of Rosehip and ginger syrup (see page 290). My favourite way of using it is with fresh mackerel and scented rice – see page 222. It is also a wonderful addition to vegetables: add one or two tablespoons to a mix of parsnips, carrots and celeriac tossed in olive oil before roasting.

Lay the rose petals out flat in the Dutch oven (or casserole dish) and leave on the cooling coals of a fire overnight to dry out (or if indoors, leave in a low oven overnight). They may need a little more time to dry out completely, in which case repeat the drying, being careful not to put the Dutch oven in coals that are too hot.

Once you have dried the petals, put all the spices into a dry frying pan and heat over a medium heat, tossing gently. When the seeds start to pop, they are nearly cooked. Toss the seeds over the fire for another few minutes, without burning them. The aim is to allow the heat to release the flavour in the spices, rather than to 'cook' them.

Using a pestle and mortar, grind the spices, in batches if necessary. Mix the ground spices into the rose petals. Store the mixture in an airtight container away from sunlight. It is best eaten within a few months of grinding.

Hawthorn sauce

a handful of hawthorn leaves
a handful of other wild
  leaves (e.g. hairy
  bittercress, wild rocket,
  watercress or dandelion)
a good pinch of salt
2–3 tablespoons brown sugar
  to taste
100ml boiling water
100ml cider or sherry vinegar

This is the wild equivalent of a mint sauce, using the nutty-flavoured hawthorn leaves in place of mint. Hawthorn leaves are at their best in April and May and some years ago were eaten in cheese sandwiches, such was their popularity. In *Food for Free* (essential reading for any PG), Richard Mabey suggests combining them with wild garlic, sorrel or hedge garlic to make the traditional sauce. I did as he suggested and it was indeed a splendid accompaniment to local spring lamb.

Chop the leaves finely and sprinkle with the salt and sugar. Pour over the boiling water, stir to dissolve the sugar and leave to cool. Stir in the vinegar, tasting after you have added about two-thirds. You can always add more water or more sugar, according to taste.

Damson sauce

1kg damsons
1 teaspoon cloves
1 teaspoon whole allspice
3 whole star anise
1 teaspoon black peppercorns
400g soft brown sugar
3–4cm piece of fresh ginger,
* very thinly sliced*
210ml cider vinegar
sea salt

It was the middle of November by the time Guy and I had made it up to Cumbria on our journey through Britain and food worth foraging was thin on the ground when, in return for a day's rough shooting, we had to cook supper for some locals. We did not have much food and I was wondering what on earth I could make that would stretch to our numbers. That afternoon I went out looking for anything that I could use. I stumbled across an old damson tree. It was astonishing to see the upper branches laden with fruit so late in the year. When twilight came at about 3.30 p.m. I was still shaking the branches with long sticks, trying to knock down the precious fruit. This sauce was the result of that lucky hunting.

It is delicious served in pancakes with the Peking poached pheasant on page 148, with braised rabbit or thinned down with a little oil and brushed over meat before you barbecue it. You could use plums if you can't find any damsons.

Halve and stone the damsons and crack about half the stones. Tie them up in a piece of muslin with the cloves, allspice, star anise and peppercorns. Put the spice bag, damsons, sugar, ginger and vinegar in a large non-reactive pan and bring to the boil. Simmer until all the sugar has dissolved and then keep cooking for another 20–25 minutes. Remove the bag and press to extract all the juices. Press the sauce through a sieve (or a food mill) and transfer back into the cleaned pan. Simmer to reduce to a jam-like consistency.

The sauce is best if you can leave the flavours to mature for several days. If stored in sterilised jars, it keeps for several months.

Juniper marinade

6–8 juniper berries
1 garlic clove, peeled
salt and pepper
a splash of sherry vinegar
100ml extra virgin olive oil

This marinade can be whipped up in five minutes. Juniper berries are delicious and their flavour goes splendidly with game. Try this marinade on any game you happen to have; it is especially good with venison, wild boar, duck and pigeon. Sit the meat in it for several hours before roasting or pan-frying. You'll be in for a treat.

Using a pestle and mortar, mash the juniper and garlic to a paste, seasoning it with salt and pepper to taste. When it is as smooth as you can get it, stir in the vinegar and olive oil.

Mayonnaise

2 free-range egg yolks
1 teaspoon Dijon mustard
1–2 teaspoons white wine
  vinegar or lemon juice
350ml mild olive oil or half
  sunflower oil and half
  olive oil
a pinch of brown sugar
sea salt and freshly ground
  black pepper

I am a big Hellmann's fan and like nothing more than a dollop on my BLT or ploughman's. However, home-made mayonnaise is in an entirely different league. Trying to compare the two is like comparing a bicycle with a car. The first is fine for a short hop but the second needs to be wheeled out for more serious distances. Freshly caught fish, foraged wild food, free-range natural ingredients are that extra distance and a home-made mayonnaise does justice to such special food. It need take only fifteen minutes to make, and you can flavour it with anything you've got up your sleeve. Why resist the temptation?

Don't be tempted to use extra virgin olive oil in this recipe. The flavour of a typical olive oil is more pronounced in mayonnaise and can make it taste bitter. If you do use only olive oil in this recipe, be sure to use a mild-flavoured one. When you've mastered the basic recipe, then try some of the variations below.

Rinse a bowl with boiling water and dry it thoroughly.

Whisk together the egg yolks, mustard and vinegar or lemon juice and then start adding the oil, drop by drop, whisking continuously to bind the mayonnaise. After a few minutes you can add the oil in a slow, constant trickle until it is all incorporated. If it looks as if it is splitting, add a teaspoon of boiling water and keep whisking, but if you use free-range eggs and add the oil slowly you shouldn't have a problem.

Add the sugar – it balances the flavours – and season with sea salt and pepper. You may need a touch more lemon juice or vinegar too.

Fennel and samphire mayonnaise Finely chop a handful of wild fennel fronds into the basic mayonnaise.

Drop a clutch of marsh samphire into some boiling, salted water for 2–3 minutes until tender. Drain and briefly dunk into some cold water before roughly chopping. Add to the mayonnaise. If you can't get samphire, substitute a mix of capers and gherkins.

Spiced mayonnaise Warm ½ teaspoon cumin seeds and 1 teaspoon coriander seeds in a dry frying pan for about 5 minutes until their flavours are released. Try not to burn them.

Using a pestle and mortar, grind the spices with half a small dried chilli and add to the basic mayonnaise.

Potted mayonnaise Use sherry vinegar instead of lemon juice. Using a pestle and mortar, grind a blade of mace, a pinch of cayenne pepper and half a teaspoon of allspice, and add to the basic mayonnaise.

Aioli Using a pestle and mortar, pound 2 garlic cloves and a handful of toasted almonds or hazelnuts to a paste. Add to the mustard and lemon juice. Continue as for the basic mayonnaise.

Wild garlic aioli Shred 3 or 4 rolled-up wild garlic leaves into very fine wisps and stir into the basic mayonnaise. If you can't find any wild garlic leaves, use hedge garlic.

Lemon mayonnaise Use 1 tablespoon of lemon juice in the mustard mix and the zest of half a lemon. This is delicious with shellfish.

Horseradish cream

½ horseradish root, peeled
200–300ml crème fraîche
 (or double cream mixed
 with lemon juice)
salt to taste

I am beginning to feel like a cracked wild food gramophone record, but home-made horseradish cream, made with freshly grated horseradish, is a world away from the bought version, which is full of vinegar and other preservatives. Serve the cream with fish, beef, tongue or boiled new potatoes. It has the perfect fiery bite. Try grating horseradish over hollandaise, too (see page 233).

Put the cream into a bowl and grate the horseradish over it. Mix the horseradish into the cream and add salt to taste.

Celeriac remoulade

Feeds 4
1 celeriac
1–2 tablespoons vinegar
a large handful of parsley
 chopped
2–3 tablespoons grated
 horseradish
zest of 1 lemon
200–300ml crème fraîche
 or mayonnaise
 (see page 294)
2–3 tablespoons capers
 (optional)
salt and pepper to taste

There will be occasions when fire is not an option, and bad weather and soggy wood can damage the morale. This is when the PG can gleefully rise to the occasion and concoct something delicious from what he or she has saved for a rainy day. I had a store of celeriac left over in Yorkshire from some digging we did. Celeriac and horseradish are both at their best in November and December and are natural partners.

I made this classic French salad, which you can eat by itself or serve with some of the home-made Duck prosciutto (see page 149) or perhaps some smoked fish (see pages 240–1). It is a really magical combination.

Peel the celeriac and slice it into very thin discs. Slice each disc into tiny matchsticks and toss them in a bowl of water with the vinegar as you slice them, or the celeriac will discolour. When you have finished, drain the celeriac and pat dry. Combine it with the parsley, horseradish, lemon zest, crème fraîche or mayonnaise and capers, if using. Season to taste with salt and pepper.

Beetroot, apple and horseradish dressing for sashimi

Finely grate two parts of peeled beetroot and apple to one part horseradish. Loosen with extra virgin olive oil, season with salt and pepper and serve as a dressing for very fresh, raw fish.

Chargrilled pumpkin wedges with mixed wild mushrooms and sage beurre noir

Feeds 6
1 small pumpkin, about 2kg
1 tablespoon olive oil
120g butter
salt and pepper
10–12 sage leaves, chopped
1 teaspoon sherry vinegar
600g mixed wild mushrooms

Guy and I travelled through Wales dogged by dreadful weather and poor hunting. Our luck was failing us, as was our morale. The only thing I had left of any value (and at this point Guy was certain I was losing my marbles) was a Kilner jar of jellied eels that I had pickled underneath the Severn bridge for a rainy day. The rainy days came with a vengeance, so there was nothing for it but to see if our luck might change.

Guy dropped me off by an honesty vegetable box scheme. Mr Evans's daughter was away but Mr Evans was game and swapped my eels for a couple of enormous pumpkins. We chargrilled them inside the wall tent on (another) rainy night with some mushrooms I foraged the next day. The supper was further proof that foraged food somehow tastes infinitely better than bought.

These mushrooms are also delicious with venison liver.

Cut the pumpkin up into generous-sized wedges – 1 wedge to feed each person. You may not need the whole pumpkin. Place the wedges in a large saucepan of boiling salted water for 10–15 minutes to parboil them. They should not be too soft or else they will not hold their shape. Drain, brush each wedge with oil and arrange them on a chargrill. They should take about 5–8 minutes a side to cook over a medium heat.

Meanwhile melt all but a knob of the butter in a small saucepan over a high heat until it starts simmering. Season it well with salt and pepper and continue to cook until you start to smell the butter browning. Swill the butter round to check that it has browned before adding the sage leaves, followed by the vinegar. Set aside.

Melt the remaining butter in a large frying pan and add the mushrooms. Stir-fry over a high heat for about 10 minutes until they look good enough to eat.

Put a wedge of chargrilled pumpkin on each plate with a mound of assorted wild mushrooms. Spoon over the sage butter and tuck in.

Baked parasol mushrooms with breadcrumbs, garlic and chilli

Feeds 6
8 large parasol mushrooms
2 garlic cloves, finely chopped
100g coarse dry breadcrumbs,
  preferably from leftovers of
  Guy's bannock bread
  (see page 172)
½ teaspoon fresh thyme
  leaves
2 dried red chillies, crumbled
2 tablespoons extra virgin
  olive oil, plus some
  for frying
5 tablespoons butter, softened
salt and pepper
bread and butter, to serve

There are few people who can resist the flavours of garlic, chilli and olive oil, especially when scattered over freshly picked parasol mushrooms. This recipe is always a winner.

Remove the stems from the mushrooms and finely chop them. Add the garlic, breadcrumbs, thyme, chillies, oil and half the butter. Season with salt and pepper. Lay the mushrooms in a large frying pan and spread the crumb mixture over them. Pour a little oil in the pan and fry over a high heat for 10 minutes. Turn the mushrooms and cook on the other side for a further 5 minutes until they turn a golden, toasted colour. Serve at once with plenty of bread and butter.

Pan-fried beefsteak mushrooms

Feeds 2
2 large beefsteak mushrooms
300ml milk or water
50g butter
1 medium onion, finely sliced
salt and pepper
bread and butter, to serve

The first week of our travels was one of the hardest. We were in Cornwall and there were gales blowing, rain and sometimes plummeting temperatures. Food was hard to come by and Guy and I were feeling distinctly down on our luck. Despite all this, someone seemed to be smiling on us. On a dejected walk through a soggy wood, we looked up at an old oak tree and saw two of the most enormous beefsteak mushrooms sprouting forth. They tasted deliciously meaty. From that point on, whenever we had a low point on our journey we headed to woods or grassy areas, hoping that something edible might stop us in our tracks.

These mushrooms go very well with Sorrel omelette (see page 269) or Chargrilled pumpkin wedges (see page 298).

Slice the beefsteaks into ½cm-thin slices. Soak them in the milk or water for 10 minutes and if possible rinse away the milk or water and soak them again in fresh liquid. The soaking takes away any bitterness from the mushrooms.

Pat the mushrooms dry and melt the butter in a heavy frying pan over a high heat. Add the onion, season with salt and pepper and cook until the onion turns translucent. Add the mushrooms and cook for 3–4 minutes a side until the slices turn golden brown. Check for seasoning and serve with hunks of bread and butter.

Mushroom and herb broth

Feeds 4–5
450g mixed wild mushrooms
40g butter
1 medium onion,
* finely chopped*
1 fat garlic clove,
* finely chopped*
1–2 teaspoons thyme leaves
2 bay leaves, fresh if possible
salt and pepper
1.5 litres game stock
* (or stock made from*
* bouillon cubes) or water*
2 tablespoons parsley,
* finely chopped*
100ml double cream
* (optional)*
slug of sherry (optional)

Soup is one of the easiest and most comforting things to make in a domestic kitchen, let alone on an outside fire. This soup takes so little time and really does nourish the weary PG after a hard day's hunting. If you like, mix the mushrooms with other ingredients. Nettles make a fine partner (see page 268), as long as they are young ones, and to make a more wholesome soup you can thicken this with potato or stale bread soaked in milk, if you have either to hand.

Chop the mushrooms roughly. Melt the butter in a heavy casserole over a high heat and add the onion. Sweat for 5 minutes before adding the garlic, thyme and bay leaves. After a few minutes add the mushrooms and cook for 10 minutes, stirring from time to time. Season with salt and pepper. Pour in the stock or water, add half the parsley and simmer, covered, for at least 20 minutes, so that all the flavours get a chance to blend.

Check the seasoning and pour the soup into cups or bowls, scattering each with a little parsley and cream, if you have it. This broth responds well to a slug of sherry too.

Snail linguine

Feeds 4
24–36 snails
280g linguine (or spaghetti)
30g butter
1 tablespoon olive oil
5 fat garlic cloves,
*   finely chopped*
1 medium onion,
*   finely chopped*
1 small chilli, crumbled
⅓ bottle of white wine
a small handful of parsley
*   leaves, freshly chopped*

For the court bouillon:
3 bay leaves
carrot, celery or onion,
*   chopped into largish*
*   chunks*
fresh thyme
1 garlic clove, peeled
1 teaspoon peppercorns

Although killing and cooking snails is not a particularly peaceful occupation (I had a terrible time in Cornwall killing even one snail for fish bait, let alone a whole batch of the poor creatures), they are the perfect forageable food, high in protein and abundant throughout Britain. I therefore feel they have to be mentioned here.

As I said, catching them and preparing them for supper is not a job for the faint-hearted. They are bewitchingly sweet, despite all the slime, and the sight of their little heads twitching about quizzically is rather heart-wrenching if you know you are keeping them for munching. This is a job I would undertake only if seriously challenged for food.

Most people say that wild snails need to be purged before eating, to rid them of any toxins they may have eaten. My grandmother's generation largely seems to think this is absolute nonsense, but snails were less exposed to chemicals in those days so I recommend purging, which means emptying the snails' digestive tracts.

First of all you must make a temporary home for your snails. A standard plastic bucket (9 litres) can house about 20–25 snails comfortably – any more than that and the snails start getting crowded. Pierce holes in the bottom of the bucket for air and place a saucer of water in the bucket. Snails are quite feisty and surprisingly strong, so when you have managed to put them in the bucket, either top it with a weighted-down lid or wrap some thick tights over the top. Start by feeding them with a diet rich in lettuce, dandelion leaves, wild fennel and other edible leaves. A mixture of leaves and herbs will not only fatten them up but also give them a delicious flavour. Make sure you clean the bucket out regularly, so that they have a clean home, and change their drinking water every couple of days, always watching out for the ones that try to scoot off.

After a minimum of 7 days of feeding, the snails need to be starved for 24–48 hours, although many people like to purge them for anything up to 2 weeks. If any of the snails look as if they have died during purging, throw them away.

Blanch the snails for 3 minutes in well-salted water, taking care not to lose them. If need be, rattle the bucket so that they disappear inside their homes; otherwise they will do their utmost to escape. Drain the snails and leave in more salty water for another 15 minutes. This ensures that they will be totally digestible. Prise the snails from their shells with a sharp object and then rinse in fresh water. Put the snails in a large saucepan with the court bouillon ingredients, cover with water, bring to the boil and simmer for 60–90 minutes. The aim is to cook the snails until they are tender. Test after an hour.

Drain the snails, reserving the water for the pasta, and leave them to cool slightly. Bring the water to the boil, add the pasta and simmer until al dente. While it is cooking, melt the butter and olive oil in a saucepan over a high heat and add the garlic and onion. Sweat for 5–10 minutes until the onion is translucent. Cut the snails in half and add to the onions with the chilli. After a couple of minutes pour in the wine and let it reduce by one-third. Drain the pasta, reserving a little of the cooking water. Add the parsley to the sauce and toss the sauce through the pasta, adding a little cooking water if needed. Serve drizzled with extra olive oil.

Escargots If you like the classic dish of snails with garlic butter, retain the snail shells and clean them by simmering them in salted water for 15 minutes. Cook the snails in the court bouillon as above and serve them in their shells with a double quantity of the sauce on page 304, melted and bubbling hot.

FURTHER INFORMATION

Shooting seasons

This list of shooting seasons for species mentioned in the Militant Gourmet chapter is a guide based on information from BASC, but should not be used as a definitive statement of current regulations. Go to BASC's website at www.basc.org.uk for more information.

Game and wildfowl

Duck and goose

inland England, Scotland, Wales	1 Sept–31 Jan
foreshore England, Scotland, Wales	1 Sept–20 Feb

Grouse

England, Scotland, Wales	12 Aug–10 Dec
Northern Ireland	12 Aug–30 Nov

Partridge

1 Sept–1 Feb

Pheasant

England, Scotland, Wales	1 Oct–1 Feb
Northern Ireland (cocks only)	1 Oct–31 Jan

Woodcock

England, Wales	1 Oct–31 Jan
Scotland	1 Sept–31 Jan

Woodpigeon

No closed season

Deer

Red deer stag

England, Wales, Northern Ireland	1 Aug–30 Apr
Scotland	1 July–20 Oct

Red deer hind

England, Wales, Northern Ireland	1 Nov–28 Feb
Scotland	21 Oct–15 Feb

Fallow buck

	1 Aug–30 Apr

Fallow doe

England, Wales, Northern Ireland	1 Nov–28 Feb
Scotland	21 Oct–15 Feb

Sika stag

England, Wales, Northern Ireland	1 Aug–30 Apr
Scotland	1 July–20 Oct

Sika hind

England, Wales, Northern Ireland	1 Nov–28 Feb
Scotland	21 Oct–15 Feb

Roe buck

England, Wales	1 Apr–31 Oct
Scotland	1 Apr–20 Oct

Roe doe

England, Wales	1 Nov–28 Feb
Scotland	21 Oct–31 Mar

Chinese water deer

(only found in England)	1 Nov–28 Feb

Muntjac

	No closed season

Minimum landing sizes

This list of landing sizes for species mentioned in the Aquatic Gourmet chapter is a guide based on information from DEFRA, but should not be used as a definitive statement of current regulations. For a complete listing, go to DEFRA's website at www.defra.gov.uk.

Bass	360mm
Clam (razor)	100mm
Conger eel	580mm
Crab (edible)	140mm
Crab (spider)	120mm (f) 130mm (m)
Crab (velvet)	65mm
Flounder	270mm
Gurnard	(no minimum landing size)
Mackerel	300mm
Mussel	50mm
Oyster	70mm
Pollack	300mm
Scallop	110mm

Websites

The MCSUK and Fish Online are both brilliant and recognised sources for providing advice on sustainable fish. Find them at:

www.mcsuk.org
www.fishonline.org

Books

There are many books out there that are waiting to become our friends . . .
we just have not met them yet. Here are a few personal favourites:

- Baden-Powell, Robert and Boehmer, Elleke, *Scouting for Boys* (Oxford University Press, 2005)
- Ball, Ian, *Secrets of Fly-Fishing for Trout* (Elliot Right Ways Books, 1998)
- Batley, John, *The Pigeon Shooter* (Swan Hill Press, 2004)
- Bezzant, David, *Ferreting: A Traditional Country Pursuit* (The Crowood Press, 2004)
- Burrows, Ian, *Food from the Wild* (New Holland, 2005)
- Coats, Archie, *Pigeon Shooting* (Andre Deutsch Ltd, 1995)
- Coats, Prue, *The Poacher's Cookbook* (Merlin Unwin Books, 2003)
- Crawford, Lesley, *The Trout Fisher's Handbook* (Swan Hill Press, 2002)
- Deeley, Martin, *Advanced Gundog Training* (The Crowood Press, 2001)
- Downing, Graham, *The Deer Stalking Handbook* (Swan Hill Press, 2004)
- Erlandson, Keith, *Home Smoking and Curing* (Ebury Press, 2003)
- Fearnley-Whittingstall, Hugh, *A Cook on the Wild Side* (Boxtree Ltd, 1997)
- Hart-Davis, Duff, *Fauna Britannica* (Weidenfeld & Nicolson, 2002)
- Humphreys, John, *The Complete Gundog* (David and Charles, 2003)
- Hutcheon, John, *Long Netting and Net-Making* (The Crowood Press Ltd, 2006)
- Mabey, Richard, *Flora Britannica* (Sinclair-Stevenson Ltd, 1996)
- Mabey, Richard, *Food for Free* (Collins, 2001)
- McCall, Ian, *Your Shoot: Gamekeeping and Management* (A&C Black, 1990)
- Moen, Frank Emil and Svensen, Erling, *Marine Fish and Invertebrates of Northern Europe* (AquaPress, 2004)
- Moxon, P.R.A, *Gundogs: Training and Field Trials* (Swan Hill Press, 2007)
- Niall, Ian, *The Poacher's Handbook* (Merlin Unwin Books, 2003)
- Phillips, Roger, *Mushrooms* (Macmillan, 2006)
- Sandler, Nick and Acton, Johnny, *Preserved* (Kyle Cathie, 2005)
- Scales, Susan, *Retriever Training* (Swan Hill Press, 1992)
- Schwab, Alexander, *Mushrooming Without Fear* (Merlin Unwin Books, 2006)
- Stanbury, Percy and Carlisle, G.L., *Shotgun Marksmanship* (Hutchinson, 1987)
- Weiss, E.A, *Comprehensive Guide to Wilderness and Travel Medicine* (Adventure Medical Kits, 1997)
- Willcock, Colin (ed.), *The New ABC of Shooting* (Andre Deutsch Ltd, 1994)
- Wright, John, *The River Cottage Mushroom Handbook* (Bloomsbury, 2007)
- Wyman, Harold, *The Art of Long Netting* (Coch-y-Bonddu Books, 1997)

ACKNOWLEDGEMENTS

Thank you so much to all who made our travels possible …

To all the Meyricks at Hinton Admiral, and to Ken and the team, for their support in the beginning, when it mattered the most; without all their help our journey, and the book, would not have happened. And thank you to the Milbanks and their beautiful red grouse – you were wonderful, fun hosts.

We are indebted to Anne and Sifty in Somerset; to Mr Evans in Wales; to Colin and his delicious saltmarsh lamb in the Gower peninsula; to John Constable, whose knowledge of pike was marvellous; to Jason Gathorne-Hardy and his long-suffering parents for making us feel so welcome at Great Glemham; to everyone at the Ardtornish Estate, particularly Colin for his dry humour and great company; and to the National Trust for allowing us to explore the British countryside.

Enormous thanks to Tommi's parents and her boyfriend Mark for endless guinea-pigging and helpful comments, and to the whole collection of friends who were subjected to tasting sessions. Thanks also to Cotswold Fish & Game and Hayles Fruit Farm for always being around to produce the ingredients.

Thanks to Mike and his superb team at Regenatec, who made it possible for us to drive our vehicle over all kinds of terrain using nothing but rapeseed oil. Thanks also go to John Crocker at Fourtec who was brave enough to lend us an unstoppable Santana; to everyone on Mull, particularly to Dawn for her wonderful illustrations; to Nick Turnbull and Kenny at the Isle of Mull Crab Company; and to the team at Isle of Mull Oysters, whose wonderful knowledge of the sea shows in everything they do. Thanks to Liam Griffin and friends in Oban for laughter whatever the weather. And special thanks to Juno, a retriever with heart, who never gave up looking – even when the land held nothing for us and the living was hard.

Many thanks to Caroline and Somerset who let us make camp; to Daisy Goodwin, Dan Adamson, Lucy Hooper and the whole team at Silver River (we mean you, Craghopper) who worked miracles even when it was blowing force 12; to Sue Murphy at Channel 4 who determined to make it happen; and to Antony Topping at Greene & Heaton and Euan Thorneycroft at A.M. Heath, our wonderful literary agents.

Finally thank you to the team at Bloomsbury for such stellar work: to Natalie Hunt, who has the patience of a saint; to Anya Rosenberg, publicist extraordinaire; to Will Webb, for the stunning design work; to Minna Fry, for her endless enthusiasm; to Lisa Fiske, for all her work on the production; and of course thank you to Richard Atkinson for helping us make this beautiful book. We particularly want to thank Jill Mead – not only did she produce the extraordinarily wonderful photographs that have brought this book to life, but she added quirkiness, huge enthusiasm and 150 per cent dedication to the job. If only everyone made work this much fun.